In the World but Not of the World

In the World but Not of the World

The Liminal Life of Pre-Constantine Christian Communities

A. Sue Russell

☛PICKWICK *Publications* · Eugene, Oregon

IN THE WORLD BUT NOT OF THE WORLD
The Liminal Life of Pre-Constantine Christian Communities

Copyright © 2019 A. Sue Russell. All rights reserved. Except for brief quotations in critical publications or reviews, no part of this book may be reproduced in any manner without prior written permission from the publisher. Write: Permissions, Wipf and Stock Publishers, 199 W. 8th Ave., Suite 3, Eugene, OR 97401.

Pickwick Publications
An Imprint of Wipf and Stock Publishers
199 W. 8th Ave., Suite 3
Eugene, OR 97401

www.wipfandstock.com

PAPERBACK ISBN: 978-1-5326-4474-0
HARDCOVER ISBN: 978-1-5326-4475-7
EBOOK ISBN: 978-1-5326-4476-4

Cataloguing-in-Publication data:

Names: Russell, A. Sue, author.

Title: In the world but not of the world : the liminal life of pre-Constantine Christian communities / A. Sue Russell.

Description: Eugene, OR: Pickwick Publications, 2019. | Includes bibliographical references.

Identifiers: ISBN 978-1-5326-4474-0 (paperback). | ISBN 978-1-5326-4475-7 (hardcover). | ISBN 978-1-5326-4476-4 (ebook).

Subjects: LCSH: Bible—New Testament—Criticism, interpretation, etc. | Church history—Primitive and early church, ca. 30–600.

Classification: BR170 R87 2019 (print). | BR170 (ebook).

Unless otherwise indicated, all Scripture quotations are from The ESV® Bible (The Holy Bible, English Standard Version®), copyright © 2001 by Crossway Bibles, a publishing ministry of Good News Publishers. Used by permission. All rights reserved.

Scripture quotations marked (NIV) are taken from the Holy Bible New International Version®. Copyright © 1973, 1978, 1984, 2011 by Biblica, Inc. ®. Used by permission. All rights reserved.

Greek text is from *The Greek New Testament*, 4th rev. ed. Edited by K. Aland, M. Black, C. M. Martinit, and B. M. Metzger. © 1993 Stuttgart: Deutsche Bibelgesellschaft, Stuttgart.

Manufactured in the U.S.A.   11/14/19

For my gracious, gentle husband, David,
whose life reflects so much of what is written here.

Contents

List of Figures and Tables | viii
Preface | ix
Acknowledgments | xiii

1 Understanding Early Christian Communities | 1
2 Liminality, Structure, and Anti-Structure | 30
3 Liminality, Jesus, and the Kingdom of God | 55
4 Liminal Community in Acts | 96
5 Liminality and Pauline Communities | 136
6 Liminality in Transition: Post-Pauline Communities | 176
7 The End of Ancient Christianity | 223

Bibliography | 233

Figures and Tables

Figure 1. Temporal Dimension of Inaugurated Eschatology | 43

Figure 2. Social Dimension of Inaugurated Eschatology | 44

Figure 3. Both/And Liminality of the Kingdom of God | 57

Figure 4. Liminal Time of the Kingdom | 65

Figure 5. Jesus' Rites of Passage | 67

Figure 6. Jesus' Rites of Separation | 68

Figure 7. Jesus' Rites of Reincorporation | 68

Figure 8. David's Rites of Passage | 70

Figure 9. Comparison of David's and Jesus' Liminality in Rites of Separation | 71

Figure 10. Liminality of Israel | 73

Figure 11. Reorientation of the Disciples' Eschatology | 101

Figure 12. Temporal Liminality in Paul's Writings | 139

Figure 13. Analogies of Temporal Liminality | 141

Figure 14. Rites of Passage and Embodied Liminality in Paul's Writings | 144

Figure 15. Rites of Passage and Three Dimensions of Inaugurated Eschatology | 151

Table 1. Turner's Characteristics of Structure and Anti-Structure | 35

Table 2. Comparison of Structural and Anti-Structural Expectations | 75

Table 3. Passages That Reflect Development of Church Leadership | 182

Preface

It is rare when a moment of clarity about an idea leads to a lifelong journey of scholarship and writing. I vividly remember the moment when the seed of this book was planted. I was in a seminar on the historical Jesus taught by Dr. S. Scott Bartchy at UCLA. He had been discussing the differences between the values of the first-century Mediterranean world and the values Jesus taught his disciples. When he summarized his lecture with a slide showing a table with contrasting lists of characteristics, I realized I had seen a similar list in Victor Turner's *Ritual Process* describing the structural and anti-structural characteristics of people in rites of passage. It was in that moment that Dr. Bartchy and I knew that this concept would be the core of my dissertation, which has ultimately resulted in this book.

However, the journey that led to this book actually started in the jungles of Southeast Asia thirty years earlier. I had been asked to help a group of pastors translate the New Testament into their language. As a young, single person, I discovered that in this collective community my resources and gifts were to be used for the good of the collective under the stewardship of the church elders. I learned more about this when I returned to the village after earning my first doctorate and the elders met to discuss how we were going to use "our" doctorate.

At the time I was a new follower of Jesus, and the elders became my spiritual mentors. I was socialized as a Christ follower into the non-Western, non-individualized Christianity they lived. In their practice of Christianity, I learned that the greatest offenses in this culture were those that disrupted the harmony of relationships in the village. Christianity was not about your morality but about how you engaged in relationships and treated people. I became aware of how much this reflected what was taught in the New Testament when we started to translate the great love passage in 1 Corinthians 13:4–8. The language we were working in did not allow for love to be translated as an abstract noun; it had to be translated as a verb with a subject and object. The way we translated the passage changed love from a personal characteristic to an action—how you treat someone. For instance, rather than the familiar "love is patient, love is kind" that appears in English versions, our translation read, "A person who loves someone is patient with them; they are kind to them." The passage was no longer about me and who I was in my Western, individualized interpretation, but rather it was about the relationships I had with other people and how I treated them. As I read the New Testament through this collective orientation, I realized that most of what Jesus and Paul taught was about relationships. The fruits of the Spirit in Galatians 5:22–23 are not just desired attributes for individuals but characteristics that communicate the relationships needed between people. We are to have new types of relationships, ones that reflect the Holy Spirit.

As I began working on this book, I found that others had sought to articulate these new types of relationships by using social models that described similar types of relationships. These studies compared the early Christian communities to sects, family, communes, and contrast society to explain how these new kinds of relationships in community were formed. Many had also used Victor Turner's concept of liminality to describe these new types of relationships. In rites of passage, people in liminality form intense bonding and camaraderie and reflect the characteristics of relationships described in the teachings of Jesus and Paul. Although I was encouraged by the insights of these models into the life of the early church, most of these types of relationships were either lived apart from society or were temporary. These models described communities which eventually became institutionalized and no longer reflected the types of relationships found in liminality.

A key turning point for me was when I was asked, "How was it possible for the early Christians to live as an egalitarian society when there was a wide range of social statuses in the church?" This became the key focus for this book. I realized that just as there were concepts of temporal liminality (living in the already not yet) and embodied liminality (living in the Spirit in the flesh), there was a third dimension, a social dimension—living liminally in structure. Turner provided the concepts to describe this social dimension of what it meant to live in-Christ in the world. Rather than only a temporary liminality or a liminality lived apart from society, the in-Christ community was to live this liminality within the structures of society. The uniqueness of the early Christian communities was they were to live these new types of relationships within the structures of their society. They were to live anti-structurally within their existing structure. This was the social dimension of in-Christ communities.

As these concepts came to fruition, I found other scholars had described similar concepts in the teachings of Jesus and Paul as well as in the experience of the early church described in Acts. I am indebted to these scholars who, although they did not use Turner's vocabulary, described similar concepts. I was heartened because I saw people articulating this liminality in structure in various ways. There was continuity from Jesus' teaching up until the reign of Constantine when the church became part of the imperial structure. This book has been greatly influenced by scholars who have written about this new way of living, and I draw heavily on their work. I found N. T. Wright's discussion on the redefinition of the people of God in *Jesus and the People of God* extremely helpful in framing how liminality was reflected in Jesus' teachings. I have used several of the concepts from Aaron Kuecker in his discussion of the Spirit as the new identity marker that transcends but does not erase ethnic markers in the *The Spirit and the 'Other.'* Two books that examined the anti-structural characteristic of early Christ followers from Jesus through second- and third-century writers were Gerhard Lohfink's *Jesus and Community* and Joseph Hellerman's *The Ancient Church as Family*. I am also indebted to many Pauline scholars who discuss what it means to live in-Christ in the world. My hope is that this book offers new language that provides a continuity of thought for these remarkable scholars.

My greatest hope is that this book allows Christ followers to refocus their attention on what it means to be the body of Christ and how that is lived out in different cultures. Paul did not deconstruct the institutions of his day but rather taught his followers how to live new Spirit-marked relationships within their structure. Far too often, people equate renewal of the church with incorporating a new type of structure for worship, leadership organization, meeting place, etc. However, renewal does not come from changing structure or introducing new institutions. It comes from changing the way we relate to one another and treat people. This will look differently in different communities and cultures.

As a missiologist, I find it encouraging that each culture has the freedom to learn how to live a new way in-Christ in their culture. Paul did not deconstruct the hierarchy of his day, rather he redefined hierarchical structure from domination and exclusion to one of service and inclusion. Jesus did not deconstruct the values of honor in his culture, rather he redefined what honor meant in his followers. Living a new way in the world means that each culture must redefine and transform the values and structures of their society to align with what is the most basic teaching of loving God and loving others.

The thesis of this book is simple. Christ followers are to live a new way within the structures of their society and thereby transform it. People should know followers of Christ not by their political positions, nor by their worship style, nor by their stand on social issues. People should know Christ followers by their transformed lives and relationships with one another and others. It was the transformed relationships of early Christians that distinguished them from the world. Christ followers can (and must) do the same today! We can live in the world but also live differently than the world in a way that reflects the teachings of Jesus Christ.

A. Sue Russell
Wilmore, Kentucky

Acknowledgments

THIS BOOK IS A revision of the dissertation that I completed at UCLA, and thus it seems fitting to publically acknowledge those who were a part of my scholarly development that influenced the outcome of this project. First and foremost with deep gratitude, I want to thank Dr. S. Scott Bartchy, who was chair of my dissertation committee and also my advisor for the journey that led to this book. It was his interest in the application of anthropological models to the study of ancient Christianity that drew me to the program at UCLA and convinced me to embark upon this journey. His insights and teaching on ancient Christianity provided the trajectory for this study. His ideas helped formulate the framework for this study, and I am grateful for the countless hours he spent not only discussing these ideas but letting me see them lived out in his own life.

I would also like to thank the other members of my committee. Dr. Ronald Mellor's stimulating classes and seminars on Roman history provided the context for this study. His gracious review of this project has been most helpful. Dr. Joel Robbins provided insights, direction, and comments about Turner and the anthropological study of Christianity in the formative stages of this project. Dr. Claudia Rapp's work on bishops in late antiquity provided insight into leadership and authority in early Christianity.

I want to give a special thanks to my fellow members of the "Bartchy Bunch" at UCLA: Kevin Scull, James Petifils, Joe Sanzo, and Pat Cullough. I cannot count the number of times they shared notes, referred me to books, and provided much needed encouragement. They were amazing travelling companions.

I would like to thank Asbury Theological Seminary for their generous sabbatical program that provided the time to update my bibliography and incorporate changes in my thinking that have been integrated into this book. I serve with a delightful community of scholars who encourage and model excellence in scholarship.

A special thank you to Nancy Hoffman, who has read this manuscript and edited it numerous times at various stages in this project. She offered helpful suggestions and made me clarify my thinking along the way. This book would not have come to fruition without her amazing attention to detail.

Finally, I want to acknowledge my lifelong traveling companion, David. Early in our marriage, he recognized in me a love for learning and encouraged me through multiple degree programs to pursue this passion. His willingness to read manuscripts, create all the figures used in this book, and patiently endure the ups and downs of the writing process is a reflection of his love, character, and commitment to me.

Chapter 1

Understanding Early Christian Communities

THE RAPID EXPANSION OF the early communities of Christ followers has been the subject of numerous studies. As Wayne Meeks notes, "The origins of Christianity have excited deep curiosity since the second century . . . Yet its beginnings and earliest growth remain in many ways mysterious."[1] The question at the heart of recent research on early Christianity is what caused this growth. What attracted people to a small sect that started on the fringes of the Roman Empire and soon spread to its farthest borders? What was it about this movement of Christ followers that attracted members across class, ethnic, and gender boundaries?

Three foci of recent scholarship have sought to answer these questions. Many scholars have suggested that the expansion of Christian communities was due to the cohesive relationships between their members.[2] They have suggested that the communities offered solidarity and brotherhood among their members. To understand this cohesiveness, scholars have studied institutions within the Greco-Roman context that offered potential models for the Christ-following communities. They focus on the similarities of early Christian communities and the composition and character of the relationships of people within these institutions. These studies include comparisons to voluntary associations,[3] synagogues,[4] households,[5] and mystery religions.[6]

---

1. Meeks, *The First Urban Christians*, 1.
2. Hellerman, *The Ancient Church as Family*, 3.
3. Ascough, *Paul's Macedonian Associations*, 110–90.
4. Harland, *Associations, Synagogues, and Congregations*, 213–38.
5. Meeks, *The First Urban Christians*, 75–77. Meeks also asserts that all four of these models provide some characteristics of the early Christian assemblies (*The First Urban Christians*, 84).
6. Ascough, *What Are They Saying*, 50–70.

Early Christian communities also believed in and practiced values that were countercultural to their social context, particularly those that reflected a renunciation of status and a broad inclusion of people across statuses. Scholars who focus on this aspect of the Christian communities propose that solidarity of these communities resulted from members living in such a way that critiqued the social norms and values of their context. Studies from this perspective seek to understand the growth of early Christian communities by comparing them to similar types of social movements that sought to critique or protest against the social institutions in their environment. These studies include comparisons with sectarian movements,[7] apocalyptic groups,[8] millenarian groups,[9] revitalization movements,[10] and social movements.[11]

A third focus of the study of Christian communities is the continuation of the cohesiveness of relationships and central values through the changing structure of the church and across time and geography. These studies trace the continuity of these characteristics from the Jesus movement through the third century. In particular are Joseph Hellerman's study of early Christian communities as surrogate or fictive kin[12] and Gerhard Lohfink's study of Christ-following communities as a contrast society.[13]

What is consistent in all of these studies is that they seek to explain the expansion and continuation of the solidarity and way of life within early Christian communities that was different from the world in which they lived. However, while each of these foci contributes to our understanding of the expansion and uniqueness of communities of Christ followers, they are not able to account for other characteristics of the communities. I propose that all three of these foci are important aspects of understanding the growth, impact, and unique characteristics of the early Christian communities. In this book I introduce a model to integrate all three of these foci into one comprehensive framework to understand and explain the growth and impact of the early Christian communities. With this framework, I then trace key characteristics of the relationships

---

7. Scroggs, "The Earliest Christian Communities," 69–92.

8. Duling, "Millennialism," 183–205.

9. Gager, *Kingdom and Commmunity*, 20–26. There are many scholars who note the apocalyptic nature of the teachings of the Kingdom of God and the Pauline communities.

10. Theissen, *The Religion of the Earliest Churches*, 163–84.

11. Malina, *The Social Gospel of Jesus*, 71–112.

12. Aasgaard, *My Beloved Brothers and Sisters!*, 118–312; Bartchy, *Call No Man Father*; Hellerman, *The Ancient Church as Family*, 92–225.

13. Lohfink, *Jesus and Community*, 157–63.

of people within communities of Christ followers from the early Jesus movement portrayed in the gospels through the writings of leaders of the second- and third-century communities.

In this chapter I explore the contribution of the three foci of study to the understanding of the growth, organization, beliefs, and quality of relationships within early Christian communities. I first examine studies that have focused on the similarities of early Christian communities with social institutions within the context of the first-century Judean and Greco-Roman world. These have been used to understand the organization and practices of the early Christian communities that reflect the social structure of their context. I then examine studies that compare early Christian communities to models of movements that critique or protest their broader social environments—what I call a critique on structure. Finally, I provide models that trace the persistence of solidarity and values of the Christ-following communities within the changing institutional structure of the communities and broader society.

Models of Early Christian Communities Reflecting Structure

Scholars have noted that because early Christian communities did not exist in a void, they adopted and adapted their organization, practices, identity, and beliefs from the models in society that were available to them. These include households, synagogues, associations, philosophical schools, and mystery religions. An early contribution to these comparisons was Meeks who compared the communities to households, voluntary organizations, synagogues, and philosophical or rhetorical schools.[14] A full-length comparison of various institutions is Richard Ascough's *What Are They Saying About the Formation of Pauline Churches*? In this book, he compares the early Christian communities to synagogues, philosophical schools, ancient mystery religions, and voluntary organizations.[15] Edward Adams provides an update on Meeks' work by reviewing selected scholars who have advanced the study of these models since Meeks' original work.[16] In addition to these studies, there are numerous monograph-length studies of each of the social institutions that these authors compare. For the purpose of this study, I briefly describe the features of the social institutions that scholars have noted are similar to the Christian communities in the

---

14. Meeks, *The First Urban Christians*, 74–84.
15. Ascough, *What Are They Saying*, xx.
16. Adams, "First-Century Models," 68–78.

first century. I focus on households, synagogues, associations, philosophical schools, and mystery religions in this section.

Households

Scholars of first-century Christian communities have focused on three aspects of the domestic unit: household, family, and siblings. Many times, the terms household and family are used synonymously in scholarship; others make a distinction. Anthropologists make a distinction between household (those who share production and consumption activities) and family (those related by birth or marriage). Households may be made up of both consanguineal and affinal kin as well as nonrelated members, such as in Greco-Roman households in which slaves, freemen, and other types of personnel were connected to a house.[17] In many cultures, there is a preference for one type of household makeup, but in most cultures, there is a variety of household types depending on the financial status and life cycle of the household. For the purpose of this discussion, I distinguish between scholarship that puts priority on the production and consumption unit (the household) and those that discuss the characteristics of kinship. In this section, I discuss studies on household and reserve discussion on kinship for a later section.

The assertion that the early church met in private homes is neither a new development nor one of controversy within studies of the first-century Christian communities. As Robert Gehring notes, "On one point nearly all NT scholars presently agree: early Christians met almost exclusively in the homes of individual members of the congregations."[18] Gehring, Bradley Blue, and others argue that the communities met in homes initially built for private domestic use and were then modified for specific assembly use.[19] Although there is a consensus on the use of houses, the significance of the household to the formation, practice, and leadership of the early Christian community is debated.[20]

Most scholars also agree on the importance of the household to society and economy in the ancient world.[21] The household was the main production and consumption unit within the larger society and provided ties for the individual within the broader society. As Gehring explains,

17. Garnsey and Saller, *The Roman Empire*, 127.

18. Gehring, *House Church and Mission*, 1.

19. Blue, "Acts and the House Church," 119–222; Gehring, *House Church and Mission*, 291; Meeks, *The First Urban Christians*, 75.

20. Adams, *The Earliest Christian Meeting Places*, 10. Adams argues that houses may not have been as extensive or exclusive as venues for early Christian meetings.

21. Goodman, *The Roman World*, 17.

"This small 'oikos of fellowship' provided a basic building block for the entire society. It was from this point outward that individuals entered relationships with one another, building the polis and, with that, the entire political system."[22] The household provided members with a sense of identity and belonging within society as a whole.

Just as the household provided the building block for Greco-Roman society, the household also served as the building block for the early Christian community.[23] Blue argues that although the gospel was proclaimed in public, the life of Christian communities took place in private.[24] The household provided an immediately available means by which people were converted and assimilated within the early Christian community. It also provided a ready means in which a unique identity could be formed—as well as the economic means—through the hospitality of the house owner to support the reinforcement of identity through private worship and meals. Ekkehard Stegemann and Wolfgang Stegemann note, "The significance of household for the recruitment of members and for the solidarity of the social relations within the community cannot be overestimated."[25]

Gehring argues that households were essential for the mission outreach of the early church. He observes that Jesus instructed his own disciples to use houses when he sent them out and notes that households were the natural unit for conversion. Gehring also asserts that using private homes allowed the early Christians to develop distinctly Christian worship and fellowship from the earliest days, which allowed a unique identity to develop through distinctive Christian practices: teaching of the word, the practice of Christian prayer, and effective *koinonia* fellowship. The household also provided a training ground for koinonia and a showplace to witness to outsiders the uniqueness of Christian fellowship.[26] He notes the impact of this fellowship for the missional outreach of the early church: "The missional expansion of the gospel was due not so much to the mission-strategic initiatives of individuals as to the powerful attractiveness of the Christian community actively practicing koinonia fellowship."[27]

There is no consensus on the role that the house owner played in the leadership and organization of the early church. E. A. Judge argues that one of the attributes of Greco-Roman households was a common cult;

22. Gehring, *House Church and Mission*, 17.
23. Klauck, *Hausgemeinde und Hauskirch*, 17.
24. Blue, "Acts and the House Church," 121.
25. Stegemann and Stegemann, *The Jesus Movement*, 279.
26. Gehring, *House Church and Mission*, 294–95.
27. Gehring, *House Church and Mission*, 94.

therefore, the conversion of the head of household was one way a new cult was introduced in new areas.[28] The conversion of the head of household led to the conversion of the whole household, which included family members, slaves, and visiting clients. Because a whole household was converted and met in the house in which it was established, not only was the head of household the host for the congregation, but many scholars argue that the heads of households continued their role as *pater* to the members of their household in the congregation and functioned as the patron to the rest of the congregation. Philip Esler notes that members in the congregation continued to reflect the social realities, the roles, and values of households in their particular location.[29]

Early Christian communities reflect many of the characteristics of households. However, scholars note that many of the other cultural institutions in the broader first-century environment were also based on household. Although households were an important part of the growth and mission of the early Christian church, this model does not contribute significantly to an understanding of the unique practices of early Christianity and the unique values and relationships found among those in the Christian communities of the first century.

Synagogues

Scholars who focus on the relationship between early Christian communities and the institutions of broader society often focus on the continuity between its roots in Judaism and its development into its own movement.[30] James Burtchaell argues that it is impossible to understand primitive Christian worship unless it is in continuity with its Jewish roots.[31] He argues that often continuity is missed in studies of early Christianity while innovation is noticed. It is easier to examine differences in early Christian practices and make that the focal point of comparisons to social institutions in the broader Greco-Roman world. He argues:

> So much of what we might consider distinctively and creatively Christian was in fact an outgrowth of its Jewish antecedents: the blending of word and gesture into sacrament, the weekly holy days, the calendar of feasts, the daily rhythms of prayer, the

---

28. Judge, "The Social Pattern," 1–56.
29. Esler, "Imagery and Identity," 133–49.
30. Barker, "The Temple Roots," 29–51; Maher, "Knowing the Tree by Its Roots," 1–28; Taylor, "The Original Environment of Christianity," 214–24.
31. Burtchaell, *From Synagogue to Church*, 190.

reading of scriptures followed by exposition, the sacred meal, ritual initiation through baptism, anointing, the laying-on of hands: this and so much else derive from the Jewish tradition.[32]

Burtchaell has argued that comparison with Jewish practices is the most logical comparison for the practices and organization of early Christianity because it was rooted in Judaism. He also argues that since first-century Judaism was diverse and complex, it could accommodate Christianity in its broader spectrum of beliefs.[33] At its core, there are several features of early Christian beliefs that demonstrate its genealogical heritage from Judaism. Justin Taylor notes that many of early Christianity's sacraments and dogmas have their roots in Judaism.[34]

The organization of synagogue communities was also very similar to early Christian communities. Like voluntary associations, synagogue communities often met in private houses. According to Ascough, the use of the term synagogue refers not to a particular meeting place but rather the organized community of Jews who met to worship together.[35] The one activity that every synagogue sponsored was meetings of the assembly. Communities met for prayer, they had common meals, and scripture was read and expounded. The reading of scripture, according to Burtchaell, had a twofold effect. First, there developed a tradition of normative beliefs through a network of synagogues. Second, since Gentiles were allowed to attend, the teaching in the assembly tended to emphasize the ethical features of Judaism. This would have served to unite people in a standard doctrine that had universal themes rather than reinforce Jewish ethnicity and exclusivity.[36]

For the Jewish community, all communal life was found in the synagogue.[37] The synagogue was not only a prayer house, but it also functioned as a school and a meeting house.[38] In addition to the religious services, a synagogue fulfilled roles such as tax collection, care for the poor, hospitality to strangers, an archive for documents, and other aspects of community life. The synagogue also had jural responsibilities and dealt with violations of the Torah and litigation between members.[39] Additionally,

32. Burtchaell, *From Synagogue to Church*, 190.
33. Burtchaell, *From Synagogue to Church*, 190.
34. Taylor, "The Original Environment of Christianity," 223.
35. Ascough, *What Are They Saying*, 13.
36. Burtchaell, *From Synagogue to Church*, 221.
37. Ascough, *What Are They Saying*, 13.
38. Cohen, *From the Maccabees*, 106. See also Goodman, *Ancient Judaism and the Roman World*, 220.
39. Levine, *The Ancient Synagogue*, 395.

the synagogue tied the members into the broader community of Jews through the collection of temple taxes and their relationships with other synagogues in the community.[40]

Although there are many similarities between synagogues and early Christian communities, this comparison is not without problems. Several challenges arise from the discussion of the synagogue itself and the lack of clear evidence of the nature of its assembly and practices in the first century. Nor does the comparison to synagogue reflect the unique character of relationships of the early Christian communities within the group and with people of the broader society. It does not explain the inclusiveness of the early Christian communities and the diversity within the communities. Additionally, many of the attributes of the character and organization of the synagogue community could also reflect the practices of other associations that met in private homes.[41] Ascough in his study of associations and the synagogues subsumes synagogue under the matrix of religious voluntary associations to account for its similarities to early Christian communities.

Associations

Groups that have been termed voluntary associations in Greco-Roman society have a wide variety of functions, memberships, and activities. Because of the diversity of associations, they are defined broadly in literature. Ascough defines a voluntary association as "a group which a man (or woman) joins of his own free will and which accepts him of its free will, and this mutual acceptance creates certain obligations on both parties."[42] Philip Harland describes voluntary associations as "social groupings in antiquity that shared certain characteristics in common and that were often recognized as analogous groups by people and by government institutions."[43] In general, associations were small, unofficial groups that regularly met together to socialize and to honor a deity. Feasting and friendship was at the heart of an association under the protection or presence of a deity.[44]

There were various types of associations based on their function. The traditional taxonomy of associations were funerary associations that were organized to provide burial for their members, religious associations that worshiped particular deities, and professional associations that

---

40. Burtchaell, *From Synagogue to Church*, 216.
41. Richardson, "Early Synagogues as Collegia," 90.
42. Ascough, *What Are They Saying*, 74.
43. Harland, *Dynamics of Identity*, 26.
44. Harland, *Associations, Synagogues, and Congregations*, 59.

were formed around the interests of a particular occupation or guild.[45] More recent discussions about associations have noted the difficulty of distinguishing funerary associations from other associations since most associations were concerned with burial for their members. John Kloppenborg suggests a taxonomy of associations based on membership: domestic, professional, and cult.[46] However, Harland argues that since many utilized houses for communal use, membership often overlapped with the household. He suggests a more productive taxonomy based on networks of members: neighborhood, guild, and cultic.[47]

In Harland's taxonomy, the neighborhood associations were made up of those who lived or worked on a particular street. Neighborhoods acted cooperatively and sometimes became an ongoing group with socio-religious purposes similar to other associations.[48] The second type of association was formed from networks of relationships in a particular guild or occupation. Location influenced the membership within these associations, and there was pressure from fellow guild members to join. Many of these associations were socio-economically homogenous. Ascough notes that the social network of occupation could be a key factor in forming the ongoing life of some of the early Christian groups.[49] The third type of association was made up of people who worshipped the same deity or who had gone through initiation into a similar mystery. The membership in these associations was mixed in both status and gender. These associations were more difficult to differentiate because many of the associations were affiliated with a particular god.[50]

Despite differences in the social networks of membership, all types of associations had a variety of interconnected social, religious, and burial functions. Activities included eating and drinking together under the protection and presence of a deity with communal feasts held on a regular basis and on special occasions. Feasting to the gods, often with meals sponsored by a patron, was one of the ways that lower-class members were able to have better food on a regular basis.[51] Much of the activity of an association focused on honoring gods and goddesses in a variety of ways including prayer, singing,

---

45. Ascough, *Paul's Macedonian Associations*, 20–23; Kloppenborg, "Collegia and Thiasoi," 16–30.

46. Kloppenborg, "Collegia and Thiasoi," 23.

47. Harland, *Associations, Synagogues, and Congregations*, 25.

48. Harland, *Dynamics of Identity*, 33.

49. Harland, *Associations, Synagogues, and Congregations*, 40.

50. Harland, *Associations, Synagogues, and Congregations*, 45.

51. Alikin, *The Earliest History of the Christian Gathering*, 19.

and dancing. Members also acted cooperatively, or with the help of a benefactor, to provide public monuments that honored their deity and thus raised the status of their associations. In this way, members could achieve a measure of honor that they could not achieve on their own.[52]

Numerous scholars have noted the similarities between early Christian assemblies and Greco-Roman voluntary associations. Wayne McCready notes, "From both the insider and outsider perspective, Christian churches might reasonably be understood as a variant on numerous voluntary associations, since they shared many common features."[53] Judge concludes that early Christian groups were not distinguishable to outsiders from other associations.[54] There were several points of similarity to associations that contribute to this comparison. First, both had voluntary membership and operated with private support. There were regular meals and special feasts that required cooperation and hospitality for meetings and meals. Second, both early Christian assemblies and associations met in private houses in which the head of household provided the use of the space and sponsored meals. Third, each had members from both genders and across social classes and provided social interaction and a sense of fraternity among the membership. They could find both emotional security as well as financial support in times of need. Fourth, both first-century Christian communities and associations provided the burial and funerary expenses of their members. Finally, some associations and early Christian assemblies sought to honor a deity through various activities, prayer, song, and dance. They believed that these deities were present in their gatherings and offered protection, and many times these deities were considered founders of their assembly.[55]

However, despite these similarities, there were also a number of differences that distinguished the early Christian communities from associations. First-century Christian assemblies had exclusive claims for membership yet inclusive membership. Although the assemblies were open to everyone regardless of ethnicity, status, or gender, membership required exclusive worship of only one God and devotion to Christ. The early Christian communities also contrasted themselves with the broader society through their lifestyle and their claims of being new people in Christ. Another difference was that the degree of intimacy and solidarity in the early Christian communities was more intense than found in most associations. Scholars have noted

---

52. Harland, *Associations, Synagogues, and Congregations*, 97–101.

53. McCready, "Ekklesia and Voluntary Associations," 59–73.

54. Judge, "The Social Pattern," 31.

55. Alikin, *The Earliest History of the Christian Gathering*, 39. He also provides a chart of comparisons between associations and Christian communities.

the use of familial terminology among associations; however, it was not to the degree and frequency that the terms were used in early Christian communities.[56] Finally, there were commonalities and links between early Christian communities in different geographical and social settings that were not commonly found in associations. Despite the social, cultural, and geographic distance, early Christian communities shared similar beliefs and lifestyles.[57] Although the organization and activities of early Christian communities may be analogous to associations, there were distinct differences of lifestyle in their exclusive devotion to Christ and in the quality of interpersonal relationships important to insiders and noticed by outsiders.

Philosophical Schools

While there are several similarities between early Christian communities, synagogues, and associations, scholars have also noted that Christianity's emphasis on ethics echoes many of the same concerns as Greco-Roman philosophical schools in the first and second centuries. Some scholars have noted the similarity of Jesus' and Paul's lives and teachings to that of a Cynic.[58] Johan Thom notes that philosophical *topoi* would have been a part of Paul's cultural repertoire.[59] Paul's teachings have been compared to Epicurean and Stoic motifs and topoi.[60] Although many studies focus on the comparison between the rhetoric and values of philosophy and early Christian communities, S. K. Stowers argues there is a more fundamental reason why early philosophical schools are similar to the way of life and solidarity of early Christian communities. He proposes that the focal point of philosophical schools is what distinguishes them from other social institutions.[61]

Stowers proposes that the early Christian communities were similar to philosophical schools not because of specific motifs from particular philosophies but rather because of the very foundation of the teachings and actions themselves. He proposes that the commitment to one underlying "big idea" was at the heart of philosophies in the ancient world, and this one "big idea" demarcated each philosophy from others and provided the foundation for the way of life that the philosophy promoted. He argues that the

---

56. Hellerman, *The Ancient Church as Family*, 23.
57. Meeks, *The First Urban Christians*, 107–10.
58. Mack, *The Christian Myth*, 41–58.
59. Thom, "Paul and Popular Philosophy," 47–74.
60. Glad, *Paul and Philodemus*, 185–332; Huttunen, *Paul and Epictetus on Law*; Lee, *Paul, the Stoics, and the Body of Christ*, 103–200.
61. Stowers, "Does Pauline Christianity Resemble a Hellenistic Philosophy?" 94.

commitment to a central ideal is what made both ancient philosophies and early Christianity distinct and mutually exclusive. According to Stowers, the foundation of the Pauline construction of ultimate good was the mutually exclusive unity with God through life in Christ.[62]

Stowers also asserts that another similarity between early Christian assemblies and philosophical schools involved the reorientation an individual went through when they embraced the one central ideal of a new philosophy. Philosophy caused a critical reflection that changed one's motivations, desires, and needs, resulting in a tension between conventional life and a post-reflection life. He argues that this change in life created by embracing the one ideal might be called a conversion—or minimally, a reorientation—to how one conducted their life in the broader society. However, rather than a new ideal, early Christians reoriented their lives around the submission to a divine being, and he proposes that the commitment to these new ideals and practices gave rise to nontraditional and radical social formation. Stowers notes, "Economic and other 'ordinary' practices must be demoted and serve only purposes that are instrumental to the virtue, friendship and intellectual practices upon which the group is to focus."[63]

Although there are a number of similarities between philosophical schools and early Christianity, Stowers also notes several differences. First, philosophical schools referred to themselves as friends and associates while Pauline groups referred to one another as fictive kin, implying a greater solidarity of the group. He also notes that Pauline Christianity was not fully integrated and consistent. Paul's audience included both Jewish and Gentile believers who had different perspectives and ways of life. Finally, philosophies did not have specific rituals that were a part of the teachings and reinforced those teachings as Christianity did.[64]

Mystery Religions

Scholars have also noted similarities between the early Christian communities and mystery religions. The term mystery religion is somewhat ambiguous because of the variety and lack of clear boundaries in its identity and practice. The mysteries, according to Walter Burkert, "were initiation rituals of a voluntary, personal, and secret character that aimed at a change of mind through the experience of the sacred."[65] Generally the mysteries

---

62. Stowers, "Does Pauline Christianity," 94.
63. Stowers, "Does Pauline Christianity," 95.
64. Stowers, "Does Pauline Christianity," 100.
65. Burkert, *Ancient Mystery Cults*, 11.

were foreign cults that flourished alongside official public religions during the Greco-Roman period.[66] Mysteries varied in their myths, rites, and practices, depending on the historical development and originating myths. Some of the ancient Greek mysteries practiced in Roman antiquity were the Eleusian mysteries, Andanian mysteries, and the mysteries of Dionysus. Those of Middle Eastern origin that were widespread included the mysteries of Isis, the Great Mother or Cybele, and Mithras.[67] Like many of the mysteries, they were agricultural-based religions that used the cycle of the agricultural year to depict the life cycle. However, there were also considerable differences in the practices of the cults.[68]

Walter Burkert notes that there were three forms of practices among mysteries that lent themselves to comparison with early Christian communities. First, mysteries that organized as associations had many of the same organizational features of the early Christian communities. Those mysteries had a place to meet and often had common property. Individuals also contributed their interest, time, and wealth to participation in the mystery. Like other associations, they may have had a patron who sponsored the mystery in their house and provided meals.[69] Mysteries that organized as associations also had common rites, meals, and sacrifices that were practiced together.[70]

Other scholars note the similarity in the religious practices of mysteries. Similar to early Christianity, mysteries were a personal form of religion. Individuals were autonomous, and it was a personal choice to enter into the mystery or to leave the mystery. Just as early Christianity had baptism as an initiation rite, so mysteries also had initiations to enter the brotherhood.[71] Like associations, most mysteries' membership included both sexes and a range of social classes. In practice, they were egalitarian and participatory.[72]

---

66. Scheid, *An Introduction to Roman Religion*, 89. Turcan, *The Cults of the Roman Empire,* notes the distinction between *religio* (national and authentic) and *superstitio* (exotic and suspect), 10.

67. For more details on the spread of cults in the Roman Empire and for attitudes and practices of the cults, see Turcan, *The Cults of the Roman Empire*; Warrior, *Roman Religion*; MacMullen, *Paganism in the Roman Empire*; and Ando, *The Matters of the Gods.*

68. Turcan, *The Cults of the Roman Empire*, 7.

69. MacMullen, *Paganism in the Roman Empire*, 122.

70. Burkert, *Ancient Mystery Cults*, 32.

71. Scheid, *An Introduction to Roman Religion*, 187.

72. Ascough, *What Are They Saying*, 72.

They often provided a common identity and community when traditional institutions failed to provide these.[73]

Finally, both early Christianity and mysteries offered an experience of the divine and salvation. Many of the mysteries were rooted in the cycle of nature and the rites aimed to secure fertility, security, and the promise of an afterlife.[74] Adherents experienced closeness to the divine through their participation in the mystery. Several of the originating myths have stories of a dying and risen deity, and through initiation, people could participate in this death and life.[75] As Geza Vermes argues about Pauline teaching, "Paul's powerful, brilliant and poetic imagination creates a magnificent drama, echoing the mystery cults of his age, in which through baptism into the death and resurrection of Jesus Christ the new initiate enters into communion with the great act of salvation by means of which the New Adam removes from human nature that universal sinfulness which resulted from the fall of the first man in the garden of Eden."[76]

Despite the similarities between mysteries and early Christian communities, there were a number of differences. Burkert notes that mysteries lacked the organization, solidarity, and cohesion that were found in Christianity and Judaism, nor was there a message of a triumph over death or of any new revelation.[77] Although individuals went through initiations together, there was no social obligation between members on a daily basis, nor did the relationships of equality extend outside the ritual spaces of the religion. Participating in mystery rites with others would not necessarily imply social obligation to fellow adherents as was expressed in Christianity.

Summary

Although there are some similarities between early Christian communities and models from the social environment that have been used to explain the uniqueness of relationships and way of life of early Christian communities, they do not explain what made early Christianity unique and why early Christianity attracted people into its communities. Specifically these models do not explain elements of the early Christian lifestyles that were radically different from their social environment.

73. Turcan, *The Cults of the Roman Empire*, 17.
74. Ascough, *What Are They Saying*, 52.
75. Theissen, *The Religion of the Earliest Churches*, 59.
76. Vermes, *The Religion of Jesus the Jew*, 212.
77. Scheid, *An Introduction to Roman Religions*, 188.

Additionally, there was considerable variation in the social compositions, geographic locations, and religious environment of the various Pauline communities. Early Christian communities in different locations may have been based on different models for their development and practice. While models from the environment can provide insight into particular practices and organization of assemblies, not one model "fits all."[78]

Models of Early Christianity that Critique Structure

The studies described above have sought to explain the similarities of early Christian communities with social institutions within the first-century social milieu in which Christianity was formed. These have focused on the organization, leadership, and the practices of the communities. However, these studies do not explain the uniqueness of the teachings, behaviors, and relationships within these communities, particularly the apparent rejection of traditional values and status relationships in the Jewish and Greco-Roman social institutions.

There are three elements of early Christian communities that are not explained by these models. First was the rejection of traditional values found in the honor and shame culture of the Greco-Roman world. Several scholars have noted that one of the unique teachings of the early Christian communities was that of status reversal, which involved both a renunciation of the display of one's status and a corresponding elevation of those with low statuses.[79] As Judge explains, "The abandonment of self-cultivation and self-preservation as an ideal person is coupled in Paul with the rejection of another notable aspect of classical ethics, their emphasis on status—the concern with relationship between people and the appropriate ordering of them as between greater and lesser."[80] C. Marvin Pate notes that new relationships within the community take priority over social status.[81]

S. Scott Bartchy also discusses this type of reversal of values by highlighting Paul's response to the Corinthians as a reversal in the honor/shame code of the Greco-Roman society. He notes, "Paul sharply contrasted his view of himself with his sense of these Corinthians' self-perception. 'We are fools for Christ, but you are so wise in Christ! We are weak, but you are strong!

---

78. Adams, "First-Century Models for Paul's Churches," 78.

79. Kee, *Who Are the People of God?*, 59; Theissen, *The Religion of the Earliest Churches*, 71–79.

80. Judge, "St. Paul as a Radical Critic of Society," 105.

81. Pate, *The End of the Age Has Come*, 201.

You are honored, we are dishonored!'"[82] Bartchy contrasts traditional ancient Mediterranean values and Paul's "new creation" as well as those same values in Jesus' teachings in order to demonstrate the continuity of the reversal of status and values between Jesus and Pauline traditions.[83]

Another defining feature of the early Christian communities was their solidarity and inclusiveness. Scholars have noted that one of the reasons for the rapid spread of the church was its solidarity and the quality of relationships within the community. Meeks recognized the solidarity of the early church: "The regular use of terms like brother and sister, the emphasis on mutual love, and epistolary reminders of the initiatory experience—all reinforce the *communitas* of the early Christian groups. Implicitly they contrast the group's life with that of 'the world,' the closed structure hierarchical society of the Greco-Roman city."[84] David deSilva also notes the solidarity and inclusiveness of the early Christian communities. He comments that baptism symbolized "the initiates' renunciation of former allegiances, affiliation and relations."[85] He argues that baptism left them marginal in relationship to society, and they entered into a place of liminality: "The rest of the believer's life is therefore to be lived out in this liminal state, in the margins between status in this world and the next."[86]

A third feature of early Christian communities was the apocalyptic worldview found in the teachings of the early Christian communities. These include end-time speculations that create a dualism: history divided into two ages, the present age and a new age that will define a different life in the future. This dualism also includes a dualism in the human race—spirit of truth and spirit of falsehood—as well as a dualism in the supernatural realm—God versus evil. There is also the characteristic of determinism in apocalyptic teachings, which is the idea that history is determined by God. Another characteristic is the eschatological woes. These are signs that indicate the end time is near, including the arrival of a savior figure who prepares the way for the final judgment of the wicked and the righteous.[87] According to George Ladd, this apocalyptic eschatology had a dynamic concept of a God who is receptively active in history and a hope that God will deliver the righteous in a future in-breaking in history.[88] Several scholars have argued

---

82. Bartchy, "When I Am Weak," 49–60.
83. Bartchy, *Call No Man Father*, 11–14.
84. Meeks, *The First Urban Christians*, 89.
85. DeSilva, *Honor, Patronage, Kinship & Purity*, 305.
86. DeSilva, *Honor, Patronage, Kinship & Purity*, 311.
87. Aune et al., "Apocalypticism," 45–58.
88. Ladd, *The Presence of the Future*, 101.

that apocalypticism in this sense is a comprehensive worldview that is reflected in the early Christian communities.[89]

Scholars have noted that many of these characteristics are similar to other types of protest movements formed out of dissatisfaction with the present social milieu or as a protest against the values and status-based relationships of the institutions of their social structure. The models most frequently used for comparisons are those that take into account the relationships and worldview of the community as well as the circumstances in which such groups would arise. In this section, I examine studies that compare early Christian communities to the sociological models of sect, millenarian group, and charismatic group. These seek to account for the unique teachings, values, and relationships of the early Christian communities as well as their boundary maintenance and responses to the broader Greco-Roman world. For the purposes of this discussion, I have limited my discussion to representative samples of studies that have sought to use comprehensive social science frameworks to explain the characteristics of the ancient Christian communities and their continuity or discontinuity over time. Since there is overlap between these models, I critique their contribution at the end of this section.

Sectarian Movements

Some scholars have sought to explain the formation, beliefs, way of life, and interaction with the broader Jewish and Greco-Roman society by comparing the characteristics of early Christian communities with the sociological study of sectarian movements. Some of these studies have traced the development of first-century Christian communities as sects from their start as Jewish reform movements of Jewish factions, while others have traced the development of early Christian communities from sects to their institutionalization.[90]

Robin Scroggs was one of the first to compare the characteristics of early Christian communities to sects. Following the work of Max Weber and Ernst Troeltsch on sects, he examines seven sectarian characteristics found in early Christian communities. The first is that a sect begins as a

---

89. Sim, *Apocalyptic Eschatology,* 1; Collins, *The Apocalyptic Imagination,* 267; Donfried, *Paul, Thessalonica, and Early Christianity,* 14; Jewett, *The Thessalonian Correspondence,* viii; Matlock, *Unveiling the Apocalyptic Paul,* 99.

90. Esler, *Community and Gospel,* 46–70; Elliott, "The Jewish Messianic Movement," 75–95. Both look at the process of the separation of the Christian communities from Judaism. MacDonald, *The Pauline Churches,* starts by assuming Pauline communities were sects and then traces their institutionalization.

protest movement. A sectarian movement is in reaction to the economic and societal repression within a particular class or society. He argues that the economic picture of early Palestine was bleak, and there was an extreme gap between the very rich minority and the very poor majority. Additionally, many people were outcast from their own society, rejected by both their religious leaders and wealthy landowners.[91]

The second characteristic is that sects reject the view of reality taken for granted by the establishment. In Scroggs' analysis, this involved the rejection by the early Christian communities of the traditional values because of their own rejection from society. They experienced hostility within their families, from the Pharisees, from the official establishment, from the wealthy, and from the intellectuals.[92]

A third characteristic of sects is that they are egalitarian. Scroggs asserts that rejection and hostility can explain the formation of the sect but not the continuation. There also needs to be a quality of life that provides fulfillment for the members. He notes that once a person was initiated into the early Christian community, the status and roles of the outside world no longer mattered since all were equal before God. The fourth characteristic is that within the sect they expected love and acceptance. Scroggs comments, "The believer realizes a quality of life within the community he has not found outside, apparently not even within his own family."[93]

Scroggs only discusses the last three characteristics briefly because to him, they are self-evident. Sects, like the early Christian communities, are voluntary associations: individuals must make a choice and are often initiated into the community. A sect commands total commitment from its members to remain distinct from the world. The way of life of the early Christian community required a socially different lifestyle from the values and ethics of the broader Greco-Roman world. And finally, some sects are Adventist. The apocalyptic nature of the early communities is well-documented. There was an imminent expectation of the final in-breaking of God's kingdom.[94] In another study, Esler also notes twenty-one features of early Christian communities that manifest salient sectarian qualities.[95]

While some scholars focus on sect formation arising out of dissatisfaction with social and economic conditions, other scholars have focused on the process of differentiation and disassociation of the early Christian

---

91. Scroggs, "The Earliest Christian Communities," 77.
92. Scroggs, "The Earliest Christian Communities," 81.
93. Scroggs, "The Earliest Christian Communities," 87.
94. Scroggs, "The Earliest Christian Communities," 88.
95. Esler, *Community and Gospel*, 79.

communities from its Jewish roots. Esler notes that sects are formed when members of a religious movement become dissatisfied with it, and they form a distinct outlook in response to the perceived deficiency. He argues that as long as the sect is part of the broader society, it remains a reform movement.[96] John Elliott observes that in Jesus' lifetime, the followers of Jesus still operated within the boundaries of Judaism as a Jewish faction, and only after the death of Jesus did the community take on the characteristics of a sect. He lists several steps of the gradual process in which the early Christian community took on the character and strategies of a Jewish sect. They include an increase in the intensity of social tension and ideological difference between the Jesus faction and the broader Jewish community, including recognizing Jesus as messiah, Torah observance, temple allegiance, and purity rules.[97]

Esler argues that one of the features that created a rupture between the Jesus movement and the broader Jewish society was the solidarity that united Jew and Gentile and allowed table fellowship between the two. This became a central feature of early Christian sectarian identity.[98] Elliot notes the final stage in the community's sectarian identity is that they distinguished themselves from the parent body.[99] As Esler notes, they called themselves *ekklesia*, not synagogue. They assumed a social identity that was distinct from Judaism.[100]

Millenarian Movements

Those who compare early Christian communities to millenarian movements focus on the apocalyptic teachings of early Christianity.[101] This framework is particularly attractive since apocalyptic ideas run through the writings of the New Testament; and according to Stephen Cook, "Groups that hold apocalyptic worldviews have definite sociological family

---

96. Esler, *The First Christians*, 13.
97. Elliott, "The Jewish Messianic Movement," 76.
98. Esler, *The First Christians*, 71.
99. Elliott, "The Jewish Messianic Movement," 90.
100. Esler, *The First Christians*, 54.
101. Duling, "Millennialism," 187. He states that the term millennialism comes from Revelation. Here he is referring to the idea of a 1,000-year reign of Christ, or chiliasm. I am differentiating millennialism (a worldview) from millenarianism (the social movement). I agree that many groups that have millennial and/or apocalyptic worldviews have characteristics that are similar to the millenarian groups studied by social scientists.

resemblances."[102] Several scholars have focused on the apocalyptic teaching and millennial hope as the reason for the early Christian communities' ethics, solidarity, and identity.[103] While the orientation is the future, it contributes to the behavior of the group in the present. John Collins argues that eschatological expectations shaped the behavior of early Christian communities. Several other scholars have noted that apocalyptic eschatology provided the framework for the Christian communities' values and behavior.[104] They sold their goods because they believed that the time was short as they waited for the eschatological judgment.[105]

David Sim notes that one of the functions of apocalypticism is that it provides hope for minority groups in crisis because of its imminent reversal of present circumstances.[106] Stephen Hunt describes this: "The dream of the Christian millenarian has been an enduring one throughout the centuries."[107] He argues that one of the most striking features of early Christianity is that it "heralds the return of the Messiah, the end of the world as we know it, and the dawning of the everlasting Kingdom of God."[108] Additionally, many of the key characteristics of millenarian groups are found in early Christian communities.[109] According to Kenneth Burridge, millenarian movements involve the adoption of "new assumptions, a new redemptive model, a new politico-economic framework, a new mode of measure of a man, a new integrity, a new community."[110]

John Gager's book, *Kingdom and Community,* also examines early Christianity from the perspective of a new world in the making, one of Burridge's descriptions of millenarian movements. In the first part of his description, Gager notes that the early Christian movement meets I. C. Jarvie's

102. Cook, *Prophecy and Apocalypticism,* 24.

103. There is also confusion over the terms related to apocalypse, apocalyptic worldview, and/or apocalypticism. Apocalypticism is a worldview that centers on "God's imminent intervention into human history in a decisive manner to save his people and punish their enemies by destroying the existing fallen cosmic order and by restoring or recreating the cosmos in its original pristine perfection." Aune et al., "Apocalypticism," 46.

104. Burridge, *Imitating Jesus*; Crossan, *The Birth of Christianity*; Luckensmeyer, *The Eschatology of First Thessalonians.*

105. Collins, *The Apocalyptic Imagination,* 267.

106. Sim, *Apocalyptic Eschatology in the Gospel of Matthew,* 63–64.

107. Hunt, "Introduction," 1–11.

108. Hunt, "Introduction," 3.

109. Ehrman, *Jesus: Apocalyptic Prophet,* 123; St. Clair, *Millenarian Movements,* 49–74; Jewett, *The Thessalonian Correspondence,* 174; Meeks, *The First Urban Christians,* 171–183.

110. Burridge, *New Heavens, New Earth,* 13.

four basic traits of millenarian cults: (1) the promise of heaven on earth, (2) the overthrow or reversal of the present social order, (3) a terrific release of emotion, (4) a brief lifespan of the movement. However, Gager adds a fifth defining feature—that of the central role of a messianic, prophetic, or charismatic leader.[111] He continues his comparisons by noting that many of the followers of Jesus were disenfranchised, which is often a characteristic of members of millenarian groups.

He also argues that the communal nature of millenarian groups describes the early Christian community as well as ethical teaching, which he claims is another important feature of the millenarian movements. He notes that the lack of leadership as well as the use of sibling terms in the early church reflects a state of anti-structure that is characteristic of all millenarian groups. He further demonstrates that the missionary impulse of the early church was a demonstration of the cognitive dissonance that occurs when the millenarian hope fades with the delay of the arrival of the kingdom.

Charismatic Groups

Closely related to studies focusing on the formation and character of early Christian communities as sects or millenarian groups are studies comparing the early Christian communities to charismatic groups. These studies focus on the effect of a charismatic leader (in this case, Jesus) on the formation of a group. In many cases, sectarian, millenarian, and charismatic groups overlap in characteristics and response to the world. However, in studies of charismatic groups, the focus has shifted from an apocalyptic worldview or social and economic repression as the cause of group formation to the leaders of the movements themselves and how they affect the formation and continuation of the group. Gager asserts that an important factor to consider in the success of early Christianity is that Jesus as a charismatic leader was a powerful attraction. He comments, "S. Angus and K. S. Latourette recognize that communal organization played an important role in ensuring Christianity's survival, but they insist that the underlying cause of its success was the figure of Jesus himself."[112]

Researchers have argued that Jesus had many of the characteristics of a charismatic leader. Vermes argues that the representation of Jesus in the gospel is a man who has supernatural abilities derived from immediate contact with God.[113] Although he places Jesus in the context of other

---

111. Gager, *Kingdom and Commmunity,* 21.
112. Gager, *Kingdom and Community,* 141.
113. Vermes, *The Religion of Jesus the Jew,* 69.

Jewish charismatic holy men, Vermes does not discuss their followers or the movements they started. Stegemann and Stegemann also describe Jesus as a charismatic leader and discuss the transition of the early church from a personally charismatic movement to an institutionally charismatic movement.[114] They claim that the charismatic makeup of the Jesus movement contributed to its expansion and increasing deviance from mainstream Judaism after Jesus' death.

Bengt Holmberg, updating Weber's thesis, uses the idea of charismatic authority to examine the extent to which a charismatic form of authority functioned within the early Christian communities. He follows the process of institutionalization by which the early church developed from a charismatic movement to one that was characterized by "routinization of Charisma."[115] Holmberg claims that no person in the primitive church had pure charismatic authority after Jesus' death. However, he claims that the church can still be considered a charismatic movement because the early Christian communities believed that they were not entirely separated from their leader. They believed that he was still alive. Holmberg also argues that the primitive community was a charismatic movement after Jesus' death because the behavior of the group was typical of a charismatic group. It still believed in an imminent end and salvation and practiced radical social morality concerning divorce and the role of women.[116]

Although Holmberg continues his discussion on what he describes as the institutionalization of the authority of the early church, he does not discuss the changes in the community and the relationships that they had with one another as the structure of the early church changes. He comments that Paul's message is not altogether revolutionary because he does not demand that early Christians give up property, nor does he attack class differences or slavery. Furthermore, he notes that Paul uses material from traditional Jewish and philosophical sources to encourage his communities to begin conforming to the broader social world.[117] Anthony Blasi also notes the transition of the communities in the writings of Ignatius. Blasi argues that in these writings there is evidence of a transformation of personal charisma to "office charisma." He argues that it is comparable to the "divine rights of kings" and that this office charisma provided for the continuation of religious entities beyond the time of the founding figures.[118]

---

114. Stegemann and Stegemann, *The Jesus Movement*, 193.
115. Holmberg, *Paul and Power*, 149.
116. Holmberg, *Paul and Power*, 150–51.
117. Holmberg, *Paul and Power*, 156.
118. Blasi, "Office of Charisma in Early Christian Ephesus," 245–56.

Critique

There have been several who have critiqued the use of the concept of sect and millenarian movements as a model to understand early Christian communities. One critique is that if early Christianity started as a revitalization movement of Judaism or a faction of Judaism that became a sect, it readily moved outside of Judaism.[119] Nor do these models explain the continuity of beliefs between the Jewish-based congregations and the congregations with a Gentile majority.

Another critique of the three models is the relationships these types of groups have to the broader society. Most sects (millenarian groups as a subset of sect) tend to have strong boundary maintenance, but the early Christian groups were open to outsiders. Another aspect of sects and millenarian groups is that they are protests against their present situations, and they separate themselves from the institutions and values that they are protesting. While early Christian communities sought to live a way of life that was different from the behaviors and values of the society around them, they were to do so while participating within that society. The early Christians were to practice this new way of living not in a separate society but within the structures of broader society. J. Paul Sampley explains, "Paul does not urge believers to flee the world, they are to live this new life, the new creation, in the midst of this age that is headed for its condemnation."[120] Early Christians were relating to one another in accordance to this new social reality while at the same time participating in the structures of the broader society. J. Brian Tucker argues that they were to be Christ followers within the context of living in the Roman first-century world.[121] They were to be a contrast society within the broader structures of society. A feature of Pauline rhetoric is his encouragement for members of his communities to remain in their present situations while participating in a new way of life.[122]

An additional difference is that although an apocalyptic worldview was at the heart of Pauline teaching, early Christian apocalyptic thought was distinct from other contemporary apocalyptic understandings.[123] In most contemporary first-century apocalyptic worldviews, history and redemption were opposed to one another—human history must be destroyed and the faithful transferred to a new heaven and a new earth. However, in early

---

119. Theissen, *The Religion of the Earliest Churches*, 27.
120. Sampley, *Walking Between the Times*, 14.
121. Tucker, *Remain in Your Calling*, 50.
122. Holmberg, *Paul and Power*, 89.
123. Sampley, *Walking Between the Times*, 9.

Christian apocalyptic thought, the two eons coexist; God had already broken into history, and they saw themselves presently living in the new age.[124] Collins notes, "The primary difference between early Christian and Jewish apocalypticism in the first-century CE was that Christians believed that the messiah had already come and that the first fruits of the resurrection had taken place."[125] Jesus did promise heaven on earth in the form of the coming of the Kingdom of God, but the self-understanding of the early Christian community was that they were already living in it.

Finally, a central distinction between millenarian groups and early Christian communities is that their new way of living was based on the perceived reality that they were already living in a new age as changed people, not just preparing for a final judgment as in millenarian groups. In contrast to the millenarian view, John Dominic Crossan concludes that Jesus' teachings about the rule of God reflected a present reality for the followers of Jesus: "The Kingdom of God, in other words, the will of God for this earth was here and now."[126] Crossan's term for Jesus' radical teaching is "eschatological ethics." He uses the term eschatology not in the sense of a future reality but in the sense of a timeless, divine reality: "Eschatology is divine reality. It is a fundamental negation of the present world's normalcy based on some transcendental mandate."[127] In Pauline communities, the new way of living was possible because of what God had done through Christ.[128] In his writing, this identity of being in-Christ was an entry into a new way of life while living in the present.[129]

A final feature of the early Christian communities is that these values did not change even as the structure of the church became more institutionalized and hierarchical in the second and third centuries. Scholars who have compared early Christian communities to millenarian movements have argued that the early Christian communities went through a process of institutionalization in which the early values and relationships were replaced with institutional values and norms. However, the unique relationships and values of the early Christian communities continued during the institutionalization of the church throughout the second and third centuries.

---

124. Sampley, *Walking between the Times*, 14.
125. Collins, *The Apocalyptic Imagination*, 268.
126. Crossan, *The Historical Jesus*, 282.
127. Crossan, *The Historical Jesus*, 282.
128. Burridge, *Imitating Jesus*, 101.
129. Tucker, *Remain in Your Calling*, 120.

Early Christian Communities Despite Changing Structure

One of the features of early Christian communities is that they maintained their values and quality of relationships despite the changing institutional structure of the church. The two studies discussed in this section demonstrate the longevity of the central values of early Christian communities well into the writings of the second and third centuries. The first study demonstrates how the relationship of siblinghood and family defined the relationships in the communities and continued through the third century. The second study demonstrates how the early Christian community remained a contrast society through the third century. Both of these demonstrate the continuation of central values and relationships through the changing structure of the church. They also demonstrate that early Christian communities lived out these unique values while engaging in the structures of their broader society rather than apart from them.

Fictive or Surrogate Kin

Several scholars have focused on the solidary that was expressed by the early Christian community with the use of sibling terminology.[130] Those who argue that the kinship terminology reflected the quality of relationships in early Christian communities contend that the relations between siblings in the Greco-Roman world were based on love rather than structural obligations.[131] They argue that the use of sibling terms signified the depth of relationship that was to be reflected in the early Christian community.[132] While competiveness and rivalry marked relationships outside the family in Greco-Roman culture, true disciples were brothers and sisters who did not seek to be "the greatest in the kingdom" or lord over others.[133] The relations between siblings were to be marked by harmony, solidarity, and cooperation.[134] According to Karl Sandnes, siblings had a strong loyalty to one another and sought to protect the family honor. There was mutual honor and respect among siblings.[135]

---

130. Monograph treatments include: Burke, *Family Matters*; Aasgaard, *My Beloved Brothers and Sisters!*; Schäfer, *Gemeinde als 'Brüdershaft'*; Hellerman, *The Ancient Church as Family*.

131. Aasgaard, "Brothers and Sisters in the Faith," 285–317.

132. Burke, *Family Matters*, 15.

133. Finlay, *The Family Metaphor in Jesus' Teaching*, xiv.

134. Aasgaard, *My Beloved Brothers and Sisters!*, 107.

135. Sandnes, "Equality within Patriarchal Structures," 130–63.

Joseph Hellerman has used the idea of family, particularly the model of patrilineal kin groups, to account for the solidarity and behavior of early Christians though the third century. Hellerman argues that the family metaphor was a significant metaphor that Jesus used to provide a model of behavior among his followers. He concludes, "Indeed, the family metaphor becomes even more pervasive in the Pauline communities of the mid-first-century C.E., a situation best explained by assuming a similar practice by the early Galilean communities of Jesus' followers."[136] He reasons that this solidarity continued with the post-apostolic writers as far as Cyprian who continued to use sibling kinship terminology in their writings. Bartchy also notes that Paul used sibling kinship terms in all of the non-disputed Pauline letters, indicating the importance of the metaphor for Christian life in the early communities of followers of Christ.[137]

However, some claim that this mutuality did not reflect radical equality between statuses in the early Christian communities. Karl Sandnes argues that the use of sibling terminology reflected an increasing equality within the structures of the Greco-Roman household. He contends that sibling relationships did not create a reversal or abandonment of the statuses, but rather "they demonstrate that egalitarian relationships were emerging within patriarchal household structures."[138] He maintains that Paul's letter to Philemon demonstrated this emerging but "not yet" equality: "A new relationship based on equality is in the making. Paul's letter to Philemon bears witness to the model of eschatological equality among believers, but it also testifies that this model did not easily overcome the inherited structures of society, not even within a Christian household."[139] Whether or not sibling terminology reflected an egalitarian structure within the church, the use of sibling terminology reflected the types of relationships that early Christians were to have with one another.

Contrast Society

Several scholars assert that the eschatological worldview and behavior provide continuity between Jesus' teaching of the Kingdom of God, Pauline communities, and post-apostolic communities. Lohfink's study on *Jesus and Community* examines the new way of life as a contrast society from Jesus' teaching through Origen. Lohfink argues that Jesus' preaching about the

---

136. Hellerman, *The Ancient Church as Family*, 71.
137. Bartchy, "The Apostle Paul's Vision of a Society of Siblings," 68–78.
138. Sandnes, "Equality within Patriarchal Structures," 163.
139. Sandnes, "Equality within Patriarchal Structures," 163.

Kingdom of God was not about a future promise but rather that his miracles demonstrated that the in-breaking of God's rule had already come. He further argues that not only were miracles closely connected to the in-breaking of the reign of God, but they were connected to those whom God was going to reign over. Lohfink states, "Inseparable from the eschatological horizon of Jesus' miracles is their relationship to the community; they served in the restoration of the people of God, among whom, in the eschatological age of salvation, no disease is permitted."[140]

According to Lohfink, further evidence of the eschatological reality of the presence of the reign of God was the Spirit of God. He writes, "The Spirit is described as God's gift to the eschatological community and even as God's power which truly creates eschatological Israel."[141] He argues that the presence of the reign of God was inseparable from the community and was inseparable from the radical way of life that was a part of the reign of God. Although Paul rarely mentions the Kingdom of God, the Spirit of God permeated his letters and defined membership and behavior of the early Christian community. This radical way of life included nonviolence, elimination of social barriers, brother/sister love, and renunciation of domination. In all ways, it was what Lohfink calls a contrast society.[142] Lohfink traces this self-understanding through the writings of post-apostolic writers.

The contribution that Lohfink and others make to the discussion of the self-understanding of the early Christian communities is that the basis of the unique relationships and way of life of early Christian communities was the worldview that the reign of God was a present reality as evidenced by the presence of the Spirit of God. Secondly, Lohfink also ties the reign of God to the people of God. The new way of life of the reign of God was to be practiced as a community. A third contribution is that they demonstrate that this contrast society was to be lived out in the broader Greco-Roman society, not as a separate society. And finally, Lohfink demonstrates that the new way of life was continuous from Jesus' teaching through the post-apostolic period, despite the developing hierarchy in the structure of the church.

A Way Forward

A brief survey of some of the models used to explain the expansion of Christianity and the quality of life in the communities of Christ followers demonstrates that while some models explain some aspects of the early

---

140. Lohfink, *Jesus and Community*, 82.
141. Lohfink, *Jesus and Community*, 82.
142. Lohfink, *Jesus and Community*, 122.

Christian communities, they do not explain others. Some explain behaviors that were congruent with other social movements in the socio-cultural contexts in which the communities were located and showed similarities in the behavior and beliefs of the early Christians. Others demonstrate the contrast in values of the Christ-following communities and strong cohesiveness but do not explain the relationship of the communities to the broader society, nor do they adequately represent some of the changes that occurred over time or the continuity in many of the characteristics of the church until Constantine.

Although comparing the early Christian communities to the structures of society is helpful in explaining some aspects of the communities, such comparisons fail to explain other aspects. The models of these three foci often conflict in trying to explain the quality of life of the people in the early movement and their relationship to the broader Greco-Roman world. They also often require additional models to understand the relationships between the teachings of Jesus, Paul, and the post-Pauline writers, which have led some to conclude that there is no continuity among them.[143]

Rather than an either/or, reflecting a social institution or living a radically new way in contrast to society, I propose that both were true. What I argue in this book is that the early Christ followers lived a new kind of way in their old social structures. Christ followers did not live apart from local institutions and broader society, but they lived a new way in their social structures. They were in the world, but not of the world.

What I introduce in this book is an anthropological framework that provides a heuristic framework tying all three of these foci into a single comprehensive model for understanding the beliefs, behavior, and self-understanding of the early Christian communities and their relationship with their broader society.[144] For this purpose I use Victor Turner's concepts of structure, anti-structure, and liminality from his study of rites of passage to provide a model in which all three foci are integrated into a single heuristic framework. This framework integrates the apocalyptic beliefs of the early communities and their unique values and relationships as well as the variations of the characteristics of local communities. Furthermore, it also explains the continuation of these values through the changing institutionalization of Christian communities.

In the next chapter, I will introduce this heuristic framework discussing Turner's concepts and terminology in detail. In the following chapters, I

---

143. See Käsemann, "Blind Alleys in the Jesus of History Controversy," 23–65; Bultmann, "Jesus and Paul," 83–201.

144. Turner, *The Ritual Process*, 97–177; Turner, *The Forest of Symbols*, 93–111.

use this framework and concepts to discuss Jesus and his teaching about the Kingdom of God. I then discuss the early communities of Christ followers as depicted in the book of Acts, Pauline writings, and second- and third-century Christian writings. I conclude by using this framework to discuss the change in the church under Constantine.

Chapter 2

Liminality, Structure, and Anti-Structure

THE HEURISTIC FRAMEWORK I introduce in this chapter is developed from the anthropological study of rites of passages in anthropology. I do not propose that the concepts and terms used in this theoretical framework were emic to the context of the early Christian communities. Nor do I suggest that writers of the primary documents of the early church reflected upon their experience in the terms that I use throughout this book. Rather I use this framework as a heuristic device in which I am able to organize what might otherwise be irrelevant and unconnected data into a consistent framework to note similar patterns of behavior and consistencies in values about social relationships in the writings of the early church. This allows a consistent framework in which to examine disparate data from different early communities and writers. This is particularly useful in comparing the characteristics of communities of Christ followers across time, geography, and cultures. I use it in this book to compare the characteristics of communities of Christ followers in different social contexts through the first three centuries of the early Christian movement.

I develop the framework using concepts from the three phases found in rites of passage that were first articulated by Arnold Van Gennep and then expanded by Victor Turner. In particular I will use Turner's concepts of liminality, structure, and anti-structure for examining beliefs, behavior, and self-understanding of the relationships within the early Christian communities and their relationship within their broader society.[1] My thesis is that unlike other groups in liminality who experience liminal relationships apart from the broader society, the unique characteristic of the early Christian community is that they were to live in liminal relationships within the structures of

---

1. Turner, *The Ritual Process*, 97–177; Turner, *The Forest of Symbols*, 93–111.

society and extend those relationships to people outside the community and as a result transform the structures of society.

In this chapter I briefly discuss the concepts from the study of rites of passage and develop the heuristic framework for this study using Turner's concepts of liminality structure and anti-structure from his study of rites of passage. I then discuss how I use the concepts in the study of the early Christian communities and define the terms I use throughout this book.

Rites of Passage

Van Gennep was the first to discuss the three-fold pattern of rites of passages.[2] He noted that when people were making a transition from one status to another—such as child to adult, single to married, living to dead—there were similar rituals that marked these transitions. As he studied these transitions cross-culturally, he found that many cultures had similar ceremonies that marked these transitions. They varied in detail, but these rites of passages had three stages: separation, liminality, and reincorporation.[3]

According to Van Gennep, all societies have distinct and separate social groups, and in some societies, the differences between these social groupings are more accentuated. He argues that within these groups there are social distinctions, for instance between nobility and peasant, adult and child, between occupations, and between territory of residence.[4] To move between these social distinctions even within groups, there are certain preparations needed to make those transitions. Some do not require ceremonies, and others do. For some of the passages, all that is needed to make the transition are the economic or intellectual resources. However, for some passages, particularly for passages between sacred and profane, societies require a ceremony for the passage, and in particular, there needs to be a period of transition.[5] The purpose of these ceremonies is to allow an individual to "pass from one well-defined position to another equally well-defined position."[6] He elaborates these ideas as follows:

> Transitions from group to group and from one social situation to the next are looked on as implicit in the very fact of existence, so that a man's life comes to be made up of a succession of stages with similar ends and beginnings: birth, social puberty,

---

2. Van Gennep, *The Rites of Passage*.
3. Van Gennep, *The Rites of Passage*, 11.
4. Van Gennep, *The Rites of Passage*, 3.
5. Van Gennep, *The Rites of Passage*, 1.
6. Van Gennep, *The Rites of Passage*, 3.

marriage, fatherhood, advancement to a higher class, occupational specialization, and death. For every one of these events there are ceremonies whose essential purpose is to enable the individual to pass from one defined position to another which is equally well defined.[7]

Rites of passage are often performed for those who are not only crossing into new social roles but also are crossing barriers between statuses—for instance between life and death or profane and sacred. He notes that many rites of passage correspond to social and biological changes in the roles of individuals from child to manhood or womanhood, but this is not always the case. Many societies have rites of passage for particular life-cycle events: birth of children, initiations, marriages, deaths, and other events that change the status and roles of people within society, such as from woman to mother, child to adult, single to married, married to widow. Rites of passage are also performed when people enter new roles with ritual and social power (such as kings, religious practitioners, or other offices) or when individuals enter a new social group (such as a secret society or ritual group).

He also observes that rites of passage have three different subcategories of rituals within the rite of passage: rites of separation (pre-liminal), transition rites (liminal), and rites of incorporation (post-liminal). He observes that these three subcategories are not developed to the same degree in every rite of passage. For instance, he notes that rites of separation may be more important in funerals and rites of incorporation in marriage. Transition rites also may be extended, such as in pregnancy, or they also may be minimal, such as in remarriage in some communities.[8] He noted that during rites of transition people learn about their new roles while transitioning into a new role. It is often during these liminal periods that rituals are performed giving the person their new status. For instance, in the transition period of birth, the umbilical cord is cut; the newborn is washed, purified, and finally named before she or he is reincorporated into society as a living human. Often in the liminal period, the novice is considered socially dead (having been removed from childhood) and is instructed in tribal law, given general education of their new responsibility, and taught the traditional myths that reinforce their new status in the structure of their society.[9] They are taught to live differently than they had in their previous status as a child. The final stage of rites of passage is the reincorporation of the individual into society with a new status and all of the privileges and obligations that are part of

---

7. Van Gennep, *The Rites of Passage*, 3.
8. Van Gennep, *The Rites of Passage*, 11.
9. Van Gennep, *The Rites of Passage*, 81.

that status. Once the threshold is crossed into the new structural status, the person cannot go back to their old status; they have died to their former status and live in the new.[10] The identification of a transitional period or liminal period in rites of passage is one of Van Gennep's major contributions to the study of rites of passage.

Liminality, Structure and Anti-Structure

Turner continued the study on rites of passage and further defined and refined the concepts in Van Gennep's study. He also began expanding the concepts of structure, anti-structure, liminality, and communitas to other periods of time when people experience relationships outside of their structural statuses. He particularly refined and elaborated the relationships within liminality and extended these studies to areas outside the context of rites of passage. These concepts form the foundation of the heuristic framework that I use in this study and are further discussed below.

Structure

To understand the concepts of liminality and anti-structure, we must first understand what Turner means by structure. Structure, according to Turner, is the "working arrangements of society and the process of ordering of actors and relations in reference to given social ends."[11] He considers structure to be the more "stable aspects of relationships that are based on the perception of the rules and meanings of the social roles."[12] The relational ties based on these statuses are those organized by social bonds of caste, class, rank, or positions. According to Turner, these create a hierarchical system in which there is "political-legal and economic separation between people in terms of more and less."[13] In structure, people behave in ways clearly defined by norms and standards based on position or status.

Status is one's social position within structure. There are usually corporate rights based on status which define a person's access to resources and people from whom resources can be obtained. Relationships in structure are based on these social positions or statuses and the rights and obligations required by these statuses. In structure, status limits and divides people into categories and are reinforced by the values of society. People in structure

---

10. Van Gennep, *The Rites of Passage*, 74–75.
11. Turner, *Dramas, Fields, and Metaphors*, 34.
12. Turner, *Dramas, Fields, and Metaphors*, 34.
13. Turner, *The Ritual Process*, 96.

relate to one another based on these social categories: Jew/Gentile, rich/poor, male/female, slave/free. We create the social "other" by defining who is in and who is out of our group based on their status.

Liminality and Anti-Structure

In contrast to structure, anti-structure is used to describe the characteristics of people within the liminal phase of rites of passage.[14] Although the liminal phase was first associated with rites of passage, Turner extended the definition to more protracted liminal phases and a broader range of conditions.[15] He follows Van Gennep in describing society as that of a "structure of positions" and liminality as an "interstructural situation."[16] He also broadened the conditions by which an individual enters liminality by expanding the definition of liminality as a phase between two states. These states were not necessarily statuses in social structure, but they could also include physical transitions between two places or could be applied to an "ecological, physical, mental or emotional condition in which a person or group may find themselves at a particular time."[17]

Turner uses liminality to describe the middle stage in Van Gennep's three stages in rites of passage, but he also included symbolic behavior indicating the transitions between states outside of rites as well. For Turner, separation that begins the entrance to a liminal period does not have to be a physical separation but can also be a symbolic separation. He describes it as consisting of "symbolic behavior signifying the detachment of the individual or group from a fixed point in the social structure or set of cultural conditions (a state)."[18] In his definition, liminality defines a person who passes through the transitory or liminal phase where they have none of the characteristics of the former state, nor the characteristics of the future state before achieving a new state.

People in the liminal phase are characterized by what Turner calls anti-structure in contrast to structure.[19] During liminality in a rite of passage, the characteristics of the people are ambiguous because they are no longer considered to have their former status, or at least they no longer have the roles that are required of their status in structure. Tom Driver notes, "Liminality

---

14. Turner, *Dramas, Fields and Metaphors*, 50.
15. Turner, *The Forest of Symbols*, 93–111.
16. Turner, *The Forest of Symbols*, 93.
17. Turner, *The Forest of Symbols*, 93.
18. Turner, *The Forest of Symbols*, 93.
19. Turner, *Dramas, Fields and Metaphors*, 45.

is characterized by a deconstructing in relationship to what Turner calls social structure."[20] Turner describes it as passing "through a cultural realm which has few or none of the obligations or attributes of the past or coming status."[21] In structure, there are rights and obligations that are defined by statuses within structure; people are expected to perform and behave in culturally prescribed ways. In liminality, people escape these structural categories. They often exhibit properties of homogeneity, equality, anonymity. According to Turner, they are betwixt and between the positions in the structural arrangements of society.[22] Status reversal is also characteristic of liminality. Within this state, servants become masters, rulers are portrayed as slaves, rich are poor, and poor are rich.

Turner observed that although their status is ambiguous and indeterminate, they are richly represented by symbols in the liminal state. They are often likened to being dead, in the womb, invisible, bisexual, or in a wilderness.[23] They are represented as having nothing that is of value in structure; they have no status, property, insignia, rank, or role in a kinship system.[24] Turner listed the contrast between the characteristics of structure and anti-structure in the following chart (Table 1).

Table 1. Turner's Characteristics of Structure and Anti-Structure[25]

Structure	Anti-structure
State	Transition
Partiality	Totality
Heterogeneity	Homogeneity
Structure	Communitas
Inequality	Equality
Systems of nomenclature	Anonymity
Property	Absence of property
Status	Absence of status

20. Driver, *The Magic of Ritual*, 158.
21. Turner, *The Forest of Symbols*, 93.
22. Turner, *The Forest of Symbols*, 93.
23. Turner, *The Forest of Symbols*, 93.
24. Turner, *The Ritual Process*, 95.
25. Turner, *The Ritual Process*, 106.

Structure	Anti-structure
Distinctions of clothing	Nakedness/uniform clothing
Sexuality	Sexual continence
Maximization of sex distinctions	Minimization of sex distinctions
Distinctions of rank	Absences of rank
Just pride of possession	Humility
Care for personal appearance	Disregard for personal appearance
Distinctions of wealth	No distinctions of wealth
Selfishness	Unselfishness
Secularity	Sacredness
Technical instruction	Sacred instruction
Speech	Silence
Kinship rights and obligations	Suspension of kinship rights and obligations
Intermittent reference to mystical powers	Continuous reference to mystical powers
Sagacity	Foolishness
Complexity	Simplicity
Avoidance of pain and suffering	Acceptance of pain and suffering
Degrees of autonomy	Heteronomy

According to Turner, people in liminality are structurally invisible because they do not fit into structurally determined categories and classifications. They are betwixt and between, neither here nor there.[26] Turner describes them as transitional beings, and they are defined by names and symbols indicating their liminal state such as initiate, neophyte, and in other cases as prophet or trickster.[27] The person in liminality is classified, yet not classified, and is often referred to as dead or at least not a part of a structural category. The person in liminality is seen as dangerous and mystical to those outside liminality. They are nearly always and everywhere regarded as polluting to those who have not been inoculated against them.[28]

26. Turner, *The Ritual Process*, 95.
27. Turner, *The Forest of Symbols*, 96.
28. Turner, *The Forest of Symbols*, 7.

Additionally, there is an absence of status markers such as property. In structure, property rights are often linked with structural distinctions; those without access to property are often reduced to the same status level.[29] There is a close connection between structure and property whether it is privately or corporately owned. This is why millenarian movements often try to abolish property or at least create a common pool. When the prophecy fails, often the movement is institutionalized, acquires property, and becomes structure.[30]

Quality of Relationships in Liminality—Communitas

Another important aspect of liminality is the quality of relationships of people in the liminal phase. Those going through transition together relate to each other not according to structured roles of the broader society but as people without structural differentiation. The formal social obligations of structure are exchanged for personal relationships.[31] They form what Turner has referred to as *communitas*, which he defines as a "mode of relationship" that involves "the whole person in relation to other whole human beings."[32] Turner describes it as the "instant mutuality when each person experiences the being of another" without the structural social differentiations.[33] He summarizes, "Communitas is when individuals although differing in mental and physical endowment are nevertheless regarded as equal in terms of shared humanity."[34]

Communitas stresses personal relationships rather than social obligations of status. It describes the intense comradeship and egalitarianism in liminality in which personal structural distinctions of rank and status disappear.[35] Oftentimes it blends lowliness, sacredness, homogeneity, and comradeship. Communitas is often expressed by people referring to each other as siblings or comrades of one another. Edith Turner comments, "When communitas appears, one is conscious that it overrides psychological and sociological constructs."[36] Communitas is thus seeing people as people, not

---

29. Turner, *The Ritual Process*, 109, 111.
30. Turner, *The Ritual Process*, 129.
31. Turner, *The Ritual Process*, 112.
32. Turner, *The Ritual Process*, 127.
33. Turner, *The Ritual Process*, 136.
34. Turner, *The Ritual Process*, 177.
35. Turner, *The Ritual Process*, 93.
36. Turner, *Communitas*, 3.

through status but relating in ways that are directed toward others that treat each person as just that, a person. She states it elegantly:

> Communitas is thus a gift from liminality. The state of being betwixt and between. During this time, people find each other to be just ordinary people after all, not the anxious prestige-seeking holders of jobs and positions they often seem to be ... People see each other face to face."[37]

Not only does communitas break down the barriers between people that status creates, but Edith Turner argues that communitas must be distinguished from solidarity. She argues that solidarity is the bond between individuals who are collectively in opposition to another group. By its very nature, solidarity creates boundaries of in-group and out-group opposition.[38] However, in communitas, this barrier is also broken down so that there is no in-group or out-group; there is only the other person. Whereas structure divides people based on status, communitas can cross ethnic boundaries as well as national and tribal divisions. Communitas is inclusive; there are no distinctions between we/they, in-group/out-group, higher/lower, betters/menials.[39] Communitas naturally proselytizes because the drive of inclusivity is to make the other become part of communitas.[40] In communitas, the "other" becomes the "we."

Liminality in the Study of Early Christianity

A number of scholars have used the concept of liminality in their discussion of the qualities of early Christian communities, particularly in Pauline writings. There are three main characteristics that have been applied in the study of Christianity. The first is the ritual of baptism as a rite separating people from their former state into a new state. Luke Timothy Johnson briefly discusses liminality and communitas in his discussion of ritual imprinting and initiation in early Christianity in the context of the religious experience of the Greco-Roman world. He applies Turner's analysis to the Pauline communities in Phrygia and argues that those who had gone through baptism as a ritual of separation understood themselves to be in transition and thus absent of status: there is neither male nor female, Jew

---

37. Turner, *Communitas*, 4.
38. Turner, *Communitas*, 5.
39. Turner, *From Ritual to Theater*, 51.
40. Turner, *From Ritual to Theater*, 51.

nor Greek, slave nor free.[41] Johnson goes on to explain that Paul advocated for a state of permanent liminality. The early Christian communities were to "live according to the principles of communitas established by the gift of the Spirit: egalitarianism, mutual upbuilding, and the positive fruits of the Spirit."[42] He argues that through the Spirit, early Christians entered into a full inheritance of God's promise through Christ. Through baptism they entered into the death and resurrection of Christ and now live in communitas, solidarity, and without status.[43]

DeSilva compares Paul's interpretation of baptism to a rite of separation.[44] He observes that Paul frequently used death to interpret the significance of baptism; initiates died to former life and to their past groups and associations. In baptism, the initiates renounced their former allegiances, affiliations, and relationships but were not separated from them. However, they also emerged as part of a new community. He also notes an important difference from Turner's model in that the rite of passage transitions an individual from one status in society to a new status within the same structure.[45] He argues however, that in baptism the rite of transition was from one society to another society. Baptism, he continues, "leaves the Christian marginal with regard to the unbelieving society, with no real place in that society any more, and assimilates them to a new community."[46]

DeSilva also notes that early Christians were living between the home they left behind and the kingdom that they were receiving.[47] They entered a place of liminality. Within liminality, they lived in a community that was marked by cooperation, sharing, and equality. He comments that they were called to embrace this liminal status, not seeking to return to their former state but rather to press on until they received honor as God's children at their reintegration into the city of God. He also argues that the life of those in early Christian communities was a state of permanent liminality. He explains, "The rest of the believer's life is therefore to be lived out in this liminal state, in the margins between status in this world and the next."[48]

The most comprehensive study using the concept of liminality for examining early Christianity is *Die liminale Theologie des Paulus* by Christian

---

41. Johnson, *Religious Experience in Earliest Christianity*, 100.
42. Johnson, *Religious Experience in Earliest Christianity*, 101.
43. Johnson, *Religious Experience in Earliest Christianity*, 101.
44. deSilva, *Honor, Patronage, Kinship & Purity*, 305.
45. deSilva, *Honor, Patronage, Kinship & Purity*, 306.
46. deSilva, *Honor, Patronage, Kinship & Purity*, 306.
47. deSilva, *Honor, Patronage, Kinship & Purity*, 311.
48. deSilva, *Honor, Patronage, Kinship & Purity*, 311.

Strecker. He notes that baptism functioned as initiation into a permanent liminality. The initiate experienced separation from their old status under the dominion of sin and death, and a new life was possible. However, Strecker argues that the baptism-initiated process was not yet completed until the *parousia*. He also notes that another aspect of baptism was that it took place in the context of community and was the incorporation into an in-Christ community. He argues that Paul emphasized the specific identity of the Lord's Supper as an expression of ritual communitas in which social differences in rank were negated.[49]

The second aspect of Turner's study of early Christian communities is the characteristics of communitas relationships within the Christian communities. According to Strecker, this was the communitas-shaped community (horizontal communitas) that is reflected in Pauline writing about the diverse people who were part of the one body of Christ. Strecker argues that for Turner, communitas is the social implementation of liminality.[50] He asserts that the common meal became a symbol of the one body and of the change in social relations that had taken place.[51] He notes that Paul emphasized the specific identity of the Lord's Supper as an expression of ritual communitas in which social differences in rank were negated.[52]

Strecker also discusses the anti-structural characteristics of people in liminality found in the Pauline communities, including the minimizing of ethnic, social, and gender distinctions.[53] He observes that there was a reversal of conventional attributes of honor and shame in Pauline communities. He argues that Paul understood himself as an embodiment of this "reversed world in which the traditional distributions of honor and shame are invalidated."[54] Meeks also attributes that the kinship language used in Pauline communities and the strong language of affection is similar to communitas, the liminal phase in rites of passage. He proposes that the use of brother and sister, the emphasis on mutual love, and the prominent role given to the Spirit all reinforce the communitas of early Christian communities, contrasting with the hierarchal structure of Greco-Roman society.[55]

The third characteristic that is discussed in regards to early Christian communities is the interaction or the dialectic relationship between the

---

49. Strecker, *Die liminale Theologie des Paulus*, 333.
50. Strecker, *Die liminale Theologie des Paulus*, 300.
51. Strecker, *Die liminale Theologie des Paulus*, 319.
52. Strecker, *Die liminale Theologie des Paulus*, 333.
53. Strecker, *Die liminale Theologie des Paulus*, 271.
54. Strecker, *Die liminale Theologie des Paulus*, 289.
55. Meeks, *The First Urban Christians*, 87.

anti-structural relationships of the Christian communities and the structural status and obligations of their place in the broader society. Meeks explains that the dialectic between structure and anti-structure appears in the tension of Pauline writings.[56] For instance, even though Paul writes that there is neither male nor female, he also writes that they must have different hairstyles and dress in accordance with the cultural standards of the day.[57]

Strecker has a different view of the interaction of the dialectic relationship between the structural and anti-structural teachings in Pauline writings. He agrees that within the Pauline communities there was minimization of ethnic, social, and gender differences. Strecker asserts that Paul's writing in Galatians 3:28, "That there is neither Jew nor Greek, free nor slave, male nor female," must be seen in the context of baptism and the initiation within the in-Christ community. However, he argues that the seemingly conservative writings of Paul about slavery and women are what Turner describes as normative communitas. In normative communitas, there is an inherent conflict between the innovative, spontaneous relationships of communitas and the normative role and statuses of structure. Strecker contends that what scholars have termed Paul's more conservative writings where he seems to support structural roles are reflections of this dialectic between structure and anti-structure in normative communitas. According to Strecker, Pauline writings reflect the argument that spontaneous communitas must have structure and standardized roles to survive. It is an inevitable process that occurs when a community seeks to maintain communitas on a more or less permanent basis.[58] However, he argues along with Turner that even with structure, groups based on normative communitas are fundamentally different from others in society. As Turner notes, "Something of 'freedom,' 'liberation,' or 'love' adheres to normative communitas."[59]

There are many points of agreement between scholars who have used Turner's framework and how I use it in this study. Early Christian communities were living between the times, or more correctly, they were living in a new age while still living in the past. Baptism was a rite of separation from the old life and initiation into the liminal early Christian community. The studies also are consistent in their understanding of the relationships within the communities as anti-structural communitas. This understanding explains status renouncement and status reversal as well as explains the qualities of solidarity and the use of sibling terminology within the communities.

---

56. Meeks, *The First Urban Christians*, 89.
57. Meeks, *The First Urban Christians*, 88.
58. Turner, *From Ritual to Theater*, 49.
59. Turner, *From Ritual to Theater*, 49.

Strecker's work has much to commend in his extended study of the liminal theology of Paul. He provides a much needed discussion on the meaning of symbols and their relationship to the liminal life in Christ. He touches upon several areas of Pauline descriptions of life in Christ and the meaning of the death of Christ, particularly as an example to believers.

I build on these studies and further refine the use of Victor Turner's concepts. What I propose is using his concepts of liminality, structure, and anti-structure as a heuristic framework for understanding the beliefs, behavior, and self-understanding of the early Christian communities and their relationship with their broader society.[60] Unlike other groups in liminality that experience communitas in rites of passage separated from the broader society and that ultimately reinforce structure, I argue that the unique characteristic of the early Christian community is that they were to live in communitas within the structures of society and extend those relationships to people outside the community and as a result transform the structures of society.

I propose that the early Christian self-understanding was that they were living in liminality. They believed that a new age had begun as marked by the arrival of the messiah and the Spirit. However, they considered themselves to be living concurrently in two ages: "this present age" and the "the age to come," the culmination of time with the return of Christ. They understood themselves to be living "betwixt and between," in the "already-not yet" of the culmination of God's promise. The reign of God promised by Christ had been partially realized, and they were participating in it, but they were also still living in their present age. This liminal time can be diagrammed as follows (Figure 1):

---

60. Turner, *The Ritual Process*, 97–177; *The Forest of Symbols*, 93–111.

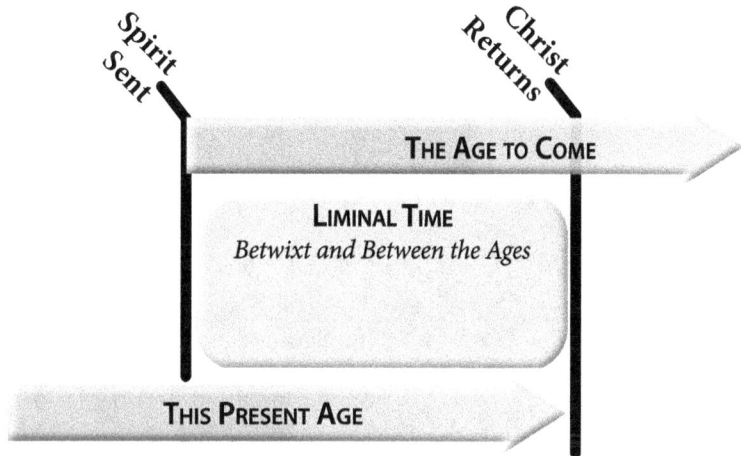

Figure 1. Temporal Dimension of Inaugurated Eschatology

Second, I argue that members of early Christian communities entered into communitas not by separation from society but by the indwelling of the Spirit. Their separation from their old statuses was marked not by separation from structure but by the Spirit. It was through the Spirit that they entered into communitas, "the unstructured egalitarian bonds between people."[61] I also contend that they did not lose their statuses; the Christian communities were not homogenous. However, their relationships with each other were anti-structural, based on individual human beings rather than status and roles within society (structure). Because liminality of early Christian communities was not defined structurally as in normal rites of passage, but temporally, people were to live in communitas and in anti-structural relationships within the structures of society. This is diagrammed below (Figure 2):

---

61. Bowie, *The Anthropology of Religion*, 168.

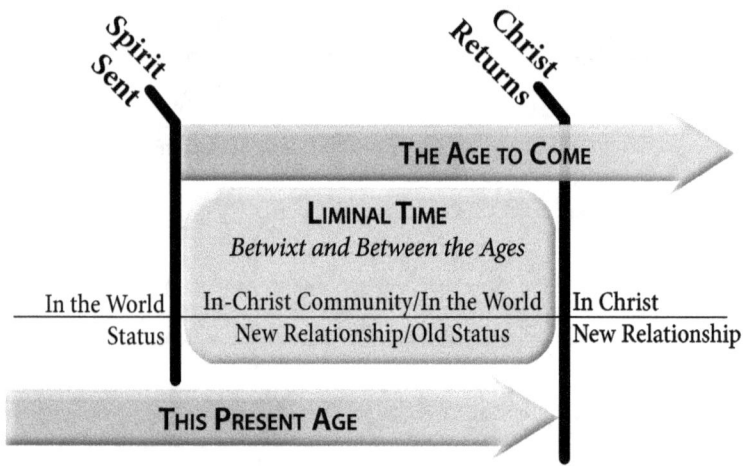

Figure 2. Social Dimension of Inaugurated Eschatology

A third important aspect of this framework is the relationship between the Christian communities and the broader society. Unlike many communities that experience communitas-like relationships that are separated from society, the early Christian communities were to extend these same types of relationships to people who were outside their communities.

In this book, I advance the discussion using Turner's model in two distinct ways. First, I provide a different analysis of the relationship between communitas and structure. I argue that the early Christians were living in a permanent liminality, but instead of living in it on the margin as Meeks suggests or as normative communitas as Strecker suggests, I argue that the early Christian communities lived communitas within the statuses and structures of society.

Another way I advance the conversation is in the breadth of my research. Whereas most studies have focused on Pauline communities, I demonstrate that the same features found in the Pauline tradition are found in the Jesus tradition and the post-Pauline traditions in pre-Constantine Christian communities. Since the early Christian communities themselves did not use the terms liminality, communitas, structure, and anti-structure, I provide the parameters for structure and anti-structure in my examination of the primary sources and their relationship to their social context as noted below.

Defining Structure and Anti-Structure in Early Christianity

There are many ways of defining characteristics of structure and anti-structure in the early Christian communities. Gerd Theissen suggested that there were two distinctive characteristics or values of primitive Christianity that defined their interpersonal relationships: renunciation of status and love for neighbor. I use these two concepts to frame anti-structural characteristics that are the focus of this study because both of these unique values are characteristics of Turner's description of communitas and contrast sharply with key values in Greco-Roman and Jewish societies.[62] The first, humility, undermines the structural positions in society, and the other, love, undermines the boundaries that separate people from one another or the limits of inclusion. In this study, I use the characteristics of humility, love, sibling, and mutuality to define the anti-structural characteristics of relationships of the early Christian communities.

For the purposes of the study, I address two dimensions of status in the ancient world to define structure. The first, honor, reinforces the vertical hierarchical relationships of status in the ancient world. The second are those values that reinforce horizontal exclusivity, which is often expressed in maintenance of ethnic boundaries. Both of these divide and separate people based on status. The first divides people based on hierarchy; the second divides people based on ethnicity. In the next section, I discuss how these structural concepts were expressed, understood, and maintained in the context of the first-century Greco-Roman and Palestinian world of the early communities of Christ followers.

Honor and Status in the Greco-Roman World

Scholars have noted that status reversal was one of the characteristics of early Christian communities. Theissen explains that there were three terms that indicated the basic value of status reversal. The broadest term was humility. This, he argues, was an internal attitude towards one's status. Those of lower status accepted their position, and those of higher status did not seek to use their position for their own benefit. The second characteristic is the renunciation of status. The renunciation of status involved not displaying the markers of status, not using their status to exploit or coerce others, nor giving up the marker of status completely. The third aspect of status reversal was the corresponding elevation of people of low

---

62. Theissen, *The Religion of the Earliest Churches*, 64.

status to a higher status, or giving greater value to lower status markers rather than high status markers.[63]

Several others have noted status reversal. Judge highlights the lack of interest in status in Pauline writings. According to Judge, status provided the appropriate ordering of individuals between greater and lesser, especially as he notes, "In classical society the quest for status itself was a noble goal of human endeavor, and admired even by those who were exploited by it."[64] The abandonment of the pursuit of status in Pauline communities was notable. Harrison notes that because people in Paul's communities were raised in the ethical values of honor and shame, Paul had to address it in his writing.[65] The reversal of status is observed in studies of Pauline writings as well as the teachings of Jesus. Several scholars note that this abandonment of status or the reversal of status was an important feature of early Christian communities. Pate also notes that new relationships take priority over social status.[66] Lohfink traces reversal of status from Jesus's teaching of the reign of God through third-century literature.[67] However, to understand the uniqueness of this reversal of status in early primitive Christianity and how it marked communitas and anti-structure, a contrast must be made with the importance of status and honor in the Greco-Roman world. In order to discuss status and honor, it is important to define how I am using terms in relationship to others across disciplines.

The first is status, one's position in society. Often status is confused with the social prestige or social ranking society gives to or perceives about a specific social status. Social status can be either achieved (that which is earned, such as doctor, lawyer, or president) or ascribed (social positions into which one is born or over which one has no control, such as gender, kin, rank, caste, and age). Social roles are those expectations, obligations, and privileges which society assigns to a particular status. For instance, the status of university professor requires the individual to fill the roles of teacher, advisor, researcher, and university community member. Performance evaluations and promotions are based on how well faculty members are able to fulfill these multiple roles and expectations. Although some statuses are human universals (e.g., age, gender, father/mother), the social roles assigned are always cultural. Social roles are derived from the social expectations and attitudes of social status. Although there are cross-cultural

---

63. Theissen, *The Religion of the Earliest Churches*, 63–71.
64. Judge, "St. Paul as a Radical Critic of Society," 105.
65. Harrison, "Paul and Ancient Civic Ethics," 75–118.
66. Pate, *The End of the Age Has Come*, 200.
67. Lohfink, *Jesus and Community*.

similarities in patterning of roles, there is ample evidence of the variety of roles for similar statuses.

In the Greco-Roman world, status described the legal position of an individual with respect to both a person's household and the broader civic community. These social statuses were often defined by birth, wealth, sex, formal education, citizenship, civic position, occupation, learned skill, birthplace, and residence.[68] These statuses were ordered in a hierarchical structure and were the basic organizing principle of Greco-Roman society. As Meyer Reinhold notes, "The hierarchical structure of Roman society evolved into one of the most hierarchical and status conscious social orders in mankind's history."[69] The ordering of these statuses was based on the value that society placed on them: what society considered honorable or prestigious. In other words, some statuses were considered more honorable or prestigious than others. The terms prestige, honor, and dignity are often used interchangeably in literature to express the public valuation of persons and their statuses.

What was prestigious and honorable, what made a person honorable, was defined by the very persons to whom honor meant the most—the upper classes.[70] The upper class in Roman society was a social position that was largely determined by birth since many in this position inherited their status. The most prestigious or honorable were the three orders of the social elite: the senators, equestrians, and the decurions.[71] Each of these had a wealth requirement, but not all acquisition of wealth was honorable. Inherited wealth and wealth from land ownership were considered the appropriate forms of wealth for these orders.[72] The rest of the free population was less stratified, but there were divisions based on other criteria. Some of these divisions include citizen versus noncitizen, free versus slave, and head of household versus those under a head of household.[73] Other factors such as occupation, residence, family name, and birthplace could also provide status among the non-elite. Power, education, and moral stature added prestige to their holders. J. E. Lendon notes that it was not just the material elements that marked a person as honorable. It was also the subtle markers: signs of a proper upbringing and education, an aristocratic manner

---

68. Hopkins, "Elite Mobility in the Roman Empire," 12–26.
69. Reinhold, "Usurption of Status and Status Symbols," 275–302.
70. Hellerman, *Reconstructing Honor in Roman Philippi*, 56.
71. Garnsey and Saller, *The Roman Empire*, 112–13.
72. Lendon, *Empire of Honor*, 37.
73. Garnsey and Saller, *The Roman Empire*, 118–23.

in accent words, and posture and bearing.[74] In reality, what made persons honorable was public opinion of them and their actions. This sense of hierarchy ruled public behavior.[75]

Status also came with expected roles and behaviors. Honor was gained or lost depending on how a person fulfilled societal expectation for a social status. According to Lendon, moral excellence was an important component of prestige.[76] The greater a man's honor, the more his behavior was scrutinized. Behavior must uphold the honor of a person's family.[77] In addition to moral excellence, persons of high standing were expected to exhibit generosity to the Roman populace. They were expected to host games and feasts and build public buildings. According to Lendon, honor could not be defined by one attribute or status; it was perceived as a quality a person had that set the person apart and above his peers.[78] All the qualities (birth, wealth, office, education, etc.) added together were required for honor.[79]

Since a person's honor or prestige was a matter of social perception, status was always on display, and behavior was public. Holding public office, one's appropriate education and speech, and one's moral stature lent prestige to the holder.[80] Status was also advertised in various ways. As Peter Garnsey and Richard Saller explain, "Since status was linked to wealth, it could be demonstrated through conspicuous consumption. For Seneca, a fine mansion and numerous slaves were among the foremost symbols commonly associated with wealth and status."[81] Status was on public display in the political and religious life of the city. Prestige and honor was demonstrated by the number of clients, the seating at public affairs, and the quality of food and drink that was served to a person at banquets.[82] Status was declared through clothing, the golden ring of the equestrian, purple outer clothing of the wealthy, the toga for the citizen, and through public benefaction.[83] Hellerman summarizes this public display of honor:

> The Romans were remarkably creative in devising ways to publicly proclaim and reinforce the social hierarchy. Clothing,

---

74. Lendon, *Empire of Honor*, 37.
75. MacMullen, *Roman Social Relations*, 112.
76. Lendon, *Empire of Honor*, 41.
77. Lendon, *Empire of Honor*, 37.
78. Lendon, *Empire of Honor*, 47.
79. Lendon, *Empire of Honor*, 42.
80. Garnsey and Saller, *The Roman Empire*, 121.
81. Garnsey and Saller, *The Roman Empire*, 122.
82. Lendon, *Empire of Honor*, 34.
83. Reinhold, "Usurption of Status and Status Symbols," 283.

occupations, seating at spectacles and banquets, and the legal system all served to remind the empire's residents of their respective positions in the pecking order of society. And the list of ways in which the hierarchy was expressed could be expanded even more.[84]

Because honor was on public display, competition for honor was a central part of Greco-Roman life. Lendon states, "Competition for honor often subsumed all other competitions and became extremely important to the participants in the competition."[85] Not only were people expected to gain honor, but they were expected to surpass competitors and the honor of previous generations.[86] Honor was a way of differentiating people who were set apart by a set of shared values. As Lendon notes, "The aristocracy was an opinion community; it granted, and was defined by, honor."[87] Statuses and qualities are not in and of themselves honorable. They are determined through the opinion of others, and in the Roman case, by the very people who had honor.[88]

There were several ways an aristocrat could add to his honor or prestige. People could grant honor to one another without losing their own prestige. Letters of recommendation or praise from extremely prestigious persons were saved and often put on public display. A greeting from a person with greater honor, prompt admission to his house, seating at his banquet, and the food that one was served would add to a person's prestige.[89] Performing and achieving accomplishments that were affirmed and valued by the aristocracy were another way of gaining honor.[90] Lendon observes, "A brilliant speech in court or in declamation, a profound knowledge of the Roman law, the destruction of a political enemy, paying off a friend's debt, the proper education of a young wife, or the possession of a remarkable ass: anything praised by aristocrats conferred glory."[91] Honor was reinforced by the deference of others. People uncovered their heads, dismounted on their approach, kissed his hand, mentioned him with respect, and praised him in speeches and writings.[92] Balanced reciprocity

---

84. Hellerman, *Reconstructing Honor in Roman Philippi*, 32.
85. Lendon, *Empire of Honor*, 34.
86. Harrison, "Paul and Ancient Civic Ethics," 87.
87. Lendon, *Empire of Honor*, 37.
88. Lendon, *Empire of Honor*, 37.
89. Lendon, *Empire of Honor*, 37.
90. Lendon, *Empire of Honor*, 49.
91. Lendon, *Empire of Honor*, 49.
92. Lendon, *Empire of Honor*, 59.

was expected between equals in status and honor. An invitation required one in return; a favor given required a favor to be returned. To not provide reciprocity placed one in the other's debt.[93]

The greatest threat to honor was insult.[94] Just as a good opinion of a great man added to the honor of a person, so an insult created dishonor or shame.[95] An insult could be given in the same manner as honor. For example, a person could be denied an invitation, given a lower seat, refused seating in public places, or given inferior food. Those who sought to establish their status over another could do so, particularly if the recipient had no power to protect his honor.[96] Insults could reinforce the ranking of honor between people, particularly between the aristocracy and the non-elite. To have honor was also to have the power to protect honor.[97] An insult that was not addressed implied weakness and less honor than the one who gave the insult. Lendon explains, "A marked disparity of prestige tended to transform the ideally equitable system of reciprocity into the enslavement of the lesser man to the untrammeled power of the honour of the greater; he must do as he is told, or take the consequences."[98]

Honor was important for not only the elite who defined what was honorable, but it was also important for the non-elite. However, honor was often defined differently. Those who were not born into a high position found honor in their city, their legal status, and their occupation. Honorable occupations were distinguished from dishonorable by specific sets of attributes: behavior required for the job, the degree of service to specific persons, the intelligence required, and the social utility of a person. The lowest in status were those that required people to gain wages through manual labor for another.[99] Tradespeople could obtain honor through offices in the work associations or by gaining enough wealth to obtain the outer symbols of honor: the house and clothing.[100] Hellerman states, "Even those who were not members of the elite class ultimately embraced, rather than rejected, the marked verticality of Roman society."[101] However, money could not replace birth. A man could use wealth to obtain some honor, but it could not

---

93. Clarke, *Secular and Christian Leadership in Corinth*, 32.
94. Lendon, *Empire of Honor*, 51.
95. Lendon, *Empire of Honor*, 51.
96. Lendon, *Empire of Honor*, 55.
97. Lendon, *Empire of Honor*, 51.
98. Lendon, *Empire of Honor*, 72.
99. Joshel, *Work, Identity and Legal Status at Rome*, 67.
100. Harrison, "Paul and Ancient Civic Ethics," 116.
101. Hellerman, *Reconstructing Honor in Roman Philippi*, 33.

compensate for a lowly birth. Sandra Joshel notes that aristocrats' claim to privilege was by birth and wealth derived from land, and they were contemptuous about families descended from the trades.[102]

Although status and honor were central features of Greco-Roman society, several scholars have noted that in the teachings of primitive Christianity, new relationships took precedence over status.[103] I argue that Christians were instructed to live anti-structurally within the structures of society. People did not lose their statuses; however, they were to relate to one another as persons rather than with the behaviors socially expected of their statuses. They were to renounce the displaying of their social position and not treat people differently because of social status. Niko Huttunen summarizes, "For Paul, God's call is to be Christian in one's social position."[104] Rather than living without status as people do in communitas, the early Christian communities were to live anti-structural lives (mutuality) while in their statuses and roles within the structure of society. What was honorable was no longer based on status but rather on love for one another. Throughout this study, communitas is marked by this denouncement of status, humility, redefinition of honor, and reversal of status.

Boundaries and Ethnicity

The second distinguishing feature of primitive Christianity, according to Theissen, was love for neighbor. Love for neighbor crossed horizontal boundaries in social relationships and is characteristic of communitas. This love was expressed by those included in the community and defined how they were to relate to one another. Communitas was expressed in inclusiveness and mutuality. In order to understand how the teaching in early Christian communities contrasted with structural ideals, I examine boundary maintenance, particularly how the concept of purity maintained exclusivity in the Jewish community.

Boundary markers vary between various groups, but all use some kind of markers to identify who is in the group and who is outside the group. Although identity can be formed through common features, language, culture, and values, most often ethnic identity and boundaries are maintained by contrast with another group or groups and by identifying what they are not.[105] According to Aaron Kuecker, ancients were keenly aware of the people

---

102. Joshel, *Work, Identity and Legal Status at Rome*, 65.
103. Pate, *The End of the Age Has Come*, 200.
104. Huttunen, *Paul and Epictetus on Law*, 29.
105. Kuecker, *The Spirit and the 'Other,'* 37.

to whom they belonged and the peoples who surrounded them. He notes, "Ancient ethnographers demonstrated an obsession with the 'other,' often describing people with increasingly animalistic characteristics the further away they lived from the socio-geographic center of the ethnographer's own in-group."[106] Often the ancient world divided people between themselves and all others: Jew and Gentile or Greek and barbarian. These ethnic identities were regularly a source of conflict and exclusion in the ancient world.[107] However, in the early church, these ethnic boundaries were quickly broken down to include both Jew and Gentile. In Luke's narrative of Acts, the early Christ-following communities reflected a multiethnic membership as well as members in a variety of social positions.

The maintenance of ethnic boundary markers in the first-century Jewish community often frames many of the confrontations between Jesus and Jewish leaders. The boundary marker within the first-century Jewish community depicted in Luke's gospel was purity. Purity in the broadest sense is a boundary marker or classificatory system.[108] The purity markers for Israel were part of the identification that they were God's special possession.[109] Israel was not only an ethnic people, but they were continually conscious of their special calling as the people of God. There was an emphasis on separating themselves from the Gentiles. According to deSilva, purity for Israel was necessary for allowing contact with God that was beneficial and not destructive.[110] In the case of Israel, specific foods, observances, taboos, and places were used to define themselves as a people set apart for God.[111] He also notes that two types of impurity threatened this purity. One was contact with anything that was impure. The other was to approach anything that belonged to God, such as blood. It is the former type of impurity, contact with the impure, that was most prominent in Jesus' discussions and disputes with Jewish authority.[112] The extreme stress on purity in social and religious arenas excluded not only Gentiles but also people who were considered unclean and barred from participation in the community of Israel, such as lepers, tax collectors, sinners.

Recent scholarship has also argued that the purity rules and symbols of Israel's special relationship with God had also become symbols of national

106. Kuecker, *The Spirit and the 'Other,'* 38.
107. Kuecker, *The Spirit and the 'Other,'* 38.
108. Neyrey, "The Symbolic Universe of Luke-Acts," 224.
109. Neyrey, "The Symbolic Universe in Luke-Acts," 250.
110. deSilva, *Honor, Patronage, Kinship & Purity,* 270.
111. deSilva, *Honor, Patronage, Kinship & Purity,* 270, 279.
112. deSilva, *Honor, Patronage, Kinship & Purity,* 253–74, 280–85.

identity.¹¹³ N. T. Wright notes that the temple cult, observance of the Sabbath, food taboos, and circumcision were key things that distinguished the Jew from the Gentile.¹¹⁴ E. P. Sanders also notes that these particular markers created a social distinction between the Jews and other races in the Greco-Roman world.¹¹⁵ He argues that the central issue in the Maccabean revolts was the defense of these markers that were threatened under the Hellenist program of Antiochus Epiphanes, who sought to force them to abandon these ancestral distinctions.¹¹⁶ According to Hellerman, nationalism was the dominant motivation for the preoccupation of Torah keeping in the post-Maccabean period.¹¹⁷ Wright concurs, stating that those who kept the Sabbath and the food taboos were emphasizing their membership in or their solidarity with the Jewish people.¹¹⁸ Not only did the emphasis on the symbols of nationalism reinforce in-group boundaries, they also defined exclusions from membership within the community. Wright explains that the Jews considered it a God-given duty to protect this boundary, thus preserving those markers of distinctions found in the Sabbath, food, circumcision, and the sanctity of the temple.¹¹⁹

The mission of Jesus and relationships of the first-century followers of Jesus must be seen in this background. Jesus did not disregard Israel's unique relationship with God. However, he also did not reinforce their nationalistic aspirations as other revival movements did. Hellerman summarizes one of the main differences between Jesus' ministry and the ministry of other renewal groups:

> Jesus was not just offering another way to maintain Jewish particularity in the highly Hellenized world of Roman Palestine. Here is where a sectarian analysis that identifies early Christianity as just another reform of Judaism loses some of its explanatory power. Unlike Pharisees, Sadducees, and Essenes, the movement started by Jesus of Nazareth ultimately transcended the boundaries of normative Judaism by relativizing those marks

---

113. Wright, *Jesus and the Victory of God*, 384; Hellerman, *Jesus and the People of God*, 112; Sanders, *Jesus and Judaism*, 102.

114. Wright, *Jesus and the Victory of God*, 384.

115. Sanders, *Paul, the Law, and the Jewish People*, 102.

116. Sanders, *Paul, the Law, and the Jewish People*, 385.

117. Hellerman, *Jesus and the People of God*, 112. Hellerman does distinguish his use of nationalism not as modern nation-state, but ethnically. In linguistic anthropology, "nationism" refers to the type of ethnic mobilization that Hellerman means here. To avoid confusion, I will use nationalism as Hellerman uses it here.

118. Wright, *Jesus and the Victory of God*, 388.

119. Wright, *Jesus and the Victory of God*, 389.

of national identity which characterized the lives of Judeans of every stripe during the Second Temple Period.[120]

Rather than reinforcing Israel's unique vocation from this defensive posture of ethnic and national identity, Jesus frames one that reflected the inclusivity of people who follow him. Wright notes, "The command to love one's enemies, and the prohibition on violent revolution, constituted not an attack on Torah as such but a radically different interpretation of Israel's ancestral tradition from those currently on offer."[121]

Conclusion

Turner's framework of structure, anti-structure, and liminality provides a basis in which we can examine early Christian communities through geography and time. The key feature of the early communities of Christ followers was the unique relationships that they had with one another and with others in broader society. Whereas structure divides people based on their social status in structure, the early Christian communities had relationships that united them based on their common identity as Christ followers. Relationships within structure were divided hierarchically and reinforced by status and values of honor and horizontally by ethnicity. We will see in the following chapters that although people retained these statuses within the communities, they were to relate to one another as if those statuses did not matter. This is the key difference between Christ followers and other groups in liminality. They did not abandon their statuses nor did they separate themselves from the world. They were to have communitas, anti-structural relationships with one another within their structural status. Furthermore, they were to extend the same kind of relationships to people outside their community. They were to live in the world but not of the world.

We will start our exploration of the anti-structural relationship of Christ followers with the ministry of Jesus recorded in the gospel of Luke. The first-century followers of Jesus did not reflect a break with the ancestral traditions of Israel, but membership was inclusive and not marked by the national identity markers of Israel. The following chapter examines how Jesus radically redefined Israel's ancestral tradition through his actions and teaching of the Kingdom of God.

---

120. Hellerman, *Jesus and the People of God*, 120.
121. Wright, *Jesus and the Victory of God*, 389.

Chapter 3

Liminality, Jesus, and the Kingdom of God

THE NATURE OF THE Kingdom of God and its messenger, Jesus, have been a significant focus of New Testament studies. The Kingdom of God is central to Jesus' message, but he never explicitly defined the term. Although most scholars agree that there was an Old Testament antecedent for the Kingdom of God, scholars disagree on the intended meaning behind Jesus' use of the term and how Jesus' audience would have understood that meaning. The answer to these questions influences how scholars understand the person of Jesus, his intentions for Israel, and the relationship of Israel to the early Christian communities. Likewise, the understanding of who Jesus was and the purpose of his ministry affects the interpretation of his teachings about the Kingdom of God.

There are a variety of ways in which the Kingdom has been understood, and there is no consensus among scholars about what Jesus intended when he taught about the Kingdom of God and how this was understood by his audience.[1] The issues are multifaceted, and for the purposes of this study, I focus on two dimensions. The first is temporal: did Jesus perceive the Kingdom as already beginning in his ministry as evidenced through his casting out demons and healings,[2] or was it still future as expressed in his prayer "Thy Kingdom come?"[3] The second dimension is its social character:

---

1. For summaries of the historical study of the Kingdom of God, see Perrin, *The Kingdom of God in the Teaching of Jesus*; Lundström, *The Kingdom of God in the Teaching of Jesus*; Saucy, *The Kingdom of God in the Teaching of Jesus*; Witherington, *The Jesus Quest*; Wright, *The New Testament and the People of God*.

2. This position is expressed is often expressed as present in a transcendent way, not as a physical restoring of Israel. See Chilton, *Pure Kingdom*; Weiss, *Jesus' Proclamation of the Kingdom of God*; Bultmann, "Forward," xi; Rauschenbusch, *Christianity and the Social Crisis*, 65.

3. Often this is expressed by those who also see that Jesus meant the restoration

was it a physical, political realm of God as expressed in Israel,[4] or was he referring to something more universal?[5]

More recently studies on the Kingdom of God have sought to integrate God's covenant with Israel and Jesus' teaching, which also included universal aspects. This position argues that Jesus was talking about Israel as the people of God but redefining how Israel was to be the people of God outside of the political and national expectations of first-century Israel. This position articulates the eschatological, messianic understanding of first-century Israel as expectations of the restoration of Israel. However, it was not in the way that Israel expected.[6] According to Hellerman, Jesus' vision of the people of God was not marked by ethnic particularity but was a surrogate family of those who obeyed the will of God. He explains, "Jesus begins to deconstruct the idea of God's people as a localized ethnos that had prevailed since Sinai in order to reconstruct the social identity of the people of God in terms of surrogate family."[7]

Wright provides a comprehensive discussion on this position in his book *Jesus and the Victory of God*.[8] Wright argues that Jesus was announcing the long-awaited Kingdom, but it was not going to look the way they imagined. According to Wright, Jesus retells the story about Israel's destiny but with a new way of being the true people of God. It is through this retelling of the story that Jesus affirms the covenant of God to ethnic, political Israel but avows the nonpolitical aspects of the rule of God. He argues that the confrontations about temple, purity, and Sabbath observance were confrontations between Jesus, who emphasized this new way of being the people of God apart from national aspirations, and those who used these to strengthen their identity as the ethnic, national, and political entity.

Wright's analysis is useful in that it helps to separate the two distinct but intertwining perspectives of the Kingdom of God: the universal rule of God and the rule of God articulated in a particular way through ethnic Israel. Rather than either/or, structure or anti-structure, I propose that the teachings of Jesus about the character of the Kingdom of God are both/and. In other words, both are true. Structure represents the aspect of the ethnic political Israel, while anti-structure is the new way of being the people. People will live a new way within their structure (Figure 3).

---

of a physical Israel. See Schweitzer, *The Kingdom of God and Primitive Christianity*, 15.

4. See Horsley, *Jesus and Empire*, 49–50.
5. See Crossan, *The Birth of Christianity*, 282.
6. Lohfink, *Jesus and Community*, 26.
7. Hellerman, *Jesus and the People of God*, 265.
8. Wright, *Jesus and the Victory of God*, 203.

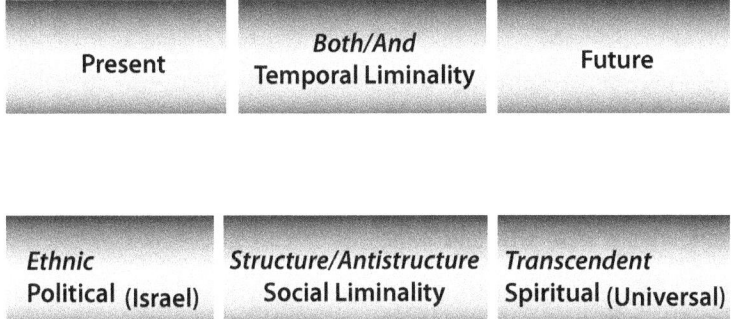

Figure 3. Both/And Liminality of the Kingdom of God

The diagram above also models the two positions of the temporal aspects of the Kingdom of God in Jesus' ministry as liminality. It takes into account the position that the Kingdom of God was present in Jesus' ministry, particularly in the exorcism of demons and in healings, as well as the future aspect, or consummation, that takes place sometime in the future in the age to come. This creates a liminality in which the Kingdom had already broken into the present age in the ministry of Jesus but was not yet fulfilled.

What I propose in this chapter is that Luke is writing his account of Jesus and his ministry after Pentecost and the incorporation of Gentiles into a Spirit-marked community as depicted in Acts 15. I suggest that he is framing Jesus' person and teaching—his teachings about the Kingdom of God and the people of God—through post-Pentecost lenses. Following Wright, I argue that Luke told the story of God's restoration of Israel and the fulfillment of his promises to her, but with a "dynamic twist." What I propose is that Luke portrayed the Kingdom of God, its agent Jesus, and the people of God in such a way that it emphasized the anti-structural aspects of Israel's understanding of her relationship with God. The time of the Kingdom, the agent of the Kingdom, and the people of the Kingdom can all be framed in liminality in which anti-structure characterizes relationships, thus allowing Luke to tell the story of God's fulfillment of his promises, but not according to structural expectations of Israel. I propose that Luke deliberately frames the relational aspects of the Kingdom of God in a way that is consistent with Pauline understanding of inaugurated eschatology. Rather than either/or characteristics of temporal and social characteristics of the Kingdom, it is both/and. As Wright notes, "To put it another way, Luke sees the eschaton, expected by many first-century Jews, as having already occurred but as being still to occur . . . Luke, then, has retold the story of Israel in such a way to subvert other first-century tellings of it."[9] By using the heuristic framework of liminality, structure, and anti-structure, I am able to focus on key features that demonstrate the continuity between Jesus tradition with the Pauline tradition and writings of post-Pauline Christian communities through the third century.

Liminality, Jesus, and the Kingdom of God

A discussion about the nature of the Kingdom of God is not complete without a discussion of who Jesus was and his intentions in announcing the Kingdom. Different scholars have sought to define Jesus by categorizing the social context in which he lived and taught. Some try to place Jesus within the context of Second Temple Judaism while others place Jesus in a more Hellenized context. Just as they have sought to understand the Kingdom of God in terms of its first-century listeners, so they have sought to understand how Jesus' audience would have perceived him as they listened to his words and saw his actions. He has been variously described as a Jewish rabbi or prophet,[10] prophet of justice,[11] prophet of Sophia,[12] God's broker,[13] divine man,[14] folk healer,[15] exorcist,[16] cynic,[17] sage,[18] itinerant charismatic,[19] and apocalyptic prophet.[20]

However, many of these descriptions do not clarify how the gospel writers understood Jesus in the broader narrative of Israel's story. Most scholars agree that Jesus saw himself announcing something about God's actions involving Israel. As Wright argues, "Jesus affirms Israel's basic beliefs, that their god is the god of creation and they are his people and that he must act to vindicate her from her enemies."[21] Wright also asserts that Jesus did not do away with the basic paradigm, but he was "redefining the Israel that was

---

9. Wright, *The New Testament and the People of God*, 382.
10. Pelikan, *Jesus Through the Centuries*, 11.
11. Herzog, *Jesus, Justice and the Reign of God*, 47.
12. Stambaugh and Balch, *The New Testament and Its Social Environment*, 104.
13. Moxnes, "Patron-Client Relationships," 241–70.
14. Koester, *Paul & His World*, 118–125.
15. Pilch, "Sickness and Healing in Luke-Acts," 181–210.
16. Witmer, *Jesus, the Galilean Exorcist*, 97–208.
17. Crossan, *The Historical Jesus*, 421.
18. Witherington, *The Jesus Quest*, 185–96.
19. Theissen, *The Religion of the Earliest Churches*, 38–40.
20. Ehrman, *Jesus: Apocalyptic Prophet*, 125–39.
21. Wright, *Jesus and the Victory of God*, 173.

to be vindicated, and hence was also redrawing Israel's picture of her true enemies."[22] A discussion of Jesus and his ministry cannot be single-faceted but must be multidimensional in order to demonstrate not only how Jesus' audience viewed him but also how the gospel writers portrayed him.

In this section, I demonstrate that the Kingdom of God, God's agent, and Israel are portrayed in liminality, and it is the anti-structural characteristics of the Kingdom of God which are emphasized. First, I demonstrate that Luke framed the Kingdom of God, inaugurated in Jesus' public ministry, as temporal liminality. Second, I argue that Luke framed the public ministry of Jesus as the liminal phase in a rite of passage, and in doing so, presented Jesus as the Davidic king in liminality. Third, I demonstrate that Luke frames Israel as a nation in her liminal phase and characterized Jesus as a prophet like Moses who taught his audience what it meant to be the people of God.

Temporal Liminality of the Kingdom of God[23]

The inauguration of the Kingdom of God in Luke's narrative is expressed in two ways: through Jesus' own announcements and through his actions. Luke's narrative provides two sets of Jesus' announcements: one at the beginning of his public ministry and the second when John's emissaries came to Jesus on John's behalf. In both of these announcements, Luke reframes the expectations of the Kingdom of God in anti-structural terms by: (1) redefining the people of God, (2) identifying the real opposition to God's rule, and (3) introducing Jesus as God's agent in Israel. By redefining these expectations, Jesus' words and actions demonstrated that the restoration of God's people had begun his ministry.

Luke places the first announcement at the beginning of Jesus' public ministry in Luke 4:16–29. While parallel passages in Mark and Matthew emphasize Jesus' rejection by his hometown, Luke places the Nazareth rejection at the beginning of Jesus' public ministry, including the announcement of the inauguration of God's restoration. By placing the announcement at the beginning of Jesus' public ministry with a similar recap of it in Luke 7, Luke emphasized the purpose of Jesus' ministry.[24] In the announcement, Jesus redefined God's plan for Israel's restoration as beginning in his own ministry.

22. Wright, *Jesus and the Victory of God*, 173.

23. My intention here is not to provide a detailed argument for inaugurated eschatology but to highlight how Luke frames the Kingdom of God as liminal.

24. Stauss, *The Davidic Messiah in Luke-Acts*, 225; Bock, *Luke Volume 1:1—9:50*, 398.

Jesus in his announcement quoted from Isaiah 61, which was understood in Second Temple Judaism to refer to the dawning of the new eschatological age, and Jesus' audience would have interpreted it as the coming of God's new age of salvation.[25] Not only would it raise expectations for God's new age, but Luke made it clear that the new age was beginning and that Jesus was God's agent announcing it. In this announcement, Jesus and God's age of salvation were closely linked together, but it comes in a way that the people did not expect. As Joel Green notes, "Through the shaping of the story he seems to cater to, and then transform normal expectations. This is an outgrowth of his portrayal of the actualization of God's redemptive aim as status reversal."[26] Jesus' announcement in Luke 4:18–19 reads:

> The Spirit of the Lord is upon me,
> because he has anointed me
> to proclaim good news to the poor.
> He has sent me to proclaim liberty to the captives
> and recovering of sight to the blind,
> to set at liberty those who are oppressed,
> to proclaim the year of the Lord's favor.

In describing the Spirit-anointed figure proclaiming the good news, Luke was evoking images of salvation, but not in an individual sense. The poor in Second Temple Judaism were not just the spiritually or the economically poor, but were in a holistic sense those who were, for a number of reasons, outside the boundaries of God's people.[27] Green notes, "By directing his good news to these people, Jesus indicated his refusal to recognize those socially determined boundaries, asserting instead that even these 'outsiders' are the objects of divine grace. Others may regard such people as beyond the pale of salvation, but God has opened a way for them to belong to God's family."[28]

Green also argues that the structural arrangement of the passage is also important for understanding the redefinition of God's plan of restoration for his people. The first half of the passage is about Jesus and those to whom he will preach the good news. Each of the first lines refers to the first person and underscores the relationship of Jesus and the people of God, those who need to be restored to God. They are the poor, the disenfranchised, and the marginalized—those who are liminal to the religious

---

25. Bock, *Luke Volume 1:1—9:50*, 405.
26. Green, *The Gospel of Luke*, 203.
27. Green, *The Gospel of Luke*, 211.
28. Green, *The Gospel of Luke*, 211.

structures. This highlights that restoration will come to those who were excluded by their structural statuses in Jewish society.[29] In the last three lines, the verb ἀφέσει (*aphesei*), "release," is highlighted. But what is meant by "release"? What one is released from redefines the expectations of God's restoration and salvation.[30] Giving sight to the blind can be interpreted in Second Temple tradition in the literal sense of healing the blind, or it can be understood in a figurative way of the spiritually blind now able to "see" salvation.[31] According to Peter Mallen, the use of the images of restoring sight to the blind and setting free the oppressed were signs of messianic salvation.[32] However, the more central question for Jewish expectations of salvation and the mission of God's agent of salvation was the question of release: from what did they need to be released?[33]

Esler argues that this passage includes the physical aspects of captivity and oppression, specifically under social and economic conditions of first-century Palestine.[34] Isaiah 61 was understood in Second Temple Judaism as bringing God's message of deliverance to those in exile. Jesus' audience would have understood the new age as drawing near—that Jesus was aligning himself with the national agenda. Esler argues, "The main task of the Messiah, over and over again, is the liberation of Israel, and her reinstatement as the true people of the creator god. This will involve military action, which can be seen in terms of judgment as in a law court."[35]

However, there are also extended meanings of captivity in Old Testament usage. In the broader semantic usage, release referred to exiles living in captivity but also referred to the sin that caused the exile or captivity.[36] In Second Temple Judaism, liberty of the oppressed also had spiritual connotations, and often this wording was used in reference to exorcism.[37] Jesus proclaimed that the inauguration of God's salvation had started through him as the agent of God's salvation in his statement, "Today this Scripture has been fulfilled in your hearing."[38] Jesus was announcing the long-awaited epoch of

---

29. Green, *The Gospel of Luke*, 210–14.
30. Bock, *Luke Volume 1:1—9:50*, 408; Green, *The Gospel of Luke*, 211–12.
31. Green, *The Gospel of Luke*, 211. He also compares it to its usage in Luke 1:78–79, 2:29–32.
32. Mallen, *The Reading and Transformation of Isaiah in Luke-Acts*, 75; Isaiah 29:18; 35:4–6.
33. Bock, *Luke Volume 1:1—9:50*, 410.
34. Esler, *Community and Gospel in Luke-Acts*, 181–82.
35. Wright, *The New Testament and the People of God*, 320.
36. Bock, *Luke Volume 1:1—9:50*, 409.
37. Green, *The Gospel of Luke*, 214.
38. Luke 4:21.

salvation had begun but it was not coming the way that they expected it.[39] The different expectations of how God would free his people and from what were pivotal in Jesus' conflicts with religious leaders.

The differences in expectations of God's restoration were demonstrated in Jesus' second announcement in response to emissaries from John the Baptist in Luke 7:18–35. The fact that the questions were from John was important in this narrative because John was a prophetic voice, the one who had prepared the people with expectations for the arrival of God's agent.[40] As Green notes, "John's voice has been established as the voice of a friend of God's purpose; if he has questions about the expression of God's purpose in Jesus' activity, then they are surely worth contemplating."[41] He of all the people in Israel should recognize the arrival of the one whose way he had prepared. But the messiah John expected was one who would bring judgment: "His winnowing fork is in his hand, to clear his threshing floor and to gather the wheat in his barn, but the chaff he will burn with unquenchable fire."[42] Because Jesus' ministry did not meet John's expectations, he questioned whether Jesus was the messiah or if there was another to come.

The context for Jesus' answer was that he was doing what he proclaimed God's agent would do: healing many people of diseases, plagues, and evil spirits and giving the blind sight. As John's disciples stood and watched these healings, Jesus answered them, "Go and tell John what you have seen and heard; the blind receive their sight, the lame walk, the lepers are cleansed, the deaf hear, the dead are raised up, the poor have the good news preached to them. And blessed is the one who is not offended by me."[43] The list of miracles is found in numerous passages in Isaiah, and in each of these passages, the force of these healings was an indication that God's day of salvation had arrived.[44] Darrell Bock notes, "The events show the presence of the eschaton, when God's rule is fully manifest."[45] In his answer, Jesus confirmed that he was the agent of salvation and that the day of salvation had come, just not the way that John expected. Jesus both redefined John's expectation and confirmed himself as the agent of God's salvation. Jesus' last statement was a blessing to those willing to change their minds about what God's salvation and agent would look like. Green

---

39. Green, *The Gospel of Luke*, 218.
40. Luke 3:1–18.
41. Green, *The Gospel of Luke*, 296.
42. Luke 3:17.
43. Luke 7:22–23.
44. Bock, *Luke Volume 1:1—9:50*, 668; Isaiah 35:5–6; 26:19; 29:18–19; 61:1–11.
45. Bock, *Luke Volume 1:1—9:50*, 668.

argues, "Jesus pronounces a blessing on any who are willing to undergo a conversion in their views of God's purpose, the in-breaking eschatological salvation, and, so of Jesus's mission."[46] This overlap between Jesus' answer to John's question and the initial pronouncement of his ministry demonstrated that the age of God's salvation had now been inaugurated, and his actions were a part of that evidence.

Jesus' actions not only showed that God's age of salvation had arrived, but they also demonstrated who the true enemy of the people of God was and how one was restored to God. In Luke's narrative, healings demonstrated how someone was released from captivity and restored to God, and they also served to identify the true enemy of the people of God. The first pericope that Luke introduces after Jesus' announcement of his ministry was Jesus' healing of a man who was possessed with an unclean spirit.[47] Luke highlights Jesus' attack on the kingdom of Satan though the demon's words, "Have you come to destroy us?"[48] The pericope that follows is the healing of Simon's mother-in-law and then the healing of many people who were sick. In Luke's narrative, the actions of Jesus (healing and exorcism) were closely linked with his announcement of the inauguration of the age of salvation.[49] For Luke, the demonstration of Jesus' freeing people from Satan's oppression was a sign that God's age of salvation had come. This was made explicit in Jesus' response to people who were accusing him of casting out demons by Beelzebub, the ruler of the demons.[50] After arguing with his accusers over the illogic of Satan casting out his own minions, Jesus said, "But if I cast out demons by the finger of God, then the kingdom of God has come upon you."[51] George Eldon Ladd argues that other uses of φθάνω make it clear that the meaning in this context is the actual presence of the Kingdom of God, not just proximity.[52] Green concludes, "In the same way, the exorcisms of Jesus are manifestations of God's liberating power, but this is to say nonetheless than that his exorcisms must be understood as the kingdom of God at work,

---

46. Green, *The Gospel of Luke*, 297.

47. Luke 4:31–37.

48. Luke 4:34.

49. In many countries of the world, illnesses of all kinds are thought to occur through either possession of a spirit or affliction caused by a spirit, and many of Jesus' healings throughout Luke are the result of casting out demons.

50. Luke 11:14–20.

51. Luke 11:20.

52. Ladd, *A Theology of the New Testament*, 63.

now."[53] The healings that delivered people from oppression by Satan affirmed his authority as God's agent of restoration.[54]

However, according to Bock, this leaves unanswered the question that John implied, "Where is the great apocalyptic judge and deliverer that is expected?"[55] For Luke, the day of the Lord, the consummation of God's kingdom, was still in the future.[56] Although the Kingdom was inaugurated in the ministry of Jesus, the consummation of it was in the future. The emphasis is not "if" there will be a day of the Lord but rather "when" it will come. All the gospels anticipate an apocalyptic consummation when the Son of Man will come in glory and gather the elect.[57] In his announcement in Luke 4:18–19, Jesus omitted in the reading of the Isaiah passage the phrase, "And the day of vengeance of our God."[58] The message of Isaiah was not only about times of refreshing and return for the people of Israel but also vindication of Israel and God's judgment upon her enemies. Jesus' message was one of hope and restoration, but also there was judgment for those who opposed God's plan, whether or not they belonged to Israel.[59] This judgment was not based on national expectations but what they did with Jesus and his message. Some of Jesus' sayings about the nature of the consummation were about the return of the Son of Man.[60] Some alluded to the future judgment and destruction of Israel.[61] Some passages were about the disciples' role in the future Kingdom or the fulfillment of Jesus' mission.[62] All of these pointed to a future judgment but just not yet.

In his gospel, Luke depicts the two temporal aspects of the Kingdom of God: first, the Kingdom of God has been inaugurated by Jesus as God's agent of salvation demonstrated by his words and deeds, and second, there will also be a future consummation and judgment. In Luke's narrative, the Kingdom of God, God's salvation through his agent, had broken into the present, but it was not yet fully consummated. It was liminal time, as shown below (Figure 4). Not only was the time of God's salvation liminal time, but Luke portrayed God's agent of salvation, Jesus, in liminality as well.

53. Green, *The Gospel of Luke*, 457.
54. Bock, *Luke Volume 1:1—9:50*, 410.
55. Bock, *Luke Volume 1:1—9:50*, 699.
56. Green, *The Gospel of Luke*, 416.
57. Green, *The Gospel of Luke*, 309.
58. Bock, *Luke Volume 1:1—9:50*, 411; Isaiah 61:2b.
59. Luke 10:13–16.
60. Luke 17:22–27; 21:25–28.
61. Luke 21:20–24.
62. Luke 22:14–22, 28–30.

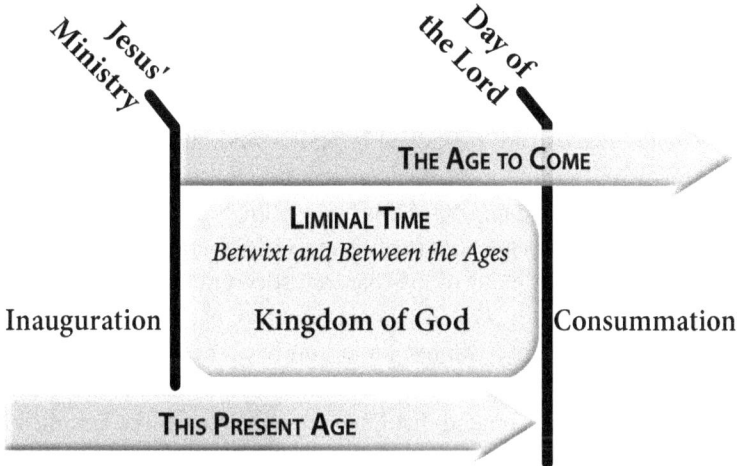

Figure 4. Liminal Time of the Kingdom

Liminality of the Messianic King
—Agent of God's Salvation

Not only did the inauguration of Jesus' ministry redefine Jewish expectations of the arrival of the Kingdom, but Luke also redefined expectations for the agent of God's salvation, the Davidic messianic king. In Luke's narrative, Jesus was portrayed as a prophet but also as more than a prophet. Luke portrayed Jesus as the long-awaited Davidic messiah. The expectations of Second Temple Judaism for the messiah were in terms of a king from the line of David. These expectations were grounded in the promises found in the oracle of Nathan.[63] The key part of this promise from which arose the messianic hope was the promise of the continuation of David's dynasty and the eternal Davidic throne. This Davidic promise became an extension to God's covenant relationship with Israel.[64] Other royal Psalms extended the role, function, and character of the Davidic descendant.[65] The expectations of the Davidic messiah began during exile with the hope for the reestablishment of the Davidic dynasty and deliverance from Israel's enemies. These hopes for a Davidic monarchy were also reflected by later prophets.[66]

---

63. 2 Samuel 7:5–17; Psalm 89.

64. Strauss, *The Davidic Messiah in Luke-Acts*, 36.

65. Strauss, *The Davidic Messiah in Luke-Acts*, 36; Psalms 2, 18, 20, 21, 45, 72, 101, 110, 132, 139, 144.

66. Strauss, *The Davidic Messiah in Luke-Acts*, 36; Haggai 2:20–23; Zechariah 9:9–10; 12:7–14.

The hopes for a Davidic messiah were renewed during the late Hasmoneon and early Roman periods with the failure of the priestly leadership. According to Mark Strauss, abuse of royal powers, an increase in Hellenizing tendencies, and subjugation to Rome led to renewed hopes for a Davidic king who would judge corrupt rulers and bring the vindication of Israel and an era of peace and prosperity.[67] He notes that the Psalms of Solomon represented the strongest expression of this hope in the Second Temple period.[68] The psalmist beseeches the Lord to raise up a son of David to rule over Israel. Strauss also notes that many of the characteristics and functions of this Davidic rule draw upon the Old Testament promises, particularly from Isaiah 11. The Spirit of the Lord will rest upon him (v. 2), he will restore those in exile (v. 12), and Israel will conquer her enemies (vv. 14–16).[69]

In this section, I contend that Luke presents Jesus as the Davidic king but not in the way that Jesus' audience expected it. I demonstrate that the point of comparison between Jesus and David was not while David was on the throne but rather while David was in liminality between his anointing and his recognition as king. By comparing Jesus to this time frame in David's life, Luke redefined the purpose and person of God's agent of salvation. In order to make the comparison, I first use rites of passage to describe phases of Jesus' life in which the majority of his public ministry was in a liminal state and compare it to David's life during his liminal period.

In Luke's narrative, Jesus' liminality began with separation from his status as Joseph's son at his baptism and ended with his reincorporation into a new status as Lord and Christ upon his ascension. This three-stage process illustrated in Figure 5 reflects Van Gennep's three stages in rites of passages: separation, liminality, and reintegration.

---

67. Strauss, *The Davidic Messiah in Luke–Acts*, 40.
68. Strauss, *The Davidic Messiah in Luke–Acts*, 40.
69. Strauss, *The Davidic Messiah in Luke–Acts*, 41.

LIMINALITY, JESUS, AND THE KINGDOM OF GOD

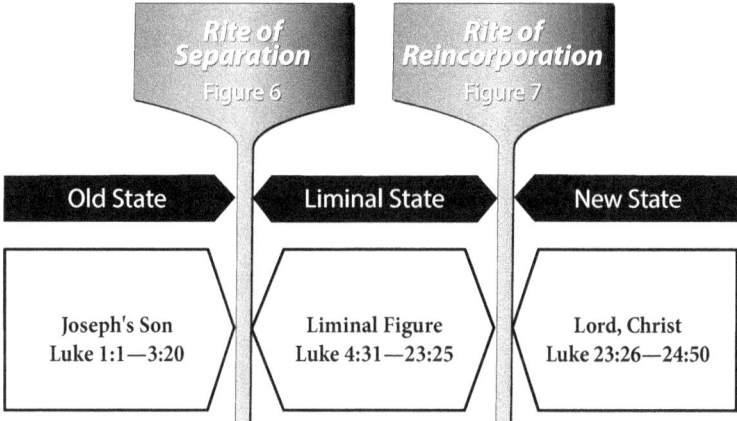

Figure 5. Jesus' Rites of Passage

Before Jesus' rite of separation, Luke spent the first chapters of his narrative describing Jesus as Joseph's son. The narrative describes his birth, his circumcision, his presentation at the temple, and then an incident of Jesus as a young man at the temple. There is little written about Jesus in his status as Joseph's son other than he was submissive to his parents and grew in wisdom.[70] In the narratives of Luke, baptism and the anointing of the Spirit mark the beginning of the rite of separation from his status as Joseph's son to his period of liminality, which covered most of his public ministry.[71] His reincorporation was upon his ascension into heaven in which he was recognized as the Christ.[72]

There were also rites of passages within the rites of separation and reincorporation that function as the bookends for the period of liminality of Jesus' public ministry. The doubling of a rite of passage occurs in many rites of passage when there is an extended period of liminality, such as betrothal. The embedded rites of passage are illustrated in Figures 6 and Figure 7 below.

---

70. Luke 2:39–40.
71. Luke 3:21–22.
72. Acts 2:36.

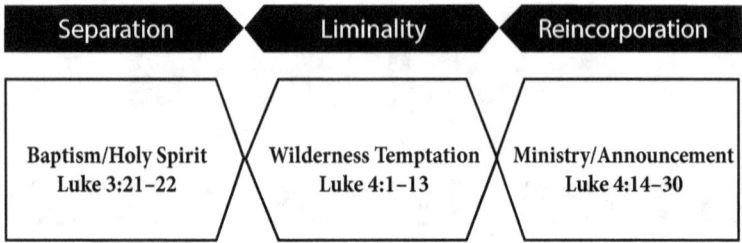

Figure 6. Jesus' Rites of Separation

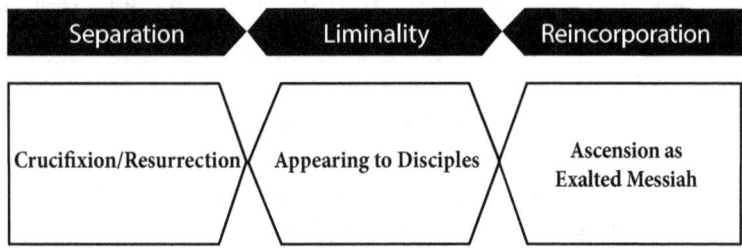

Figure 7. Jesus' Rites of Reincorporation

The rites of passage within the rites of separation included the baptism and anointing of the Spirit as separation, the wilderness and temptation as a period of liminality, and the reincorporation of Jesus into the liminal phase of his public ministry. There is also a rite of passage from the liminal phase of his public ministry that included his death and resurrection as separation,[73] his appearance to the disciples for forty days as liminal, and his ascension into heaven as reincorporation with a new status as the exalted messiah. Jesus' public ministry as liminality was bookended with rites of passage that were both forty days long.

Luke portrayed Jesus as a prophet during his public ministry, but his narrative also portrayed Jesus as more than a prophet. Throughout Jesus' birth narrative, Luke included themes identifying him as the Davidic king. First, it was explicit in the annunciation in Luke 1:26–38. The Davidic lineage was confirmed because Mary was engaged to a man who was a descendant of David (v. 27). The revealing of who the child would be presented the key elements of the Davidic promise: a king from the line of David to whom God would give the throne of his father David (v. 32), which would be an eternal throne over a restored Israel (v. 33), and this king would reign over

---

73. It could be argued for another embedded rite of passage: crucifixion as separation, the grave as liminality, and reincorporation into liminal state of his resurrection.

the house of Jacob forever without end (v. 33). The second explicit mention of Jesus as a Davidic messiah was in Mary's response in which she tied the promise of her child's identity to the promise God had given Abraham and his covenant to Israel, which would be fulfilled by the Davidic king who was to come.[74] A third allusion to the Davidic messiah was in Zachariah's prophecy. In his speech, he announced that God would restore Israel through a "horn of salvation" in the house of David.[75]

Luke's narrative of Jesus' birth also alluded to his identity as the Davidic messiah. Luke reminds the reader of Joseph's lineage when he returned to Bethlehem, the city of David, because he was from the lineage of David.[76] In the announcement to the shepherds, there was another reference to the role of this descendant of David. The angels told the shepherds that a Savior was born in the city of David.[77] In the presentation at the temple, Jesus' identity as messiah was confirmed through both Simeon and Anna. Simeon declared that in Jesus he had seen the salvation of the Lord.[78]

Peter Mallen argues that Luke used these allusions so that from the beginning of Luke's narrative, authoritative voices identified Jesus as the Davidic messiah who will rule on David's throne.[79] The Davidic king was expected to act as God's agent to deliver Israel from her enemies and oversee ethnic renewal.[80] Thus, through the infancy narratives, Jesus was introduced as the one who will fulfill the Old Testament promises to David.[81] However, although the infancy narratives framed Jesus as the Davidic king to bring salvation to Israel, Luke did not portray Jesus as a king during his earthly ministry.[82] It was only after the resurrection that Luke returned to the theme of identifying Jesus as the Davidic king. As David Ravens notes, "It is the resurrection that is the turning point from anointed prophet to the expected Messiah of the end-time and therefore a change in the role of the χριστός."[83]

---

74. Strauss, *The Davidic Messiah in Luke-Acts*, 97.

75. Luke 1:69.

76. Luke 2:4.

77. Luke 2:11.

78. Luke 2:25–32.

79. Mallen, *The Reading and Transformation of Isaiah in Luke–Acts*, 173.

80. Strauss, *The Davidic Messiah in Luke–Acts*, 114.

81. Strauss, *The Davidic Messiah in Luke–Acts*, 124.

82. Koester, *Paul & His World*, 115. Koester also notes this same pattern in Matthew.

83. Ravens, *Luke and the Restoration of Israel*, 119; Luke 24:26, 46; Acts 3:18; 17:3; 26:23.

Between the infancy narratives announcing Jesus as the Davidic messiah until the resurrection where Luke depicts Jesus as the reigning Davidic messiah at the right hand of God, there are no explicit references to Jesus as the Davidic messiah in Luke's narrative. However, placing David's career in the framework of a rite of passage and comparing it to Jesus' rite of passage, it becomes apparent how Luke reframed the Davidic expectations and Jesus as the Davidic messiah (Figure 8).

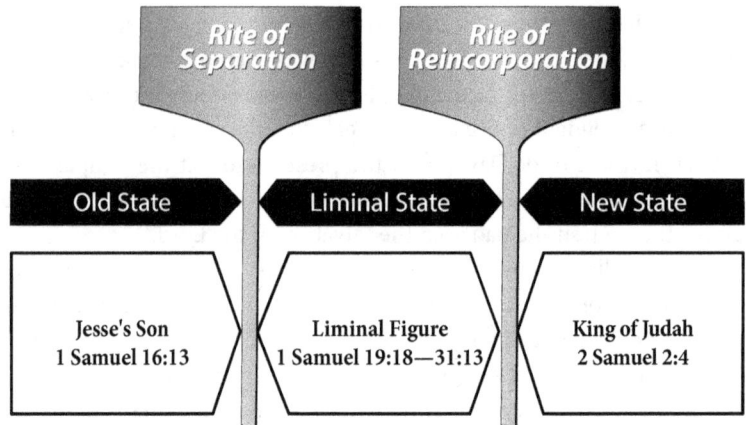

Figure 8. David's Rites of Passage

David's life, like Jesus' life, can be illustrated as a rite of passage as noted in Figure 8 above. In 1 Samuel 16, Samuel anointed David as the king of God's choice, and the narrative states that the Spirit came upon David and was with him from that point onward. Luke did not frame Jesus' ministry to the period when David was recognized as king over Judah. Luke framed Jesus as the messiah to David's liminal period between his anointing by Samuel and his recognition as king. David left Saul's court and wandered as a hunted fugitive with his band of followers as Saul plotted against his life. Jesus spent most of his public ministry wandering around the countryside with his band of followers, and sometimes there were plots against his life.[84]

The narrative of David also provides a further comparison to Jesus in the rite of separation. Like Jesus, David's rite of passage has an extended rite of separation which has a rite of passage within it. In 1 Samuel 16:14, the Spirit left Saul, and David was separated from his household and brought into Saul's court to minister to Saul. During this liminal period, David killed Israel's enemy Goliath, proving his character. Finally, David

---

84. Wright, *The New Testament and the People of God*, 380.

fled Saul's household because Saul sought to kill him. He entered a period of liminality in which he had been anointed as king but was yet to be recognized as king.[85] Placing Jesus' rites of separation and period of liminality in the wilderness alongside David's rites of separation and period of liminality, these similarities are observed:

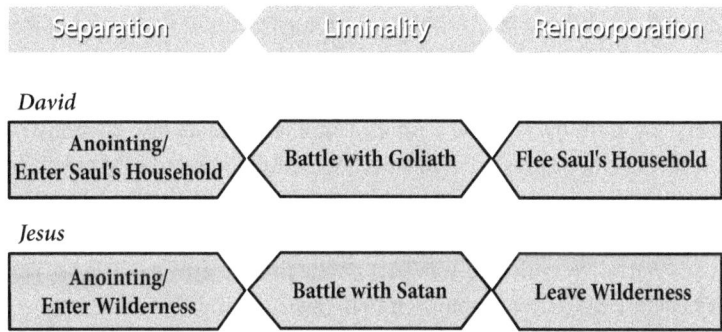

Figure 9. Comparison of David's and Jesus' Liminality in Rites of Separation

In this juxtaposition, one can see the similarities and how Luke framed Jesus' wilderness experience to correspond to David's period in Saul's household. Both David and Jesus, after they were anointed and received the Holy Spirit, entered a liminal period. David entered Saul's household; Jesus entered the wilderness. In both cases, they fought Israel's enemy: David conquered Goliath, and Jesus resisted Satan. In this way, Luke identified who the true enemy of Israel was—not the nations, but Satan. Just as David fought the enemy of Israel on behalf of all of Israel, so Jesus fought Satan on behalf of Israel.

There are also points of comparison to Jesus' ministry that demonstrate the anti-structural nature of his public ministry. First, during his liminal period, David's leadership authority was not based on positional authority but rather by his mighty deeds. Jesus' authority was not based on a position in structure but rather was demonstrated by his mighty deeds. Although being chased by Saul, David continued to fight the enemies of Israel, just as Jesus fought Satan. David's liminality also defined Israel's relationship to her enemies. Twice David had the opportunity to take the throne by killing Saul, and twice David refused and did not let his men take Saul's life. David loved his enemy and made a pact with Saul's son Jonathan that he would not take vengeance on Saul's bloodlines, but rather he would take care of them. He refused to take the kingdom by force but trusted in

---

85. 1 Samuel 19:18.

God to protect him and fulfill his promise. Using this part of David's narrative, Luke redefined the expectations for the Davidic messiah. Jesus did not lead Israel to vindication over her enemies but taught his followers to love their enemies. Jesus refused to establish a kingdom by force but rather was crucified at the hands of his enemies.

As stated above, Jesus was identified in the birth narratives as the Davidic messiah who was designated in scripture to fulfill the hopes of Israel. However, Luke did not narrate Jesus as the conquering king but as the king who was anointed but not recognized and not enthroned during his earthly ministry. By framing Jesus as a king in liminality, Luke also demonstrated that suffering and death were also a part of the fulfillment of God's plan. Mallen notes, "What is surprising is the juxtaposition of the Messiah with the servant's role of suffering and death, especially as described in Isaiah 53."[86] In Luke's narrative, suffering was part of the liminal aspects of Jesus' rite of passage before his reincorporation into his status as the Davidic king.

Liminality of the People of God

The third aspect of liminality in Luke's narrative was the liminality of God's people. The liminality of God's people was depicted in two different ways in Luke's narrative. First, it is in Luke's use of a Moses typology in the description of events in Jesus' public ministry. For instance, Moses spent forty days fasting in the wilderness just as Jesus spent forty days fasting in the wilderness; God provided bread for Israel in the wilderness just as Jesus provided bread to the people. Although Luke framed Jesus as a prophet like Moses, scholars understand the comparisons between Jesus and Moses differently. Wright suggests that Luke uses the Moses comparison to reflect a new exodus which was accomplished in the life, death, and resurrection of Jesus.[87] Green suggests that the comparison lies in the wilderness during the temptations of Jesus. In this case, Jesus plays a representative role of Israel, but where Israel failed to prove faithful, Jesus proved his fidelity to God.[88] Both of these are possible and compare the Moses typology to a liminal state in Jesus' life. Wright compares it to the liminal state in the rite of reincorporation (Figure 7); Green compares it to the liminal state in the rite of separation (Figure 6).[89] While these are possible authorial intents, I argue that Luke's comparison of Jesus to Moses is during the liminal state of Jesus'

---

86. Mallen, *The Reading and Transformation of Isaiah in Luke–Acts*, 131.

87. Wright, *The New Testament and the People of God*, 388.

88. Green, *The Gospel of Luke*, 190–94.

89. Wright, *The New Testament and the People of God*, 388. Wright compares it to the shorter rite of passage of the death, grave, and resurrection that is part of this rite of reincorporation.

public ministry. This aligns with the second aspect of Luke's depiction of the people of God in liminality which is the comparison of Israel's liminal state in the wilderness to Jesus' liminal state of his public ministry (Figure 10). In order to demonstrate this, I place the exodus of Israel in a framework of rite of passage and then compare it to Jesus' rite of passage.

The rite of passage for Israel started when Moses met with the elders of Israel in Exodus 4:29–31. Moses then battled Pharaoh from Exodus 5 through Exodus 14 at which point Israel passed through the Red Sea and Pharaoh was defeated. Exodus 15 began Israel's liminal period of wilderness wanderings which continued until Joshua led them over the Jordan in Joshua 3:17. Below is a diagram of Israel's rite of passage and their liminal state in the wilderness in which they were betwixt and between two statuses. They were no longer slaves in Egypt under the domination and oppression of Pharaoh, but they had not yet crossed the Jordan into the territory that would define them as a nation. While in the wilderness they were in a state of liminality. They had been consecrated as God's people, but they had yet to learn to live as God's people. During this time, they followed the authority of Moses as God's agent. Like other groups in liminality, they learned the *sacra* of God: its knowledge, its objects, and its actions in the detailed instructions of life as a people and cultic practices in the worship of God (Figure 10).

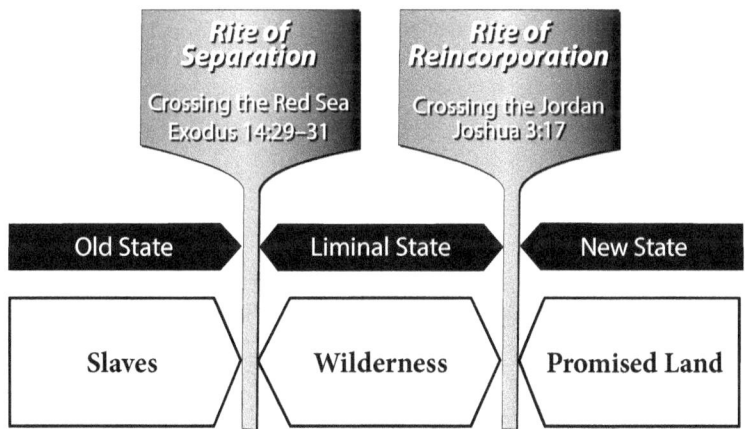

Figure 10. Liminality of Israel

There was also an extended rite of separation that began when Israel was ready to leave until when Pharaoh was defeated, which can be compared to Jesus' extended rite of separation. Moses fought Pharaoh for control of Israel; Jesus battled Satan. After defeating Pharaoh, Moses freed Israel from slavery; in the new exodus, Jesus freed Israel from the captivity and oppression of Satan. Second, both Jesus and Moses performed mighty deeds, and their authority came from God as his agent, not from a position in structure. Exodus 15 records that it was through this great power to fight the Egyptians that people feared the Lord, "and they believed in the Lord and in his servant Moses."[90] Moses' authority came from his closeness to God and the mighty deeds that God did through him. Jesus' authority came from the Spirit of God and from the mighty deeds he did. Both were agents of God who acted on God's behalf. The extended rite of separation also highlights the true enemies of Israel: in the first exodus, Pharaoh, and in the new exodus, Satan.

Using rites of passage as a heuristic framework allows a comparison of Jesus' public ministry to a liminal period in the life of Israel and demonstrates how Luke reframed the people of God and defined Jesus' public ministry in anti-structural terms. Luke framed Jesus in his public ministry in the role of the Moses-like prophet and the people of God as Israel during her liminal period in the wilderness.[91] The people of God in Jesus' ministry were in liminality. In the wilderness, Israel's identity was not found in a geographic territory or as a political entity (structural). Rather, her identity as a people was marked by the presence of God and her obedience to God as a people (anti-structure). In the wilderness, Israel learned to be God's people. Moses instructed them in the actions and behavior expected of God's people; Jesus also instructed them in the actions and behavior expected of God's people.

Luke also used the motif of the new exodus to tell the story of Israel's deliverance with Jesus as the agent of God's deliverance. Just as God led the Israelites through the wilderness, the first-century Jews hoped for deliverance and restoration. Charles Scobie notes, "It has long been recognized that the numerous allusions to the exodus in the Second Isaiah form the basis of the portrayal of the future age of salvation, on the principle that the past deliverance is a type of future deliverance."[92] That deliverance came, but not in the way they expected it. In comparing Jesus and his public ministry to Moses and the exodus, Luke was able to retell the story of the people of God, but with a "dynamic twist." Just as Moses delivered the people of God from captivity, so too, Jesus was delivering them from their true enemy, Satan. In Luke's narrative, framing Jesus' public ministry as liminal subverted nationalistic expectations and demonstrated that Israel's need for deliverance was not from the nations but from the true source of their oppression and captivity, Satan

---

90. Exodus 14:31.

91. Scobie, "A Canonical Approach to Interpreting Luke," 327–49.

92. Scobie, "A Canonical Approach to Interpreting Luke," 338; Isaiah 42:13; 43:16–19; 48:21; 51:10; 52:12, etc.

Summary

This section demonstrated that three aspects of the Kingdom of God can be framed in liminality. First, the Kingdom of God as Jesus taught it was in temporal liminality. It was inaugurated in the ministry of Jesus, but there was also a future consummation. Second, the agent of God's salvation was in liminality. Placing Jesus' life into a framework of rites of passage demonstrated that Jesus' public ministry was in a liminal phase. Comparing this to David's life highlighted how Luke identified Jesus as the Davidic king, the expected messiah and deliverer, but not in the way that Israel expected the king. Jesus' public ministry compared to David's period of liminality in which he was betwixt and between; he was anointed as Israel's future king but not enthroned as king. It was only after Jesus' death that he was recognized as the exalted Davidic king.

Finally, the people of God were in liminality. The liminal phase of Jesus' ministry was compared to Israel's liminal phase in wilderness. The people of God were experiencing God's presence, but they were not yet a nation. They had experienced deliverance, but their identity was based on a relationship with God rather than geographic territory. Placing Israel's life in a framework of rite of passage demonstrates how Luke retold Israel's story and reframed their expectations for a new exodus from their enemies. Jesus as the new Moses was leading Israel on a new exodus, but their enemies were not the nations, but Satan. The framework of liminality provides a framework to compare the structural expectations of Israel for her deliverance and the anti-structural characteristics of Jesus' own redefinition of God's deliverance and the people of God. The features of structure and anti-structure are compared in Table 2.

Table 2. Comparison of Structural and Anti-Structural Expectations

	Structure Ethnic Israel	**Anti-Structure** God's rule
People of God	Bloodline, ethnic	Obedience to God
Identity Marker	Circumcision, Sabbath, food	Relationship with God
Way of Life	Structural expectations	Anti-structural relationships
Enemy	Nations	Satan
Problem	Oppression by nations	Alienation from God
Solution	Vindication over nations	Restoration to God

The discussion in the last section demonstrated how Luke reframed expectations of deliverance from structure to anti-structure. In the next section, I demonstrate how Jesus defined the people of God and the expectations of behavior for the people of God with the anti-structural characteristics of people in liminality.

The People of God

As demonstrated in the preceding section, Luke in his narrative framed the Kingdom of God, Jesus in his public ministry, and the people of God in liminal states. In liminality, life and relationships are defined by anti-structure rather than structural status and position. However, unlike many rites of passage in which the liminal states are lived separated from structure, the people of God lived liminal lives within structure. They did not separate from their statuses in society while in liminality, but they were to live out these anti-structural relationships within the structures of society. In the following section, I demonstrate that anti-structural characteristics defined who belonged to the people of God, how they related as people of God, and the behavior of leaders within the people of God.

Who Is "In"—Redefining the People of God

The people of God in first-century Israel were defined by bloodline and circumcision. The boundaries and identity of the people of God were symbolized in the temple, the Torah, the land, and maintaining a way of life, including right praxis particularly related to temple and Torah, which were important for maintaining Jewish identity.[93] These practices distinguished Israel as a unique people within the broader context of Greco-Roman society. Hellerman observes, "The evidence is quite conclusive. Greco-Roman writers identified circumcision, Sabbath-keeping, and adherence to the levitical food laws as those practices that marked out Judeans as socially distinct from their pagan contemporaries."[94] Hellerman notes that purity, particularly concerns about Sabbath and food laws, became a symbol for the Pharisees as a way of maintaining their socio-religious boundaries and exclusiveness.[95] The Temple was a national symbol for Israel.[96] These

---

93. Wright, *The New Testament and the People of God*, 233, 35. Wright also outlines the retelling of Israel's story line in his discussion of Israel's worldview, 215–43.
94. Hellerman, *Jesus and the People of God*, 19.
95. Hellerman, *Jesus and the People of God*, 112, 207.
96. Hellerman, *Jesus and the People of God*, 171–72.

symbols and practices all defined who was "in" and who was "out" of the people of God, the "true Israel."

However, Wright argues that in Jesus' ministry as the agent of God, he was reconstituting Israel around himself.[97] The characteristics of people who were "in" in Jesus' people of God were defined not by structural characteristics but by anti-structural characteristics of obedience to his word and restoration to God. In Luke's narrative, Jesus emphasized anti-structural criteria over structural criteria such as bloodlines for defining the people of God. In Luke 8:19–21, Jesus' mother and brothers came to him, and he was told that they were waiting for him. He answered, "My mother and my brothers are those who hear the world of God and do it." In this passage, Jesus defined who was part of his family—not by bloodline but by obedience to the word of God. Similarly, in Luke 11:27–28, a woman in the crowd shouted, "Blessed (honored) is the womb that bore you, and the breast at which you nursed." Jesus responded that it was not kin relationships that made one blessed (honored) in his group, but, "Blessed (honored) rather are those who hear the word of God and keep it." Here, people were honored, i.e., favored by God and Jesus' followers, not because of a particular kin relationship, but because of their obedience to God's word. The anti-structural criteria of obedience to God's word defined who were the people of God, rather than structural conditions of national identity. It does not change the structural relationship (they are still Judean or kin), but it redefined how one was included in the reconstructed people of God.

In a similar manner, there were no structural boundaries to gaining membership in the people of God. There was no out-group or in-group based on some kind of structural characteristic. While inclusion into Israel involved the right genealogy, inclusion into the new people of God required a right relationship. Membership extended to all who obeyed the word of God and to all who did his work. As the people of God, the marginal were no longer on the margins. Those on the margins of religious life in first-century Palestine included the lame, the crippled, lepers, tax collectors, and women. Jesus' people of God not only included people from the margins, but also included people in positional structure. Jesus ate with sinners, tax collectors, Pharisees, lawyers, and women. Jesus healed a widow's son, unclean women and men, a synagogue ruler's daughter, a centurion's slave, a Gentile, the blind, the crippled, and the lame.[98] There were no boundaries

---

97. Wright, *Jesus and the Victory of God*, 131.

98. Luke 4:17–25, 29–31, 33–35, 38; 7:1–10, 11–17, 36–49; 8:26–33, 35–43; 13:10–13.

to those who could obey his word: both the marginal and those who were in positions within the structure were included.

Just as there were no structural boundaries for inclusion, so there were no cliques within the people of God. When Jesus' disciples tried to stop someone outside their group from casting out demons in Jesus' name, Green notes, "They had engaged in boundary-marking on the basis of conventional notions of perceived honor."[99] In his answer to the disciples, Jesus redefined the in-group as all who were obeying and doing his work: "Do not stop him, for the one who is not against you is for you."[100] The unnamed exorcist was doing the work that Jesus did in the name of Jesus. Although the disciples failed to include him because he did not fit a perceived in-group status, Jesus based the in-group on those who were following his word and doing his work.

On the other hand, there were those who thought they were "in" by structural categories but now found themselves "out." The criteria for inclusion and exclusion were not based on position in structure but rather on those who followed Jesus. Those who thought they were included because of ascribed or achieved structural status found themselves excluded. While they may have been honored for their structural statuses, these were not what made someone part of the people of God. This understanding of structure and anti-structure provides a framework for interpreting the trope of blessings and woes at the beginning of Jesus' sermon to the crowds in Luke 6:20–26.

In this passage, there seems to be reversals of status for the poor and the rich. However, it is not so much a reversal of status but rather a redefinition of honor, specifically who were honored in the new people of God. And it is not based on their status. The characteristics that follow can be attributed to those basic conditions of rich, or honored in society, and poor, those who are not honored in society.[101] The poor were not just economically poor but were those marginalized in the broader world.[102] They were the ones who were suffering injustice in the world, often at the hands of the rich who abused their power.[103] They were the ones who were disadvantaged and experiencing misery.[104] In terms of honor and shame, they were the shamed ones, those who lacked honor within structure because of their status as

---

99. Green, *The Gospel of Luke*, 392.

100. Luke 9:49–50.

101. Goheen, "A Critical Examination of David Bosch's Missional Reading of Luke," 229–D67.

102. Green, *The Gospel of Luke*, 265.

103. Stein, *Luke*, 204.

104. Goheen, "A Critical Examination of David Bosch's Missional Reading of Luke," 244.

poor. The rich were those who had a structural status, who were honored and who often oppressed the poor.[105]

I reverse the order of the trope and discuss the attributes of the rich first, to highlight their contrast with the poor through the lenses of honor, shame, and marginalization. In the Luke 6 passage, Luke lists four woes of those who are rich and then three of their characteristics: well fed, laughing, and spoken well of by others. Each of these characteristics were attributes of wealth and a criteria or result of honor. In the Greco-Roman world, wealth was one of the attributes of honor, particularly land ownership.[106] The quality of food and those to whom you served it were also part of the symbols of prestige that were honored.[107] Bock claims that the laughter to which Jesus referenced was not one of joy, but Bock argues that γελάω denotes a laughter of arrogance, boastfulness, and rejoicing in the misfortune of others. He concludes, "Thus, the picture is of a person of worldly ease who is indifferent because of self-satisfaction."[108] Finally, a good name was an important criteria for honor. To be praised by another, particularly one of high status, was one way of gaining traditional honor in structure.[109] The people who met these criteria were the ones favored by the world's standards.

Reversal of fortunes was a common trope in the ancient world, but the significance in this context as Jesus began to speak about the people of God was that it served to redefine who were the people of God.[110] In the contrasts of blessings and woes, those who thought that their place in structure afforded them favor with God or that their place in structure was a result of God's favor, discovered that those criteria did not define the people of God whom Jesus was reconstituting. What the society honored was not what God honored. As Green observes, Jesus "is replacing common representations of the world with a new one."[111]

Jesus defined the people of God by different standards. The people of God were those on the margins, the dishonorable, and the ones who mourned and were hated because of their commitment to the purposes of God. These were the people who received God's favor and were honored by God: those who did not orient themselves around their own striving to receive honor. Those who thought they were "in" because of structural honor

---

105. Bock, *Luke Volume 1:1—9:50*, 624.
106. Lendon, *Empire of Honor*, 36.
107. Lendon, *Empire of Honor*, 46.
108. Bock, *Luke Volume 1:1—9:50*, 585.
109. Lendon, *Empire of Honor*, 49.
110. Green, *The Gospel of Luke*, 265.
111. Green, *The Gospel of Luke*, 265.

found themselves "out." It was the anti-structural qualities, relationship to Jesus and obedience to his word that made a person part of the people of God and honorable in God's people.

Inclusion into Jesus' people of God was not based on being a part of ethnic Israel. Instead, membership required an acceptance of the invitation to be restored to God. In the parable of the banquet, Jesus clarified that there were many who thought they were included but rejected the invitation to participate in the reconstituted people of God.[112] When those who were invited did not accept the invitation, thus dishonoring the master, the master invited those who were on the margins of society to dine with him. Those who believed that they were included based on their position in structure (Israel chosen by God) had no place in the Kingdom. In the liminal Kingdom of God, membership was based on a relationship with God: those who accepted his invitation to dine with Him.[113] Those who thought they were "in" because of structural qualities found themselves "out" because they ignored the anti-structural invitation.

The last example of redefinition of honor is a narrative that juxtaposes those who were honorable according to their status in structure with those that are honorable in Jesus' people of God. This provides an illustrative case of the interaction of structural and anti-structural attributes considered honorable. Jesus made a contrast between the behavior of a repentant woman and the behavior of his host, a Pharisee, during a meal.[114] The way that Luke unfolds the narrative highlights the contrast of the structural status of the two people who interacted with Jesus. Jesus had been invited to eat at the home of Simon, a Pharisee and an honorable person by the standards of his peers. The woman was described in great detail. Green notes, "She is depicted more fully than any other person we have encountered."[115] She was described as a sinner, a woman of the city, and possibly a prostitute by social status.[116] She was considered unclean, but more importantly in this context, she was the polar opposite of Simon's purity-based honor. She was the epitome of a dishonorable person according to the standards of the Pharisee.

The next scene described her actions toward Jesus. Luke unfolded the narrative as she wets Jesus' feet with her tears and wipes them dry with her hair while kissing his feet and anointing them with the ointment she had

---

112. Luke 14.
113. Luke 14.
114. Luke 7:36–50.
115. Green, *The Gospel of Luke*, 306.
116. Green, *The Gospel of Luke*, 309.

brought with her. Her actions can be interpreted as erotic, which was congruent with her status.[117] However, as Green notes, "Her behavior is open to divergent interpretations that can only be disambiguated with a larger system of meaning or a worldview."[118] Simon interpreted the actions of a dishonorable woman as dishonorable, and Jesus as dishonorable by his association with her. However, Jesus interpreted them as gratitude from a grateful woman as demonstrated in his parable of the debtors. Only then does Luke contrast these actions with Simon's own actions.

Simon as the host demonstrated his attitude toward Jesus by forgoing the expected etiquette of a host to a social equal; he neglected to provide Jesus with water for washing his feet, a kiss of greeting, and oil for his head. In fact, such neglect would have been considered as an insult to Jesus' honor.[119] Here the redefinition of honor is clear. The honorable person according to their status in structure acted dishonorably toward Jesus, while the dishonorable woman according to her structure in status acted honorably in her extravagance toward Jesus. It was the person who acted honorably toward Jesus who was restored to God rather than the person who had honorable status. Jesus restored the woman to fellowship with God and within the community by proclaiming, "Your sins are forgiven."[120] It was not a person's status in structure that made someone a part of the people of God, but rather their actions toward Jesus and his invitation to be restored to God. Anti-structural criteria defined who were included in Jesus' people of God rather than structural criteria.

Relationships of the People of God— Anti-Structural and Allocentric[121]

The relationships between the people of God were also redefined by anti-structural criteria. In the Greco-Roman world, hierarchically ordered statuses defined relationships. People seeking honor used their interactions with others to increase their social esteem in the eyes of others, or in other words their honor.[122] The competition for honor was egocentric. Each

---

117. Green, *The Gospel of Luke*, 310.
118. Green, *The Gospel of Luke*, 311.
119. Lendon, *The Empire of Honor*, 134.
120. Bock, *Luke Volume 1:1—9:50*, 707.
121. Kuecker's use of allocentric in *The Spirit and 'the Other'* provided a concise concept to describe the relationships in the Kingdom of God. I use it throughout.
122. Malina and Neyrey, "Honor and Shame in Luke–Acts," 25.

sought to increase their own honor, sometimes at the expense of others.[123] Additionally, within the Jewish community, their structural symbols of identity and their practices to maintain their identity created an ethnic boundary between themselves and others. Boundary maintenance and even solidarity within a group relies on an "us" versus "them" evaluation, or ethnocentrism.[124]

However, the relationships between people in liminality are characterized by communitas. There are two dimensions that reflect communitas: anti-structure and allocentricism. Anti-structure implies that in-group/out-group boundaries, status, and rank no longer define relationships within the community. People still maintain their statuses in structure, but relationships among people and between people and God were no longer based on these ranks, groupings, or statuses. In liminality, there is a suspension of the normal distinctions of rank and status. People relate to one another not by position in structure but as humans. Boundaries that were maintained because of ritual, rank, status, or ethnicity no longer affect the interaction between individuals in a liminal state. The second characteristic is allocentricism, a commitment to the interests of others. The people of God were expected to relate to one another as equals and to serve the interests of others. One of the ways this was expressed was the use of sibling terminology.

There are several who have characterized the relationships in the people of God in terms of brother/sister relationships.[125] The relationships within the family were based on love, and there is the practice of generalized reciprocity rather than the balanced reciprocity that is found in relationships within the broader society. The relationships between siblings are among the closest friendships in the Greco-Roman world.[126] The relationships of the people of God were compared to these anti-structural relationships found in sibling relationships. Siblings were expected to cooperate rather than compete and were not to seek honor at the expense of a sibling.[127]

The allocentric, anti-structural interpersonal relationships of the people of God were antithetical to the competition and seeking for one's own gain that defined the honor and shame game in the first century. First, they had no status. Jesus compared those who enter the Kingdom of God to a child: "Truly I say to you whoever does not receive the Kingdom of

---

123. Malina and Neyrey, "Honor and Shame in Luke-Acts," 29.

124. Kuecker, *The Spirit and the 'Other,'* 155.

125. Hellerman, *The Ancient Church as Family*; Lohfink, *Jesus and Community*, 43, 154–57.

126. deSilva, *Honor, Patronage, Kinship & Purity*, 166.

127. deSilva, *Honor, Patronage, Kinship & Purity*, 167.

LIMINALITY, JESUS, AND THE KINGDOM OF GOD

God like a child shall not enter it."[128] In stating that people must enter like a child, Jesus was stating that people enter without their status. They were to humble themselves and not count on their structural position to become a part of the people of God.

Second, they were not to seek honor for themselves. The actions of people according to anti-structural criteria were to be different. The people of God were not to compete for honor. They were not to be like those in structure who sought honor, particularly at the expense of another. In first-century Palestine, those in structure sought honor and praise for the position that they held in structure.[129] They sought seats of honor in synagogues, vied for seats of honor at dinners, and desired to be greeted with respect in the marketplace.[130] However, honor was redefined in the people of God wherein it did not come from domination, position, and self-exaltation but from service, honoring others, and humility. As Luke records, "For all who exalt themselves will be humbled and those who humble themselves will be exalted."[131] Those who sought to honor others were the ones who were honored in the people of God. They were to be humble in regards to one another and allow others to honor them and give them positions and status rather than seek it for themselves.[132]

They also did not gain honor through comparison to others, defining who was "in" and who was "out" by their performance. Practices that honored one's self or honored one's group were not allowed within the people of God. Just as inclusion was redefined in liminality, so were the practices that defined exclusion. In the structure of Judaism, "righteousness" was obtained through purity, or boundary maintenance, and orthopraxy (right performance of religious ritual, including tithes, fasting, prayer, and sacrifices). These practices focused on the symbols of Judaism, Temple, and Torah that maintained Jewish identity.[133] However, in Jesus' people of God, community practices were defined by loving each other and loving God.[134] The defining identity for people within Jesus' people of God was love. What made the person acceptable to God was not outward performance but the inward condition of the heart.[135] Relationship with God and

---

128. Luke 18:17.
129. See Malina and Neyrey, "Honor and Shame in Luke–Acts," 25.
130. Luke 11:42–48.
131. Luke 14:11 (NIV).
132. Luke 14:7–11.
133. See chapter 2 for a fuller discussion.
134. Luke 7:27.
135. Luke 11:39–40.

with each other rather than individual piety as defined by structure was considered righteous and pleasing to God.

Jesus illustrated this in his parable of the Pharisee and tax collector in Luke 18:9–14. As Green notes, Jesus set up a distinct polarity between these two men; the Pharisee separated himself from the other and sought honor in his own piety, which he compared to the low-status other, the tax collector. In this story the Pharisee has seemingly won the competition and God's favor through his actions as noted by his prayer: "God, I thank you that I am not like other men, extortioners, unjust, adulterers, or even like this tax collector. I fast twice a week; I give tithes of all that I get."[136] The tax collector on the other hand recognized his state of unworthiness, that he was not honorable. Green notes in Jesus' telling of this parable that he idealized the behavior of both. Green observes, "One claims superior status for himself by comparing himself with and separating himself from others, the other makes no claims to status at all, but acknowledges his position as a sinner who can take refuge only in the beneficence of God."[137] Jesus summarized, "For everyone who exalts himself will be humbled, but everyone who humbles himself will be exalted."[138] In liminality, there was no place for comparison to others, seeking honor or prestige by comparison to others, which only alienated people from others and from God. Those who competed for honor found themselves praised by men but alienated from God.

Not only were people in anti-structure not to seek honor, but they were also not to defend their own honor. Jesus taught, "Judge not and you will not be judged, condemn not and you will not be condemned; forgive and you will be forgiven."[139] In the ancient world, the greatest threat to honor was the insult. This could come from failure to greet someone, damage from an opinion of someone else, failure to be invited to an event, or the neglect of any of the actions that were required towards an honorable person.[140] Insult also insinuated weakness or the inability to defend one's honor.[141] According to Lendon, there was a need to act defensively since honor also depended on having the power to defend it. Lendon explains, "To avoid contempt you must lash out."[142] But in liminality, there was no need to defend honor because status had lost its importance in the people of God. In liminality, people

---

136. Luke 18:11–12.
137. Green, *The Gospel of Luke*, 649.
138. Luke 18:14.
139. Luke 6:37.
140. Lendon, *Empire of Honor*, 49.
141. Lendon, *Empire of Honor*, 51.
142. Lendon, *Empire of Honor*, 51.

related to one another as persons, not on the basis of status. Revenge that sought to retaliate for an offense was replaced by forgiveness.

A third characteristic of Jesus' people of God was that those with structural status were to use it for the benefit of others. Love was a defining characteristic of the people of God. Because relationships within the people of God were anti-structural, they were also allocentric. There was no room for egocentricism or those who were ethnocentric. They were to use their status in structure not to gain honor for themselves, but to honor others. For instance, those who had wealth were not to use their wealth to honor themselves but use it for the good of others. In structure, people who were born into wealthy families were ascribed honor and so sought to maintain that honor.[143] However, in the Kingdom, wealthy people were instructed to sell possessions and seek the Kingdom.[144] People had possessions, but they were not to use them to gain status and honor. Nor were people to treat others differently because of the wealth they possessed. They were not to give only to those who could give back in order to gain prestige, but they were to give without thought of return.[145] In structure, people gained status by who came to their feasts, what food they served, and what kind of entertainment they provided.[146] Giving feasts and receiving invitations to feasts were ways that people could gain prestige and honor.[147] However, Jesus taught that when they gave feasts, they should provide for people who were not in their "in" group. They were also to give freely to all people without thought of return.[148]

Finally, those in Jesus' people of God were to extend this same kind of honor and love to people who were outside their group. Within structure, people love and respect those who are within a particular status-based in-group, whether it is based on ethnicity, religion, or kinship. However, in the people of God, there was a suspension of boundary markers, whether they were based on kinship, purity, or other characteristics. Love was no longer constrained but was to be extended to everyone, including those who were considered enemies. Jesus said, "But I say to you who hear, love your enemies and do good to those who hate you, bless those who curse you, and pray for those who mistreat you."[149] In structure, those in the group must be loved,

---

143. Lendon, *Empire of Honor*, 36–39.
144. Luke 18:18–30; see also Luke 12:16–21, 23–34.
145. Luke 14:13–14.
146. Lendon, *Empire of Honor*, 50.
147. Lendon, *Empire of Honor*, 49.
148. Luke 6:35–40.
149. Luke 7:27–28.

those outside the group may be hated.[150] However, in Jesus' people of God, its members were to love enemies as friends, and there were to be no structural markers that divided one group from another.

Jesus' story of the Good Samaritan demonstrates the unboundedness of love that was expected of the people of God.[151] The context for the story of the Good Samaritan was a conversation between Jesus and a lawyer. The question the lawyer asked Jesus was, "What must I do to inherit eternal life?" Jesus did not answer the lawyer's question. Instead Jesus asked the lawyer a counter-question, "What is written in the Law?" He essentially was asking, "What does God require?" The lawyer responded with two familiar passages from the Torah. The first was from Deuteronomy 6:5, part of the Shema that was recited twice a day, and the second part of the answer was Leviticus 19:18, which was in the context of several tangible ways in which people were to love their neighbor.[152] Jesus commended him and told him to go and do as he had answered, but the lawyer then asked, "Who is my neighbor?" The question in essence asked for limits on the extent to which he had to love.[153] Green notes, "Different attitudes toward these foreign intrusions developed into a fractured social context in which boundaries distinguished not only between Jew and Gentile but also between Jewish factions. How far should love reach?"[154]

Jesus answered with a parable, starting it with an ambiguous "certain man." The audience was not told anything about the man—his ethnicity, social class, or religion. He was just a man. The lawyer and Jesus' audience could not automatically justify the actions of the priest and the Levite as simply following socially acceptable forms of action. Green notes, "The impossibility of classifying this person as either friend or foe immediately subverted any interest in a question of this nature."[155] The unknown man was overwhelmed by bandits and was left for dead. His state was such that he could not help himself. Green continues, "Stripped of his clothes and left half-dead, the man's anonymity throughout the story is assured; he is simply a human being, a neighbor, in need."[156]

Here, once again, Jesus provided a stark contrast between the behavior of those who were considered honorable in social structure and one who

150. Bock, *Luke 1:1—9:50*, 588.
151. Luke 10:25–37.
152. Green, *The Gospel of Luke*, 422.
153. Bock, *Luke Volume 9:51—24:53*, 1027.
154. Green, *The Gospel of Luke*, 429.
155. Green, *The Gospel of Luke*, 429.
156. Green, *The Gospel of Luke*, 429.

was considered dishonorable by his status. The first two travelers to see the man in the road were representatives of the Temple elite. Bock notes that the identification of the two who passed by as officials of Judaism is a generalized condemnation of official Judaism that placed purity over compassion, of those who saw the world as us-them.[157] Green describes the issue:

> Priests and Levites shared high status in the community of God's people on account of ascription–that is not because they trained or were chosen to be priests but because they were born into priestly families. They participated in and were legitimated by the world of the temple, with its circumspect boundaries between clean and unclean, including clean and unclean people. They epitomize a worldview of tribal consciousness concerned with relative status and us-them cataloguing.[158]

After a quick succession of Jewish leaders who saw the man but passed by, the audience was introduced to the Samaritan. A Samaritan was the last person that a Jew would consider a neighbor. There was mutual hatred between Jews and Samaritans. To the Jews, Samaritans were outsiders geographically, socially, religiously, and culturally and were considered unclean and therefore to be avoided. Bock observes, "For a Jew, a Samaritan was among the least respected of people."[159] They were the epitome of dishonorable persons to a Jew.

However, the actions of this dishonorable person were extravagant in his honorable behavior toward this unknown man. In his parable, Jesus elaborated and prolonged the care that this so-called "dishonorable" Samaritan gave to a stranger: (1) he approaches him, (2) binds his wounds, (3) anoints him with oil and wine, (4) loads him on his mule, (5) takes him to an inn, and (6) provides for his care.[160] In contrast to the two Jews, the Samaritan gave generously and did everything he could to take care of this unknown man. In Jesus' final question, he demonstrated that it was action, not boundaries, that determine a neighbor: "Which of these three do you think proved to be neighbor to the man who fell among the robbers?"[161] The lawyer responded, "The one who showed mercy on him." And Jesus said to him, "Go and do likewise."[162]

---

157. Bock, *Luke Volume 9:51—24:53*, 1030.
158. Green, *The Gospel of Luke*, 429.
159. Bock, *Luke Volume 9:51—24:53*, 1031.
160. Bock, *Luke Volume 9:51—24:53*, 1032-33.
161. Luke 10:36.
162. Luke 10:37.

Jesus' counter-question was not "Who is my neighbor?" but "Who acted like a neighbor?" The implication was that for the people of God, a neighbor was not defined by structural status, such as geographical, social, or kin ties; rather a neighbor was defined in terms of the one who had need. The man in Jesus' parable did not have an identity. His ethnicity, his geographical hometown, and his religion remained unknown in his anonymity. He was simply a person, someone who needed a neighbor. Bock summarizes, "Neighborliness is not found in a racial bond, nationality, color, gender, proximity, or by living in a certain neighborhood. We become a neighbor by responding sensitively to the needs of others."[163] Stein likewise asserts, "Jesus sought to illustrate that the love of one's neighbor must transcend all natural or human boundaries such as race, nationality, religion, and economic or educational status."[164] The anti-structural quality of liminality meant there were no structural criteria that defined insider/outsider boundaries. Nor did structural criteria determine the extent to which to extend relationships marked by the qualities of communitas.

Authority and Leadership

Just as honor was redefined in Jesus' people of God, so was leadership and authority. In structure, a leader's authority is derived from their position in structure, but in liminality, authority is based on the person, their embodiment of the values of the community, their service on behalf of the community, and their knowledge of the *sacra*.[165] Jesus' authority was based on his relationship with God as God's agent, his anointing with God's Spirit and his mighty deeds done for the benefit of God's people. He, like Moses, was God's agent in teaching the people of God the knowledge, actions, and rituals that were required for their new life as the people of God.

Loyalties are also redefined for the people of God. Leaders in liminality have complete authority over the initiates in liminality.[166] Among Jesus' people of God, loyalties to structural roles and obligations were secondary; the first loyalty was to God and the agent of God in communitas. Several have noted there were no fathers in the new community because they were symbolic of patriarchal domination.[167] In liminality, there is also a suspension of all kinship rights and obligations. When someone wanted to

---

163. Bock, *Luke Volume 9:51—24:53*, 1035.
164. Stein, *Luke*, 319.
165. Turner, *The Ritual Process*, 103.
166. Turner, *The Ritual Process*, 103.
167. Bartchy, *Call No Man Father*, 9–10; Lohfink, *Jesus and Community*, 45.

complete their kinship obligations before following Jesus, saying, "Let me first go bury my father," Jesus responded, "Let the dead bury their own dead. But as for you, go and proclaim the kingdom of God."[168]

Authority and actions of leaders was also redefined in the people of God. Leaders in communitas were not to use that authority to serve themselves; they were to be servants of all in the community. In seeking honor, Pharisees and other religious leaders exalted themselves and used their position to dominate others.[169] Jesus rebuked them saying, "Woe to you lawyers also! For you load people with burdens hard to bear, and you yourselves do not lift a finger to ease them."[170] In the liminal people of God, leadership was redefined not as one who dominated, but as one who served others. When the disciples argued over who would be greatest, Jesus compared the characteristics of leaders in structure and leaders in anti-structure: "The kings of the Gentiles exercise lordship over them, and those in authority over them are called benefactors. But not so with you. Rather, let the greatest among you become as the youngest, and the leader as one who serves."[171] The disciples desired to be great, yet Jesus responded that the leader was the one who served.[172]

Summary

Using the framework of liminality highlights how Luke reframed the story of Israel and the expectations of her restoration and deliverance. In Luke's story, Jesus did not fulfill the structural expectations of the promise of God but rather redefined the people of God—who they were, their interpersonal relationships, and leaders—by anti-structural characteristics. Just as relationships between people in liminality are characterized by communitas, so the relationships of the liminal people of God to God and to each other were characterized by communitas. The criteria for inclusion into the people of God were anti-structural, not based on status in structure but by obedience to the word of God's agent. The relationships between people among the people of God were anti-structural and allocentric. Finally, leadership in the people of God was not defined by position in structure but by the presence of God's Spirit manifested through deeds and service to the community. In the next section, I demonstrate that the conflicts between religious leaders

---

168. Luke 9:59–60.
169. Bartchy, *Call No Man Father,* Chapter 3, 7–11.
170. Luke 11:46.
171. Luke 22:24–26.
172. Luke 22:24.

and Jesus arose when structural concerns of identity undermined the anti-structural priorities of Jesus' people of God.

Conflicting Kingdoms—Anti-Structure and Structure

There were several instances in which Jesus had conflicts with the religious leaders over their practices or his praxes. These did not indicate that Jesus was rejecting structure. There were instances in which Jesus supported both the political and religious structures of his day. For instance, when the religious leaders sought to test him with the question "Is it lawful for us to give tribute to Caesar?" his response was to "render to Caesar things that are Caesar's and to God the things that are God's."[173] In this case, Jesus was not making a statement about the legitimacy of Roman rule over Israel, but rather paying tribute was part of living under Roman rule.[174]

There were also instances in which Jesus directed people to participate in the required cultic practices. For instance, when Jesus healed a man with leprosy, Jesus instructed him to follow the normal procedures for reinstitution into the community: "Go and show yourself to the priest and make an offer for your cleansing, as Moses commanded, for a proof to them."[175] Although not the focus of this pericope, it does demonstrate that Jesus did not invalidate the structural rituals of cultic practice.[176] The Levitical practices were required to restore the man to the community.[177] Other evidence of Jesus' participation in structure was his attendance at synagogues and participation in Passover.[178] Sanders argues, "His mission was to Israel in the name of the God of Israel. He thus evidently accepted his people's special status, that is, the election and the covenant. It is equally clear that he accepted obedience to the law as the norm."[179] Jesus did not reject the religious structures. However, I argue that the confrontations with the religious leaders were because of competing agendas when the leaders prioritized structural

---

173. Luke 20:25.

174. Luke 20:22–26; Bock, *Luke 9:51—24:53*, 1613. I agree with Bock in that Jesus is not making a statement about the legitimacy of Roman rule over Israel, rather the fact that they did rule.

175. Luke 5:12–16.

176. Green, *The Gospel of Luke*, 237; Bock, *Luke Volume 1:1—9:50*, 477. Bock notes that Jesus already made human contact, which violated the law, but this is consistent with Jesus' willingness to cross boundaries for someone's good.

177. Green, *The Gospel of Luke*, 238. A similar incident is also found in Luke 17:11–19.

178. Luke 4:16–28, 42, 6:6–10, 22:14–23.

179. Sanders, *Jesus and Judaism*, 336.

concerns of identity over anti-structural concerns of restoration to God. I demonstrate these competing agendas in two areas, conflicts over personal purity and conflicts over the Sabbath (national purity).

Purity

For some Jews, there was a connection between the purity codes and political aspirations.[180] To be Jewish meant the observance of the Temple cult, observance of the Sabbath, food taboos, and circumcision. These were practices that distinguished Israel from the nations, and to lose these was to lose their uniqueness as the people of God. These were to be obeyed and defended in order to insure the life of the true Israel.[181] As Wright notes, "It was a matter of guarding Israel from paganization, and, more positively, attempting (if and when occasion allowed) to throw off the pagan yoke altogether."[182]

In Old Testament usage, purity primarily had to do with one's ability to participate in the Temple cult.[183] However, Shaye Cohen asserts that during Hasmonean rule, purity had become a political symbol and to some extent a symbol of protest against the Temple and the priesthood.[184] Bartchy notes that the Pharisees regarded their tables as surrogates for the Temple and therefore maintained the purity required of priests, which meant their food had to be properly tithed, prepared, and served.[185] For the Pharisees, purity became a marker of national identity. Bartchy explains, "The Pharisees longed for the time when all of Israel would live in such a state of holiness. They believed that Israel's identity and blessed future depended on it."[186]

In Luke, the conflicts with Jesus were not about the purity laws themselves but when structural concerns took priority over anti-structural concerns. For instance, Jesus rebuked the Pharisees not for their concerns about purity of the outer body, keeping impure or unclean objects from entering or touching their body, but lack of concern for the inner heart. Jesus stated, "Now you Pharisees clean the outside of the cup and of the dish, but inside you are full of greed and wickedness. You fools! Did not the one who made the outside make the inside also?"[187] There were several instances in which

---

180. Wright, *Jesus and the Victory of God*, 384.
181. Wright, *Jesus and the Victory of God*, 384.
182. Wright, *Jesus and the Victory of God*, 384.
183. deSilva, *Honor, Patronage, Kinship & Purity*, 248–49.
184. Cohen, *From the Maccabees to the Mishnah*, 157.
185. Bartchy, "Table Fellowship," 796.
186. Bartchy, "Table Fellowship," 797.
187. Luke 11:37–40.

Jesus confronted the Pharisees about the gap between their inner heart and outer performance. He confronted the Pharisees saying, "But woe to you Pharisees! For you tithe mint and rue and herbs of all kinds, and neglect justice and the love of God; it is these you ought to have practiced, without neglecting the others."[188] Jesus did not reject the structural religious practices of the Pharisees, but they were to practice love for people, the anti-structural focus, within the context of those structures.

A second area of conflict was over Jesus' table fellowship. According to Hellerman, meals were vitally important because they were a vehicle for reinforcing social structure and preserving the boundaries between ethnic and social groups.[189] Luke records an incident in which a tax collector named Levi gave a great feast for Jesus and invited a large number of people, including fellow tax collectors.[190] The Pharisees and scribes asked the question, "Why do you eat and drink with tax collectors and sinners?"[191] The contrast between the Pharisee's table fellowship was clear. Their purity concerns excluded the very sinners who were eating with Jesus. The social implications reflected their rejection of "sinners" as being part of the true Israel whom God will rescue. However, Jesus' answer reflected the conflict between structural and anti-structural characteristics of the people of God. Jesus' agenda was to restore people to God, and who better than the tax collectors and sinners, considered the most alienated from God. As Jesus explained, "Those who are well have no need of a physician, but those who are sick. I have not come to call the righteous but sinners to repentance."[192] These sick needed the healing of the restoration that Jesus brought as God's agent.

Sabbath

Another set of controversies between religious leaders and Jesus was over the Sabbath. Luke recorded four stories concerning the Sabbath controversies, three of which involved healings while one was a direct confrontation over authority. The importance of the Sabbath reflected the post-Maccabean worldview that if all in Israel kept the Sabbath, then God would free them from their enemies and lead them from exile.[193] Their implied question in all of these confrontations concerned who had the authority to interpret the

188. Luke 11:42.
189. Hellerman, *Jesus and the People of God*, 202.
190. Luke 5:27–31.
191. Luke 5:30.
192. Luke 5:31–32.
193. Hellerman, *Jesus and the People of God*, 143.

appropriate actions on the Sabbath, or as Green comments, "Who knows and represents the will of God?"[194] It was also another example of contrasting concepts of the people of God. Was keeping the Sabbath to promote national identity in hopes of eventual freedom from oppression by the nations, or was keeping the Sabbath part of the salvific purpose of God and the best way to declare the freedom and restoration of his people?[195]

Luke recorded two confrontations in rapid succession in Luke 6:1–11. In both cases, "And it came about on a sabbath" is fronted, indicating that the temporal aspect is in focus and the focal point of the controversies that follow.[196] In the first incident, Jesus' disciples were plucking grain with their hands and eating it on the Sabbath, which was unlawful according to the Pharisees' interpretation. Jesus answered them by referencing a time when David seemingly did something unlawful while being obedient to God.[197] Wright also argues that it is significant that Jesus refers to a parallel incident that occurred during David's liminal phase when he was anointed but not yet enthroned.[198] David was legitimately king but not yet recognized. Wright asserts that this sets the context for the interpretation of Jesus' reference to himself as the Son of Man who has authority over the Sabbath. Wright states, "It fits the mindset of Jesus that he should refer to himself obliquely, for those with ears to hear, as the one anointed but not yet enthroned, as the one who would be vindicated when YHWH finally did for Israel what he intended to do."[199] Jesus as God's agent had the authority to determine what was appropriate on the Sabbath.

The incident immediately following this passage in Luke's narrative finds Jesus teaching in a synagogue on the Sabbath where there was a man with a withered hand. There were scribes and Pharisees watching to see if Jesus would heal on the Sabbath. Green notes that this was not a life-threatening situation, so it would not necessarily supersede Sabbath compliance. Green comments, "These regulators function as barriers to the healing of this man, and in fulfilling this role they represent the synagogue and Sabbath as entities segregating this needy man from divine help."[200] Jesus queried his audience, "I ask you, is it lawful on the Sabbath to do good

---

194. Green, *The Gospel of Luke*, 252.
195. Green, *The Gospel of Luke*, 252.
196. Green, *The Gospel of Luke*, 253.
197. Green, *The Gospel of Luke*, 254.
198. Wright, *Jesus and the Victory of God*, 394.
199. Wright, *Jesus and the Victory of God*, 394.
200. Green, *The Gospel of Luke*, 255.

or to do harm, to save life or to destroy it."[201] The use of "to save" in describing the healing of the man's hand harkens back to Jesus as an agent of God's restoration.[202] While the Pharisees understood the Sabbath in structural terms (maintaining national identity), Jesus framed it in anti-structural terms (restoration to God).

Another incident where the conflict over structural views of the people of God and anti-structural views of the people of God were highlighted is an episode of a healing of a woman on the Sabbath. In Luke 13:10–17, the story opens with Jesus teaching in the synagogue in which there was a woman with a disabling spirit. Jesus says, "You are freed from your disability," and she was healed. However, the ruler of the synagogue confronted Jesus about healing on the Sabbath. Jesus responded, "And ought not this woman, a daughter of Abraham whom Satan bound for eighteen years, be loosed from this bond on the Sabbath day?" In these statements, Jesus contrasted the anti-structural nature of God's domain with the structural. The woman's problem was oppression from a spirit. She was freed from that spirit. Israel's true enemy was Satan, and the Sabbath was a meaningful day to be freed of the oppression of Satan and to be restored to fellowship with God.[203] This particular incident demonstrated that God's restoration was already occurring, and it did not involve fulfilling political expectations.[204]

In the confrontations of Jesus with the Pharisees over purity and the Sabbath, the different agendas are highlighted. The Pharisees kept the purity taboos and Sabbath in part to maintain their national identity and agenda. It created a separation from the broader Greco-Roman world as a unique people chosen by God. They maintained faithfulness to these practices in the hope that God would rescue the true people of God from oppression by the nations. The confrontations occurred when structural concerns of national identity took precedence over the anti-structural purpose of restoring people to God.

Conclusion

There has been much scholarly discussion on the nature of the Kingdom of God, both its temporal dimension (present or future) as well as its social dimension (ethnic or universal). What I have proposed is that Luke writes his gospel from a post-Pentecost perspective and framed his narrative

---

201. Luke 6:9.
202. Green, *The Gospel of Luke*, 256.
203. Bock, *Luke Volume 9:51—24:53*, 1218.
204. Hellerman, *Jesus and the People of God*, 144.

reflecting this. The Kingdom was presents in the ministry of Jesus, but it was also future. Socially ethnic Israel would be included, but it would also be universal. I have used Turner's model of structure, liminality and anti-structure to compare and contrast those dimensions in Luke's gospel as he framed Jesus' person, ministry, and new people of God. I argue that by framing Jesus' ministry in the liminal state of rites of passage, Luke was emphasizing the anti-structural attributes of the people of God. I also showed how anti-structure provided a framework to understand the membership, interpersonal relationships, and authority in the people of God whom Jesus gathered around himself. I also argue that Jesus was not against the structural cultic practices of first-century Judaism but confronted them when they were prioritized over the anti-structural restoration. In the next chapter, I demonstrate that these same features of liminality, structure, and anti-structure describe the membership and practices of Jesus' followers after the resurrection of Jesus as depicted in the book of Acts.

Chapter 4

Liminal Community in Acts

I HAVE PROPOSED THAT Luke framed his gospel narrative anticipating the events that occur in Acts.[1] In his gospel, Luke narrates how Jesus redefined the expectations of Israel for God's restoration. The new way of being the people of God was anti-structural; belonging was no longer defined by structural markers of Jewish identity but by obedience to God's word. The characteristics of the interpersonal relationships of the people of God and the authority within the people of God reflected the anti-structural characteristics of people in the liminal state of rites of passage.

Luke continues his narrative in Acts and introduces the Holy Spirit, who is the central figure in redefining the new anti-structural people of God. There is a scholarly consensus that the antecedent for his understanding of the Spirit comes from the Old Testament.[2] However, there are differing opinions as to which function Luke is emphasizing in his narrative.[3] Scholars have argued that Luke frames the Spirit in his narrative as a spirit of holiness in the ethnical preparation for the eschatological age,[4] a spirit of prophecy,[5] and associated with realized eschatology and a

---

1. I am following the current trend of recognizing the literary unity between Luke and Acts.

2. Turner, *Power from on High*, 86–137.

3. There are several in-depth surveys of the various positions that have been taken in scholarship. See Menzies, *Empowered for Witness*, 18–43; Turner, *Power from on High*, 20–85; also Kuecker, *The Spirit and the 'Other,'* 1–13.

4. Keener, *Acts 1:1—2:47*, 532. Keener notes that the Spirit as a spirit of holiness is found in Qumran scrolls 1QH VIII, 20; 4Q255, 21; 4Q257 III, 10.

5. This view reflects several scholars, including Gunkel, *Die Wirkungen des heiligen Geistes*; Menzies, *Empowered for Witness*; Cho, *Spirit and Kingdom*; Shepherd, *The Narrative Function of the Holy Spirit*; Hur, *A Dynamic Reading of the Holy Spirit*.

remnant of the people of God.[6] Some scholars have argued that all three are at the heart of Luke's narrative intent.[7]

In this chapter, I follow Aaron Kuecker who suggests that the role of the Spirit in Luke's narrative is much broader. He asserts that Luke uses the Spirit as a new identity marker for the new people of God.[8] I also describe the three dimensions of inaugurated eschatology that are initiated by the Spirit. First, the Spirit introduces a new age; there is the temporal dimension. Second, the Spirit creates a new person with a new identity, one who is embodied by the Spirit. And finally, there is the social dimension. The Spirit creates a new people. The Spirit of God is the new identity marker of the people of God, a liminal community that is anti-structural and allocentric. Just as a new age begins in the old, the new anti-structural community is formed without leaving the structures of society. The new people of God were to live anti-structurally in structure.

In this chapter, I use the framework of liminality, structure, and anti-structure to demonstrate that the new community Luke envisions is in liminality. I argue that the criteria for becoming a part of the people of God, the characteristics of interpersonal relationships of the people of God, and authority within the people of God as Luke presented in Jesus' public ministry continue in the book of Acts. Although the characteristics of the people of God remain the same, there are three fundamental changes that occur in the book of Acts. First, there is a transition of leadership from Jesus to the disciples. Second, Jesus is no longer present as the Davidic messiah in liminality, but he is depicted as the enthroned, victorious Davidic king. In Acts, Luke presents Jesus as the promised messiah who has come but who also will return again, creating temporal liminality in which the new age begins but awaits a future consummation. Third, Luke introduces the Spirit of God as the marker of the beginning of the restoration of the people of God, the means of incorporation into the reconstituted people of God, and the identity marker for the people of God.

To develop this argument, I divide the chapter into four sections. The first section focuses on the creation of the Spirit-marked community. The second examines the characteristics of the new community. The third and fourth sections describe how Luke uses the Spirit to show the inclusion of people,

---

6. Keener, *Acts 1:1—2:47*, 529; Isaiah 44:3, 59:12; Ezekiel 36:27–28, 37:14, 39:29; Joel 2:28—3:1; Isaiah 32:15, 42:1, 59:2, 61:1; Zechariah 12:10. Turner, *Power from on High*, also suggests that the Spirit had an ethnical dimension as well as Wenk, *Community-Forming Power*.

7. Dunn, *Baptism in the Holy Spirit*, advances the argument of a new epoch.

8. Kuecker, *The Spirit and the 'Other.'*

first those at the margins of Jewish society and then the Gentiles. I begin by describing the creation of the Spirit-marked liminal community.

Spirit-Marked Liminal Community— A New People of God

In the first five chapters of Acts, Luke focuses on the formation of the Spirit-marked liminal community. There are four things that Luke demonstrates within the initiation of the community. First, he frames the new community in liminality. It was a community that was experiencing the blessings of the restoration of Israel through the resurrected messiah as demonstrated by his Spirit. However, it was also awaiting a future consummation of these promises. Second, he establishes the disciples as the leaders of the people of God whose authority came from their calling and relationship to the Davidic messiah. Third, Luke describes the new people of God as defined by anti-structural criteria—those who believed Jesus was the resurrected Davidic messiah and were incorporated into the people of God through the Holy Spirit. Finally, Luke highlights the opposition to the people of God. Those in structural positions of authority confronted the anti-structural authority about who had the right to define and lead the people of God. In order to discuss each of these aspects of the people of God in this section, I examine the preparation of the liminal community, the initiation of the liminal community, and then the opposition to the liminal community.

Preparation for the Liminal Community—New Leaders

The preparation period for the liminal community starts when Luke's narrative resumes in Acts 1:2 and ends with the initiation of the community at Pentecost (Acts 2:1). The main focus of this period is the transition of the disciples from followers to leaders. Using Turner's framework of rites of passage, I outline how the disciples went through the three stages of a rite of passage that changed their status from followers to leaders in the new community. Two of these stages occurred before Pentecost: separation and transition/liminality.

The beginning of the rites of passage commences with a rite of separation that is described in Acts 1:4–5 when Jesus ordered his disciples to go to Jerusalem and wait for the Holy Spirit. Luke's placement of the discussion of the Kingdom of God in Acts 1:3 and the promise of the outpouring of the Holy Spirit provide the context for the disciples' question in Acts 1:6. Within this context, Luke places the disciples' question, Κύριε, εἰ ἐν τῷ χρόνῳ τούτῳ ἀποκαθιστάνεις τὴν βασιλείαν τῷ Ἰσραήλ? The use of ἀποκαθιστάνεις is significant for Luke's framework since it was commonly used in the Septuagint and by Josephus to describe the historic hope for national restoration.[9]

The Kingdom of God was closely linked to the outpouring of the Spirit in the hopes for the restoration of Israel.[10] The return of the Holy Spirit to Israel was an integral component of what the prophets had written concerning the messianic kingdom.[11] However for many, the outpouring of the Spirit also had strong nationalistic expectations.[12] Ben Witherington argues Luke is showing that many of the early followers of Jesus believed that he, as the messiah, would restore control of the land to Israel.[13] Kuecker also concurs that it is probable Luke is depicting here the disciples as continuing to hope for national and political liberation.[14] "The assumption appears to be that 'Kingdom of God' (Acts 1:3) and 'Kingdom of Israel' (Acts 1:6) are co-terminus."[15]

Jesus did not directly answer the disciples' question. He neither confirmed nor rejected their idea of the restoration of Israel but left it open to possible future fulfillment. He did not reject the validity of the question but rather the timing of it.[16] As David Pao argues, "While it must not be denied that the futuristic aspect is present in the Lukan conception of the restoration of Israel, the beginning of the process in Acts has to be acknowledged."[17] The focus of this part of the narrative is what their role in the present fulfillment will be. Jesus continued, "But you will receive power when the Holy Spirit has come upon you, and you shall be my witnesses in Jerusalem and

---

9. Kuecker, *The Spirit and the 'Other,'* 99. He also notes Exodus 4:7, 14:27; Jeremiah 15:19, 16:15, 23:8, 24:6, 50:19; Hosea 11:11; Esdras 6:26; 2 Maccabees 11:25; Josephus, *The Antiquities of the Jews*, 11.2, 14, 58, 63, 88, 92, 144, 12.228, 13.261, 14.313.

10. Witherington, *The Acts of the Apostles*, 109.

11. Ger, *The Book of Acts*, 24; Isaiah 32:15–20, 44:3–5; Ezekiel 39:28–29; Joel 2:28—3:1; Zechariah 12:10—13:1.

12. Polhill, *Acts*, 84.

13. Witherington, *The Acts of the Apostles*, 110.

14. Kuecker, *The Spirit and the 'Other,'* 99; Stott, *The Message of Acts*, 41.

15. Kuecker, *The Spirit and the 'Other,'* 99.

16. Fuller, *The Restoration of Israel*, 12. There is ambiguity in Jesus' answer that has led to various opinions of the future of Israel. Witherington argues that Jesus' answer is just a delay in the national restoration of Israel—that it will come, but not yet (*The Acts of the Apostles*, 110–111). Polhill, argues that Jesus did not reject the concept of the "restoration of Israel," but instead, he depoliticized it, and the disciples were to be part of the "restored Israel" (*Acts*, 84). It is not the scope of this work to enter into the discussion of whether Jesus' answer referred to the timing of a future restoration of a political kingdom of Israel or only referred to a different kind of restoration in the near future.

17. Pao, *Acts and the Isaianic New Exodus*, 96.

in all Judea and Samaria, and to the end of the earth."[18] Just as Luke's gospel redefined people's expectations of the Kingdom of God, the narrative in Acts reoriented people's expectations of what the restoration of Israel would look like. The restoration would begin, but it would not look the way they expected it. According to Turner, there are three allusions in Isaiah that refer to different aspects of the restoration of Israel. The first is Isaiah 32:15, "Until the Spirit comes upon you," which anticipates the restoration of Israel. The second is in Isaiah 43:10–12 in which the restored Israel, God's servant, is given the commission to be "my witnesses." The last is in Isaiah 49:6, "to the ends of the earth," which is the extent of the witness.[19] Max Turner states, "All three together unequivocally point in the direction of Israel's restoration."[20] Turner also observes that the coming of the Spirit signified the end of the desolation of Israel and the coming of a new age.[21] The vocation of the Isaianic servant who was to raise up Jacob and restore the remnant of Israel falls to Jesus' disciples.[22]

In Luke's narrative, it is only after Jesus gave them their commission that he was taken into heaven and they were given the promise of his return. While they were not told details concerning when or what the future culmination would look like, they were told that there was to be a future completion of God's blessings. Turner notes, "If there is ambivalence in [Acts] 1:7–8, then, it is not a denial of an important future for 'Israel,' but a change of emphasis from Israel's kingship to her task as servant bringing the light of God's salvation to the nations."[23]

Luke brings out three aspects of the restored people of God in this part of the narrative. First, Jesus completed his reincorporation to his status as the resurrected, exalted, and enthroned Davidic messiah. Second, the disciples are reoriented to a new concept of the restoration of Israel and are given their commission within this process, which is to be witnesses. Third, Luke provides a two-stage eschatological framework for the restoration process, beginning with the Spirit's arrival and concluding with

18. Acts 1:8.
19. Turner, *Power from on High*, 301.
20. Turner, *Power from on High*, 301.
21. Turner, *Power from on High*, 301. Pao also reads Acts 1:8 in this way and argues that the geographic designations in Acts 1:8 refer to three different theopolitical categories. He contends that the three categories signify the three stages of the Isaianic New Exodus which signifies the arrival of a new era: the dawn of salvation upon Jerusalem, the reconstitution and reunification of Israel, and the inclusion of the Gentiles within the people of God (*Acts and the Isaianic Exodus*, 94).
22. Turner, *Power from on High*, 301.
23. Turner, *Power from on High*, 301.

a future consummation. The restored people of God will be a people in transition, or in liminality, as they experience the blessings of restoration in the present while waiting for the future consummation at Jesus' return (Figure 11). With the ascension of Jesus into heaven, the disciples return to Jerusalem and separated themselves from the broader society. They enter a liminal phase of their rite of passage until they are reincorporated as leaders at Pentecost in Acts 2.

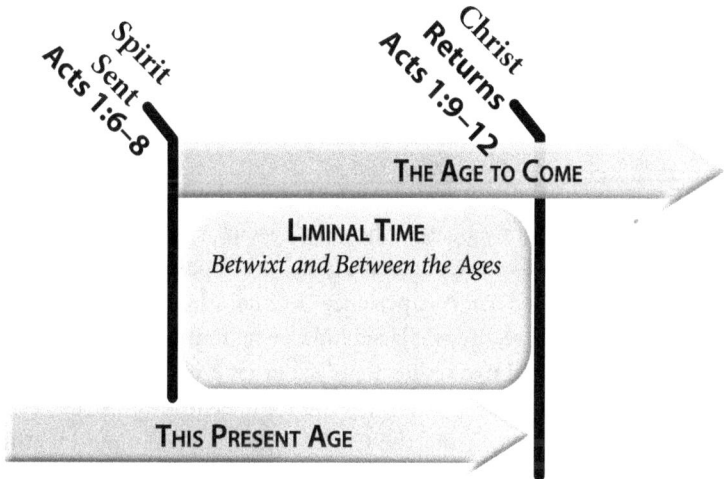

Figure 11. Reorientation of the Disciples' Eschatology

The main focus of the disciple's liminal period (Acts 1:12–26) is the replacement of Judas. Acts 1:12–14 provides the context for the replacement ritual within this liminal period. Each of the eleven disciples is named, highlighting the missing disciple from the list. Luke also marks by name those whom the reader may not expect to be among them: the women, Jesus' mother Mary, and Jesus' brothers. Luke records that there were about 120 in the upper room experiencing the communitas of liminality: "They are of one accord and praying together."[24]

The primary explanation for the replacement of Judas Iscariot was the eschatological importance of the twelve disciples, representing the restoration of Israel and promises in Luke 22:28–30.[25] In Luke's narrative, Judas was portrayed as a traitor who turned aside from his privileged election as an apostle: "He was numbered among us and was allotted his share in this

---

24. Estrada, *From Followers to Leaders*, 115.
25. Estrada, *From Followers to Leaders*, 171.

ministry."[26] Not only did Judas turn aside from his privileged position, but he aligned himself with the enemies of Jesus.[27] Thus, he needed to be replaced to restore the representative number of the twelve tribes of Israel.

However, in addition to the eschatological function of the twelve, there are other sociological and narrative reasons why this episode has importance at this particular junction. Of the sociological reasons, betrayal of a trust—particularly with one who had shared meals together—was one of the most heinous offences in antiquity.[28] There was considerable shame impugned on the group of the disciples as a result of the betrayal.[29] The portrayal of Judas as a traitor rather than just a failed disciple helped alleviate this shame. Peter also reframed this shame as part of a divine necessity, "the scripture had to be fulfilled,"[30] just as the shame of the cross was a divine necessity to accomplish God's will.[31]

The replacement of Judas also highlighted the enemies of the new community. This becomes clear when the disciples' rite of passage into their public ministry is compared with Jesus' rite of passage into his public ministry. In Jesus' wilderness experience (liminal), he faced Satan. In the disciples' rite of passage, they replaced Judas, who represented the enemies that they would face. Luke writes that "Satan entered into Judas," (Luke 22:3) clearly indicating that Satan was the force behind Judas' betrayal.[32] Judas changed allegiance from the Christ-centered group and identified with those who opposed God's plan, particularly the chief priests, officers of the temple, and the elders who later would also oppose the apostles.[33] Just as Jesus represented a corporate identity of God's servants, so Judas represented the corporate identity of those who persecuted and opposed God and God's messiah.[34]

The transition period of the rite of passage closes as the disciples complete the replacement of Judas. The disciples chose two candidates who had been proven trustworthy members of their circle. The new disciple joined the other servants τὸν κλῆρον τῆς διακονίας ταύτης, ("was allotted his share in

26. McCabe, *How to Kill Things with Words*, 202; Acts 1:17.
27. McCabe, *How to Kill Things with Words*, 206; Acts 1:16.
28. Keener, *Acts 1:1—2:47*, 757; Johnson, *The Acts of the Apostles*, 38.
29. Keener, *Acts 1:1—2:47*, 758; Estrada, *From Followers to Leaders*, 178. Estrada also argues that it was not just shame on the Jesus group as a whole but also calls into question the reliability of the apostles as leaders.
30. Acts 1:16.
31. Keener, *Acts 1:1—2:47*, 758.
32. Estrada, *From Followers to Leaders*, 178; Luke 22:3.
33. Estrada, *From Followers to Leaders*, 160; Luke 22:52.
34. McCabe, *How to Kill Things with Words*, 203, 208.

this ministry," ESV) witnessing about the Davidic messiah and the restoration of Israel.[35] They were now ready for reincorporation into their new status as the leaders of the people of God.

Initiation of the Community—A New People of God

Pentecost marked the initiation of the restoration of Israel as well as the reincorporation of the disciples in their new status as the leaders of this reconstituted people of God. These two events cannot be separated. The anointing of the Spirit and the proclamation at Jesus' reincorporation defined his public ministry. The anointing of the Spirit and the disciples' proclamation mark their reincorporation to their new status as the leaders of the people of God and defined their public ministry. Peter's proclamation served to define the Spirit's role in incorporating people into the new community, the liminal aspects of the new community, and how one became part of the new community.

The anointing of the Spirit on the community at Pentecost was rich in symbolic meaning for Israel. The day of Pentecost originally commemorated the spring wheat harvest, but later it was celebrated as the anniversary of the giving of the Law to Moses and God's appearance on Mount Sinai.[36] Wind and fire used to describe the arrival of the Spirit in Acts were used in the Old Testament to describe God's presence in the midst of Israel.[37] Steven Ger explains, "Luke's description of this manifestation resembles the description of God's Shekinah glory manifest on Mount Sinai and filling the temple upon its dedication."[38] For Israel, it meant the Spirit was once again manifesting himself in the midst of Israel.[39]

The Spirit's arrival on those gathered in the upper room marked the initiation of the community of God as well as the reincorporation of the apostles to their public ministry. Whereas Jesus proclaimed, "The Spirit is upon me," and embodied God's restoration plan, the apostles proclaimed the meaning of "The Spirit is upon us" as the beginning of God's restoration.[40]

---

35. Acts 1:17.

36. Witherington, *The Acts of the Apostles*, 131; Johnson, *The Acts of the Apostles*, 45–47.

37. Polhill, *Acts*, 98; 1 Kings 18:38–39, 19:11; Isaiah 66:15; Exodus 3:2, 19:18.

38. Ger, *The Book of Acts*, 38; Exodus 19:18; 2 Chronicles 5:14.

39. Ger, *The Book of Acts*, 38.

40. There is disagreement upon whom the Spirit fell at Pentecost. Some claim that it only included the 12, arguing that it is the closest antecedent in the text and the title Galilean (Acts 2:6) would mark the apostles. Estrada, Ger, and Menzies argue that the Spirit filling was for a specific prophetic ministry. Keener argues that the preceding

According to Keener, the quotation from Joel 2:28–32 is programmatic for Acts as Isaiah's quotation in Luke 4:18–19 was for Jesus' ministry. Through this passage, Peter explained what the people of God would look like, who was included, and how someone could join the new people of God.[41] Luke uses the Spirit in three ways in this passage.

First, the outpouring of the Spirit marks the beginning of the new age and the in-gathering of Israel. Peter announced that the manifestation of the Spirit that they saw was a fulfillment of Joel 2:28–32 in which God was beginning the restoration of Israel. However, the new people of God would be a community in transition; they were receiving the promises of God, yet there would be a future completion of the promises. Peter made several modifications to the Joel prophecy that highlighted the liminal nature of the new community. The first modification was the addition of ἐν ταῖς ἐσχάταις ἡμέραις.[42] Peter made a direct connection between what was currently happening at Pentecost and the day of the Lord. Keener notes that the phrase "in the last days" was a biblical phrase for the period of Israel's restoration which was heralding fixed in eschatological time.[43] Luke's narrative indicates that the messianic age had dawned in the resurrection of Jesus, but the apocalyptic language in Joel also pointed to a future consummation.[44]

The beginning of the restoration had begun, but at the same time, the day of the Lord ushering in God's final judgment upon the world had not yet happened. The pouring out of the Spirit indicated the in-breaking of the day of the Lord, yet it was not fully consummated. Keener observes, "Peter's last days fit the expectation that the disciples had entered an interim era

---

context fills the meaning of what it meant to be together and who was a part of that group and that the group included the 12 apostles, the women, Mary the mother of Jesus, and his brothers (Acts 1:14) with the total of those who were gathered together in one accord totaling about 120 (Acts 1:15). Peter does not describe the apostles' leadership in his speech but rather the formation of a new community.

41. Keener, *Acts 1:1—2:47*, 872. Keener also argues, "Choice of a new explicit programmatic passage for his second volume does not nullify the use of Isaiah 61 in his first volume, as if Isaiah's eschatological justice emphasis were meant to be forgotten" (*Acts, 1:1—2:47*, 794). He also states that there are social implications and effects of the outpouring notably in Acts 2:44-45 and 4:32-35, but this is not the central focus of the volume. Keener notes, "What the two programmatic texts have in common is God's Spirit empowering God's agents for the mission that God has given them" (*Acts*, 796).

42. Kuecker, *The Spirit and the 'Other,'* 120. Kuecker also notes that "in these last days" in Isaiah 2:2 marks the final exaltation of Zion that prompts the nations to stream toward Jerusalem.

43. Keener, *Acts 1:1—2:47*, 875; Isaiah 2:2; Hosea 3:5; Micah. 4:1; Daniel 2:28.

44. Bock, *Acts*, 112; Witherington, *The Acts of the Apostles*, 140-143; Keener, *Acts 1:1—2:47*, 916-919. Some authors explain the signs of the Joel quote in Acts 2:19-20 as pointing to the signs of the resurrection. See Bruce, *The Book of Acts*, 62.

between the first and second comings of the Messiah, called to testify to the nations by the eschatological gift of the Spirit."[45] During this interim era, the community was in liminality, experiencing the promises of God but waiting for their future completion.

Second, the Spirit incorporated into and identified those who were part of the new restoration of Israel as they entered into the liminal community.[46] The Spirit fell equally upon members of each basic status within the ancient world: men, women, young, old, slave, and free.[47] Keener states, "Joel's prophecy declared the eradication of any gender barrier in the Spirit of prophecy."[48] Matthias Wenk also observes that Pentecost represented the fulfillment of Luke 3:16 when the conditions for membership in the covenant people were redefined. He concludes, "Another major purpose of Peter's quote is to serve as a description of the prophetic community as the renewed community in which the people who are given no status in this world are given the highest recognition by God being accorded the long-hoped-for Spirit of prophecy."[49]

Third, the Spirit marked a new universal identity as God's people that transcended any other identity. Kuecker notes that Peter adds the pronoun "my" to the two uses of slaves in Joel's prophecy and argues that he was no longer referring to slaves in the socio-economic sense but slaves belonging to God. Kuecker notes the significance of this change: "This is similar to the reorientation of identity initiated by Jesus in Acts 1:8 ($\mu o \nu$ $\mu \acute{\alpha} \rho \tau \upsilon \rho \varepsilon \varsigma$) and like Isaiah, sets both $\delta o \tilde{\upsilon} \lambda o \varsigma$ and $\mu \acute{\alpha} \rho \tau \upsilon \rho \varepsilon \varsigma$ as key metaphors for those properly related to God."[50] The people of God were now marked by the Spirit as the key factor of identity for the in-group of the Spirit. Membership was not marked by structural identity markers, but rather anti-structural—the Spirit who was a central part of the narrative of Acts. As Kuecker observes, "Not only does the outpouring of the Spirit eliminate barriers in the community based on ethnic boundaries, it also eliminates barriers based on other social status."[51] Just as this liminal identity was expressed within an ethnic identity, so too the liminal identity was expressed within the social hierarchy. However, although there was a new identity marker that incorporated people

---

45. Keener, *Acts 1:1—2:47*, 879.

46. Keener, *Acts 1:1—2:47*, 879.

47. Even within the most egalitarian and nonstructured societies, there still is basic division based on age and gender.

48. Keener, *Acts 1:1—2:47*, 882. Keener notes that Joel's prophecy also challenges class barriers, citing the reference to slaves.

49. Wenk, *Community-Forming Power*, 236.

50. Kuecker, *The Spirit and the 'Other,'* 121.

51. Kuecker, *The Spirit and the 'Other,'* 121.

into a new community, unlike other groups in liminality, the people of God were not separated from society. They lived within the structures of society, but they related anti-structurally as a people in liminality within their current structural social statuses.

The entrance into the liminal people of God was anti-structural. Just as in Jesus' ministry someone became a part of the restored Israel through obedience to him, in Acts people became a part of the community through obedience to the word of Jesus, the risen, exalted Davidic messiah. Peter's speech proclaimed that Jesus was the Davidic messiah and that he was the reason the new age described in Joel had begun.[52] Peter used Psalm 16 to demonstrate that Jesus was the Davidic messianic claimant and that his identity was established by his resurrection as David's eschatological heir.[53] In Acts 2:33, Peter declared that Jesus was exalted at the right hand of God, using the verb ὑψωθείς, "to lift up or exalt." In Luke's narrative, Jesus was the exalted Davidic messiah who poured out the Spirit that began the restoration of Israel over which he was king. Bock notes, "The Spirit's outpouring fulfills the promise pointing to the last days and to the Messiah's mediation of salvation from God's side."[54]

In summary, the coming of the Spirit had marked two events. First, it marked the reincorporation of the disciples from followers of Christ to leaders of the new community. The second event was the initiation of the new community and the beginning of God's restoration. Peter's speech defined the new people of God in several ways. First, the Spirit initiated this new community which was a community in transition, or liminal. The restoration had begun, but it was waiting for a future completion. Second, people become a part of the new people of God through their obedience to Jesus, the exalted Davidic messiah who sent the Spirit. Finally, those who believed were incorporated through the Spirit into the new community in which status and ethnicity no longer defined relationships between people. Relationships in the people of God were now characterized by communitas. They were both anti-structural and allocentric. However, they were to be lived out in their structural statuses.

The people of God in Acts are defined by anti-structural characteristics as they were in Jesus' ministry. The structural leaders of Israel questioned Jesus about his authority to redefine the people of God by anti-structural criteria. Just as Jesus was confronted by leaders in structure, shortly after the

---

52. Keener, *Acts 1:1—2:47*, 957–59.
53. Turner, *Power from on High*, 275.
54. Bock, *Acts*, 131.

community was formed, the apostles were also confronted by structural leaders about their authority to redefine and lead the new people of God.

Opposition to the People of God— Anti-Structure vs. Structure

In Acts 4:1–22 and 5:17–41, Luke presents the Jewish authorities' opposition to the new people of God. The temple leaders in particular represented the structural expectations for the restored Israel. They also had positional authority within the cultic structure of Israel. The apostles' authority was based on anti-structural criteria, including their calling as agents of the risen Davidic messiah. They did not have personal authority but rather Jesus' authority, which he had delegated to them as his witnesses. In his narrative, Luke frames the question of authority regarding who can define and lead the people of God as a conflict between the Jewish leaders and Jesus, the exalted king and Davidic messiah. The confrontation demonstrated that opposing the Davidic messiah, his agents, and his community was opposing God.

Luke orders the narrative so that the reader is reminded of a similar confrontation between Jesus and structural authorities that took place when Jesus healed a lame man.[55] The confrontation about the authority of the apostles in Acts occurs after the healing of a lame man in front of the temple gates in Acts 3:1–10. Luke describes the lame man in vivid terms: as one who was lame from birth, helpless, and poor, highlighting his helplessness.[56] Alan Thompson notes, "The lame were often associated with the blind, deaf, lepers, and poor—typical social outcasts," who are marginalized and often excluded from the cultic life of Israel.[57] Luke provided similar typologies in Jesus' announcements in Luke 4 and Luke 7. Luke then very deliberately contrasts the man's condition after healing: he walks and leaps and praises God. The narrative stresses the completeness of the cure and the healing.[58] According to Bock, by using the verb ἐξάλλομαι which was used in Isaiah 35:6 to describe eschatological blessings, "The lame will leap like a deer," Luke describes this healing in such a way that it indicated the in-breaking of the eschatological blessings.[59] Luke records that the crowd was "filled

---

55. Luke 5:17–26.
56. Thompson, *The Acts of the Risen Lord Jesus*, 153.
57. Thompson, *The Acts of the Risen Lord Jesus*, 154.
58. Peterson, *The Acts of the Apostles*, 165.
59. Bock, *Acts*, 170; Thompson, *The Acts of the Risen Lord Jesus*, 156; Peterson, *The Acts of the Apostles*, 165.

with wonder and amazement at what had happened to him"[60] and "utterly astounded."[61] Their responses echoed the crowd's response at Pentecost to the eschatological signs: "What does it mean?"[62]

Peter's explanation to the crowd related the act of healing the lame man to Jesus the Davidic messiah. Peter described how Jesus' life and death fulfilled God's promises of the restoration of His people.[63] He declared that it was through Jesus, the exalted Davidic messiah, that the eschatological restoration of Israel had begun (and the healing was a sign of that). By referring to Jesus as the Holy and Righteous One, he used messianic titles found in intertestamental sources.[64] He also argued that in Jesus, God had fulfilled his promise made to Moses that another prophet would come in the last days, the days in which Israel's restoration would begin.[65] In Peter's two speeches, Luke demonstrated that Jesus fulfilled the messianic promises of God: Jesus was God's exalted one, the Holy and Righteous One, a prophet like Moses, and the Davidic king.[66] To participate in the blessings and become part of the eschatological community, they had to turn to Christ as the messiah.[67] David McCabe argues, "The fate of Israel is decided based on their response to the prophet like Moses."[68]

There are two separate confrontations related to this particular healing and issues of authority: Acts 4:1–22 and 5:17–41. The opponents who arrest the apostles and call into question their authority—the chief priests and the temple guards—were the same opponents in Luke's passion account.[69] Luke includes several categories of Israel's structural authority when the apostles were brought for questioning before the rulers, elders, and scribes along with the high priest. The question the structural authority asked was

60. Acts 3:10.

61. Acts 3:11.

62. Acts 2:12.

63. Bruce, *Acts*, 82.

64. Witherington, *The Acts of the Apostles*, 177; 1 Enoch 38:2, 46:3, 53:6; Psalms of Solomon 17:53.

65. Bruce, *The Book of Acts*, 87.

66. Thompson, *The Acts of the Risen Lord Jesus*, 157. In this narrative there is a promise of future consummation. Peter speaks of a future sending of Christ, which will complete the fulfillment of God's promise. For Luke, the end time is different from the beginning of the restoration that has already begun. Johnson notes, "Luke does not yet see this as yet, the restoration of all things, which will involve the return of the Messiah as the son of man." (*The Acts of the Apostles*, 74).

67. Acts 3:24–26.

68. McCabe, *How to Kill Things with Words*, 181.

69. Johnson, *The Acts of the Apostles*, 178.

in sharp contrast to the crowd's response. The authority's question was not "What does it mean?" Rather it was a question of authority over Israel: "By what power or by what name did you do this?"[70]

Peter's response was that the authority they had was Jesus' authority, which was demonstrated by God's exaltation of him and the fulfillment of God's restoration promises through him as the healing of the lame man demonstrated.[71] Peter argued that it was allegiance to the glorified Christ that determined membership in the true people of God.[72] The power and authority of the apostles was derived through him.[73] Peter also implied that those who condemned Jesus were in rebellion against God's plan, just as those who opposed the new community were opposing God: "This Jesus is the stone rejected by you, the builders, which has become the cornerstone."[74]

The second encounter in 5:17–41 was an intensification of the first, and the contrast between the structural authority and the apostles' authority in Christ was more vividly displayed. There is also an amusing interplay between structural and anti-structural authority. The high priest had the apostles arrested (structure) and put in prison, and God intervened through an angel (anti-structure). The structural leaders ordered the apostles not to speak about Christ (structure), while the angel told them to speak about Jesus (anti-structure).[75] Luke frames the narrative to demonstrate that the apostles' authority came from God. The apostles were following God's direct orders. In the confrontation with the structural authorities, Peter made it clear that if the leaders opposed them they were opposing God. The measured response of Gamaliel, a high status structural authority, conceded Peter's argument: "for if this plan or undertaking is of man it will fail; but if it is of God, you will not be able to overthrow them. You might even be found opposing God."[76] Luke in this confrontation demonstrated that those who opposed the people of God opposed God's plan and action. The answer to the question of who had authority over Israel was God. God was restoring Israel through his Davidic messiah (anti-structure), but it was not the way they expected (structure).

---

70. Acts 4:7.
71. Johnson, *The Acts of the Apostles*, 81; Bock, *Acts*, 157; Acts 4:8–12.
72. Acts 4:17–20.
73. Peterson, *The Acts of the Apostles*, 186.
74. Thompson, *One Lord, One People*, 81; Acts 4:11.
75. Acts 5:19–21.
76. Thompson, *One Lord, One People*, 163; Acts 5:38b–39.

Summary

The introductory section of Acts served several purposes in Luke's narrative. First, it demonstrated that the people of God were a people in liminality. They were experiencing the blessings of restoration but awaiting a future completion. Second, it showed that they became a part of the people of God not by structural criteria (belonging to Israel) but by anti-structural criteria (obedience to the exalted Davidic messiah). Third, it demonstrated that the people were incorporated by the Spirit, and the Spirit was the new common identity marker of the people of God. Finally, Luke legitimized the anti-structural authority of the disciples to lead the restored people of God. Those who opposed the anti-structural community opposed God. After establishing the community, Luke provides windows into how the Spirit-embodied communitas provided a new way of living.

Spirit-Embodied Communitas—A New Way of Living

While the narrative of Luke focuses on the initiation, expansion of, and opposition to the people of God, the summaries of Acts (Acts 2:42–46, 4:32–37, 5:12–16) highlight two aspects of life in Spirit-marked community. First, they highlight the communitas between people of various statuses within the community. Second, they demonstrate the submission of the initiates to the ritual leader, Jesus, and to his agents, the apostles. In this section, I discuss the values of the community as they lived in communitas and then provide two examples of high-status people within the community, one that reflected the values and one that opposed the values of the community. Finally, I discuss the authority of the leaders within the community.

Communitas

The early Christian communities were not homogenous either by status or by ethnicity.[77] However, as people in liminality, their interpersonal relationships were characterized by communitas. Their primary identity was the same: they became part of the people of God through their obedience to Jesus, the exalted Davidic messiah; they were incorporated into the community by the Spirit; and the Spirit was their primary identity marker. The unity they experienced came from a common obedience and submission to the authority of the messianic king.[78] However, unlike people

---

77. Meeks, *The First Urban Christians*, 52.
78. Thompson, *One Lord, One People*, 69.

in the liminal state of a rite of passage, they did not leave the structures of their society but instead lived out these anti-structural relationships within the structures of society.[79] Sharing possessions and common meals were concrete examples of the anti-structural, allocentric, interpersonal relationships in the community.

There are many antecedents in ancient literature for the idea of holding all things in common. Hans Conzelmann argues that Luke's picture of sharing property in the early community of Christ followers is idealized and that the information comes from knowledge about real or idealized communistic groups.[80] Keener notes that Luke uses shared, common idealized vocabulary such as παντα κοινὰ and ψυχὴ μία in his description of the early community.[81] Conzelmann asserts that the idealized communal portraits are associated with utopian ideals such as those found in Plato's *Republic*.[82] Descriptions of holding all things in common are also found in idealized descriptions of other communities in antiquity such as the Essenes and Pythagoreans.[83] Keener states, "Cynics, Stoics, Pythagoreans, and others regarded sharing all possessions as an ideal for society, though they did not believe that, given human frailty, all of society would practice it."[84]

Common property was not only an ideal of some religious brotherhoods but also an ideal of friendship in the ancient world. The same idealized vocabulary was used in proverbs about friends.[85] According to Keener, Stoics claimed that friendships were partnerships in life, and the best ones were founded by those of equal status and wealth.[86] The expectation was that friends should share, but friends that shared were of equal status. While Greco-Roman culture called patron-client relationships "friendships," these served to reinforce differences in status.[87]

Few doubt that Luke draws on many models to describe the communitas of the early community of Christ followers. However, rather than an idealization of life in the community, Bartchy argues that Luke writes what

79. Thompson, *One Lord, One People*, 69. Thompson discusses the idea that there are both universal and particularistic elements in the community. The universal are the anti-structural elements lived out in the particularistic structural statuses.

80. Conzelmann, *Acts of the Apostles*, 24.

81. Keener, *Acts 1:1—2:47*, 1013.

82. Conzelmann, *Acts of the Apostles*, 24.

83. Conzelmann, *Acts of the Apostles*, 36.

84. Keener, *Acts 1:1—2:47*, 1016.

85. Bartchy, "Community of Goods in Acts," 309–18; Keener, *Acts 1:1—2:47*, 1017; Witherington, *The Acts of the Apostles*, 162–63.

86. Keener, *Acts 1:1—2:47*, 1017.

87. Keener, *Acts 1:1—2:47*, 1017.

he actually believed had taken place among the community.[88] I propose that in alluding to idealized types, Luke not only described the community but demonstrated how the early community of Christ followers exceeded even ancient ideals.

For instance, in idealized communities such as the Qumran community, sharing of goods was mandatory, often brought about by abolishing private property or as a requirement for joining the community.[89] However, within the community of Christ followers, people retained ownership of their property, and there was no rule or obligation to share. Instead, people did not consider their property their own, but to be used for the good of the community to help others. They were to have an allocentric attitude toward property. In the restored people of God, property and wealth served the life of the community and using them for the community was both a result of the unity and contributed to the unity of the community.[90] It marked the common submission of all in the community to God.

The second idealization was the use of friendship language in which friends shared all things in common. Many have noted that in the ancient world, friends were only among social equals.[91] In employing this language, Luke was demonstrating the anti-structural characteristic of communitas. Within the community, people in communitas were social equals because their primary status was that of a follower of Christ marked by the Spirit. However, in the community of Christ followers, even that expectation of exchange was exceeded. In friendships, balanced reciprocity was expected in the ancient world. If a friend could not repay, they lost honor, and the equal friendship turned into a relationship of patron-client.[92] However, in the Christ community, even those who had wealth and acted as patrons for the group laid the gifts at the apostles' feet, subverting any expectations of gaining honor for themselves.

In the early communities of Christ followers, exchange occurred without expectation of return. This kind of generalized reciprocity was something that happened among kin.[93] Bartchy proposes that the early Christian communities considered themselves fictive kin and practiced generalized reciprocity not based on blood ties. Just as Jesus redefined family as those who obeyed his word, the community was a family of those

---

88. Bartchy, "Community of Goods in Acts," 312.
89. Bock, *Acts*, 223.
90. Kuecker, *The Spirit and the 'Other,'* 139; Thompson, *One Lord, One People*, 69.
91. Keener, *Acts 1:1—2:47*, 1017.
92. Keener, *Acts 1:1—2:47*, 1017.
93. Bartchy, "Community of Goods in Acts," 313.

who obeyed his word and followed the practices expected of kin—namely loyalty, truthfulness, and generosity.[94] This reinforced the mutuality of persons in the community.[95]

Common meals were another tangible way in which communitas was expressed, and the early Christian community exceeded the expectations of their broader society.[96] Keener notes the importance of meals throughout the ancient world: "Grounding of the meal in the same κοινωνία that produced the sharing of possessions in common (as opposed to merely patronal benevolence) contrasted starkly with the usual purpose of meals in the rest of the urban Mediterranean world."[97] In the Mediterranean context, meals reinforce social boundaries and social hierarchy. In the early communities of Christ followers, meals included whole families from different social statuses, men and women alike. The community practice of meals suggests intimate interaction and mutual acceptance among members of all statuses.[98] Keener explains, "Early Christians dining together in Jerusalem with both men and women from different families would not have been unique, but it would have been noticed."[99] Whereas meals in the Greco-Roman world reinforced structure, meals in the early Christian community reinforced the anti-structural nature of relationships in the community.

The use of material possessions, either sharing or selling, was a dominant theme in the summary statements about the life of the early Christian community. In the first two summaries totaling twelve verses, seven are devoted to material possessions. For Luke, there was a direct link between the use of material possessions and one's loyalties. This was made clear in the two narratives about high status people within the community.

Exemplars of High-Status Members

The description of shared possessions provides an ideal of how high-status people in the early Christian community were not to regard their possessions as their own but use them for the good of the community. It was also an example of how to live anti-structural lives within the structures of society. Luke provides further illustrations of the practice of these values with examples of high-status people, one positive and the other negative.

---

94. Bartchy, "Community of Goods in Acts," 313.
95. Finger, *Of Widows and Meals*, 224.
96. Acts 2:46b.
97. Keener, *Acts 1:1—2:47*, 1006.
98. Bock, *Acts*, 151.
99. Keener, *Acts 1:1—2:47*, 1007.

Both provide lessons on the relationship between material wealth, unity, and heart attitude. The first one presented in Acts is the positive exemplar of the practice of community values.

The story of Barnabas must be placed in the context of Acts 4:32. The passage describes the communitas; people were of one heart and mind, and no one among them claimed that anything belonged to themselves. This did not mean that they no longer owned the property. Rather it was not to be used for self-interest, such as to gain honor for themselves. Barnabas was a positive example of a high-status person who lived up to these ideals.

Luke describes Barnabas as a high-status person with a moderate amount of prestige. He was from Cyprus so would probably have been part of the diaspora community and spoken Greek. He was a Levite so had prestige in the structure of Judaism. As a Levite, he had both wealth and education which also would have contributed to his honor.[100] Finally, he owned land, another contributing factor to his honor in structure. After detailing all of the structural aspects of honor, Luke adds a final description. Within the community, he was called Barnabas, which means "son of encouragement." Kuecker argues that by introducing Joseph by his nickname, Luke clearly marks Barnabas' function within the community. He states, "Barnabas' new name describes his allocentric identity within the context of his social group."[101] He was honored by the community for his contributions to the life of the community.

What his name indicates, Barnabas proceeds to do. He sells a tract of land and places the money at the apostles' feet.[102] There are two important aspects of this action that mark it as exemplary for a high-status person. First, he was allocentric; he gave without any conditions or expectation of return. Placing it at the feet of the apostles for them to distribute transferred any honor for the gift to the apostles. He did not consider his property his own but rather to be used for the service of his community. Kuecker states, "Rather Barnabas' goods are unconditionally available for the mitigation of poverty in the community."[103] Second, he was anti-structural. Placing the money at the feet of the apostles indicates his submission to the authority of the apostles. Although he structurally had more honor than the apostles, he did not seek to be treated differently within communitas. Instead, like everyone else in liminality, he was obedient to the ritual leader, Christ, and

---

100. Peterson, *The Acts of the Apostles*, 206.
101. Kuecker, *The Spirit and the 'Other,'* 140.
102. Acts 4:37.
103. Kuecker, *The Spirit and the 'Other,'* 141.

his agents, the apostles. Barnabas embodied both the allocentric and antistructural characteristics of the community.

The second exemplar that Luke provides was a high-status couple, Ananias and Sapphira, in Acts 5:1–11, but they are characterized as the anti-Barnabas. Whereas Barnabas reflected the ideals of the early Christian community, they are the polar opposite. They are, as Kuecker notes, the anti-exemplar or the villain.[104] Many of the characteristics Luke attributed to Judas as a traitor to the Jesus group are portrayed by Ananias and Sapphira in their traitorous acts to the people of God. In contrast to the narrative about Barnabas, Luke provides no background description of Ananias and Sapphira except that they were husband and wife. Luke briefly described their actions: they sold a piece of property, kept some of the proceeds, brought only part of this money, and laid it at the apostles' feet. The action itself was not the problem since they were not compelled to sell their field or to give all of the money to the community as was indicated in Peter's response. The majority of Luke's description details how the couple's actions threatened the community.

There are three accusations that provide insight for why Ananias and Sapphira were the villains in the story and how their actions threatened the community. First, Peter claimed that their actions demonstrated that they were not part of the Spirit-filled community, but instead they allowed Satan to fill their hearts. Like Judas, they aligned themselves with those who opposed God's plan and community.[105] They were traitors and liars because they had chosen to associate themselves not with God's community but with Satan.[106] Behind their lie, there was the strategy of another power who wanted to destroy God's people.[107]

Second, they kept back part of the money for themselves. This in and of itself was not wrong, but they lied about it. They had put their possessions above the community and sought self-gain from their possessions. They sought honor and human praise that they did not deserve because they lied about what they had done.[108] According to Keener, possessions themselves were not the cause of their actions, but rather how they used their possessions was a symptom of their focus.[109] Instead of using their wealth to serve others (allocentric), they sought to use their possessions for

104. Kuecker, *The Spirit and the 'Other,'* 141.
105. McCabe, *How to Kill Things with Words*, 213.
106. McCabe, *How to Kill Things with Words*, 211.
107. Marguerat, *The First Christian Historian*, 166.
108. Bartchy, "Community of Goods in Acts," 316.
109. Keener, *Acts 1:1—2:47*, 146.

self. This self-serving drive for honor was the opposite of the allocentric, anti-structural characteristics of the community. In doing so, they not only demonstrated that they were not part of the community, but their actions betrayed the trust and values of the community.

Finally, Ananias and Sapphira's actions threatened the unity of the people of God. Unity in the community came from submission to Christ and obedience to him.[110] The sharing of property and meals demonstrated this unity.[111] Their lie and egocentric behavior threated the unanimity of purpose within the community. Because their actions threated the people of God and God's divine purposes, their actions brought divine judgment and death. McCabe summarizes:

> The cosmic struggle between the Holy Spirit and Satan, waging in the exchange between Peter and the deviant couple, results in a final victory and an ultimate defeat. As the corpses of Ananias and Sapphira are carried across the threshold of the door (Acts 5:9b), they are removed from the locus of God's presence. In this incident, unique within Luke-Acts, failure of the divine harmony results not in mere expulsion from the community household or relational space, but ultimately in extermination.[112]

Authoritative Leadership

Not only does the incident demonstrate exemplars of good and bad behavior of high-status people in the community, it also reinforced the authoritative leadership within the community. The relationships between people in liminality are characterized by communitas. However, the relationship between the initiates and their leaders is one of complete submission. Within the early Christian community, the people of God were expected to have complete submission to Christ as the messianic king. They also were to be in submission to the agents he had chosen, the apostles. McCabe asserts, "The community is not a democracy. It is, rather, a following of the 'way of the Lord,' a people coming together under the representative leadership of the apostolic successors of Jesus, representing his rule and

---

110. Thompson, *One Lord, One People*, 56.

111. Thompson, *One Lord, One People*, 72.

112. McCabe, *How to Kill Things with Words*, 82. It should also be noted here that Peter asks Ananias and Sapphira independently about their actions. Luke emphasizes the allocentric characteristics of the community by treating women as independent, equal, moral agents.

proclaiming the message of his resurrection-exaltation to divine power."[113] The apostles' authority was not positional authority deriving from a position or status in structure, but rather it was derived from their relationship with the exalted Messiah and his commissioning. As other ritual leaders in communitas, they were to use their authority not for themselves but for the good of the community; they were to embody the values of the community. In the encounter with Ananias and Sapphira, Peter as an agent of Christ excludes those who rebelled against Christ and the values of the people of God. McCabe states, "Peter was authorized to speak on behalf of God, and his verbal confrontation with the deceptive Ananias resulted in the death of this wicked detractor."[114]

The apostles' authority in the community was also demonstrated in apostolic teaching. In Acts 2:42, Luke states that the community devoted themselves to the apostles' teaching. Luke does not provide the content of that teaching, but since the new community was a way of life, the apostles most likely taught about the new way of life as the restored people of God. Since they had been with Jesus, they exercised skill authority over the community as they shared the repertoire of knowledge they gained from their tutelage under Christ. Their authority was confirmed in signs and wonders which demonstrated their close connection with Jesus.[115] This demonstration of their authority was also manifested in their confrontation with structural authority.

The most vivid example of the apostles' authority was people placing money for distribution at the apostles' feet. Bock points out that there are similar phrases in the Old Testament that designate submission.[116] Johnson notes that Luke's favorite symbol for relationship and power is the use of possessions, and the apostles were at the very center of the distribution of shared resources. As Johnson observes, "No more graphic image can be imagined for the community's recognition of the apostle's authority."[117] However, their authority was not to be used for themselves, but they redistributed resources for the good of the community.

---

113. McCabe, *How to Kill Things with Words*, 211.
114. McCabe, *How to Kill Things with Words*, 216.
115. Peterson, *The Acts of the Apostles*, 43.
116. Bock, *Acts*, 218; Joshua 10:24; 1 Samuel 25:24, 41; 2 Samuel 22:39.
117. Johnson, *The Acts of the Apostles*, 91.

Summary

The short summary statements in Acts provide a small window into the life of the community in transition, in liminality. Like other groups in the liminal phase of rites of passage, they experienced communitas; their relationships were both anti-structural and allocentric. However, because they were not separated from society, they lived those anti-structural relationships within their structural statuses. Luke provides two examples of people who had high status in structure, one who exemplified the anti-structural characteristics of communitas and others who did not. Luke also illustrated the legitimacy and exercise of the authority of the apostles, who as representatives of Christ, sought the good of the community through authoritative teaching, distribution of goods, and confrontation against threats to the community. The first five chapters of Acts focused on the initiation, characteristics, and authority of and opposition to the anti-structural people of God, demonstrating continuity between Jesus' ministry and the ministry of the apostles. The next sections focus on how the people of God shift their identity orientation from primarily an ethnic one to the allocentric Spirit identity.

Spirit-Marked Community—Israel

Up until this time in the narrative, the people of God, although members through anti-structural criteria, still find their common identity in their ethnic identity as Israel. The narrative events had occurred in Jerusalem, the center of Israelite identity. At this point, the anti-structural and structural identities of the community overlap. So far in the narrative, there have not been any challenges to that overlap in identities; the people of God were comprised of a smaller subset of Israel.

In Acts 8–15, these overlapping identities are challenged as God directs the movement of his people out from Jerusalem, the ethnic heart of Israel, to the "other."[118] Luke uses the Spirit in this movement outward towards the "other" in two ways. First, the Spirit initiates movement toward the "other," and second, the Spirit confirms the incorporation of the "other" into the community.[119] Each movement outward, each new "other" who was incorporated, challenges the overlap of the community's structural and anti-structural identities until the community must decide: which is the salient

---

118. Kuecker, *The Spirit and the 'Other,'* 106.
119. Kuecker, *The Spirit and the 'Other,'* 106.

identity for the people of God. In this section I discuss the in-gathering of the "other" within Israel and in the next, the incorporation of the Gentiles.

Diaspora: Acts 2:5–12

The beginning of the in-gathering of the "other" actually started at Pentecost with the Jews from the diaspora who were part of the audience that included "Jews living in Jerusalem, devout men from every nation under heaven."[120] Kuecker notes that although they were all considered Jews, they were marked by their country of origin, implying that they retained some of their native ethnic identity while they lived in Jerusalem.[121] Luke provides a list of fifteen nations starting clockwise with Jerusalem at its center. Keener notes that the listing of nations is reminiscent of the table of nations in Genesis 10, which is immediately followed by the story of the tower of Babel and the confusion of languages.[122] There was an eschatological expectation that in the eschaton, God would reverse its effects: "For at that time I will change the speech of the peoples to a pure speech that all of them may call upon the Lord and serve him with one accord."[123]

However, at Pentecost, God did not make communication possible because of a common language but united people within their ethnolinguistic particularisms. Three times, twice before the table of nations and once after, Luke records the multiethnic audience hearing the disciples speaking in their own dialect (τῇ ἰδίᾳ διαλέκτῳ; Acts 2:6, 8).[124] Kuecker observes, "Luke describes that the Spirit makes what can best be described not as a miracle of impossible communication made possible but rather a miracle of universal particularity."[125] The Spirit created a common identity, but it was expressed through their own ethnolinguistic particularity. Kuecker argues, "The Spirit not only creates a common identity, but the Spirit also powerfully affirms the validity of ethno-linguistic particularity."[126] When this group was incorporated into the community by the Spirit, they did not lose their ethnolinguistic identity (structure). Their primary identity in the

---

120. Acts 2:5.
121. Kuecker, *The Spirit and the 'Other,'* 114.
122. Keener, *Acts 1:1—2:47*, 835.
123. Zephaniah 3:9.
124. Acts 2: 6, 8 (which I cite in the text) UBS4 has τῇ ἰδίᾳ διαλέκτῳ. Verse 2:4 uses the phrase ἑτέραις γλώσσαις, as well as 2:11.
125. Kuecker, *The Spirit and the 'Other,'* 117.
126. Kuecker, *The Spirit and the 'Other,'* 118.

community is marked by the Spirit (anti-structure), but they live out this identity through their particular ethnolinguistic identity.

Samaritans

The second non-Galilean group Luke records as part of the in-gathering of the people of God was the Samaritans.[127] There are several layers to this story because of the complex relationship between Judean Jews and Samaritans.[128] The Samaritans were considered part of the northern kingdom that had rebelled against the house of Israel, but there was a longstanding hope for the reunited Israel under a Davidic king.[129] However, there was deep hostility and exclusivity that had separated the Jews and the Samaritans for generations.

The relationship between Israel and the Samaritans was unique because they both contested the same ethnic identity as the true people of God. The Samaritans considered themselves Israelites, and according to Josephus, traced their lineage from Joseph: Ephraim and Manasseh.[130] The Samaritan narrative of the division between themselves and the Jews in Judea was that they (the Samaritans) were the direct descendants of a faithful nucleus of ancient Israel. Israel's apostasy occurred when the nation's cultic center was moved from Mt. Gerizim to Shiloh and eventually to Jerusalem. In the Samaritan point of view, it was the Judeans who were the interlopers and innovators, while they remained true to the religion of Moses.[131] The Samaritans viewed themselves to be the true remnant of Israel, while Israelites were followers of Eli, who had set up a cult in Jerusalem that was a rival to the true national center at Mt. Gerizim.[132] From the Israelite point of view, the Samaritans were the descendants of Jeroboam's rebellion against the house of David.[133] According to Kuecker they were syncretistic Assyrian

---

127. Cohen, *From the Maccabees to the Mishnah*, 162. Cohen notes that the name has two different referents. The first were those who dwelt in the district of Samaria, and the second was the religious community centered in Shechem and Mount Gerizim. The latter were considered a part of Israel with different accounts as to their separation.

128. Ezekiel 37. The historicity of the two accounts of the origins of the Samaritans (Judean and Samaritan accounts) are challenged in recent scholarship. However, what is informative for this discussion is the tension that the different self-understandings had on contested identities and boundary maintenance. See Hellerman, *Jesus and the People of God*, 188–97, and Kuecker, *The Spirit and the 'Other,'* 154–56.

129. Thompson, *The Acts of the Risen Lord Jesus*, 114.

130. Josephus, *The Antiquities of the Jews*, 11.340.

131. Thompson, *The Acts of the Risen Lord Jesus*, 151.

132. Kuecker, *The Spirit and the 'Other,'* 154.

133. Thompson, *The Acts of the Risen Lord Jesus*, 113.

resettlers who worshipped Israel's God, and they were half-breeds and heretics.[134] As Kuecker observes, "Samaritan and Israelite origin narratives reflect conflicting identities based on contested claims to be the same ethnic social identity: 'True Israel.'"[135]

Philip's interaction with the Samaritans was a significant step in Luke's narrative. As Kuecker comments, it was the first time Luke uses the Spirit to mark former out-group members as part of the Spirit-marked Jesus community and incorporate them into the liminal community.[136] It was also the first time a new ministry had been started by someone who was not part of the original twelve. Philip, one of the seven appointed to leadership by the apostles in Acts 6, is described as a man of good repute, full of the Spirit and of wisdom. When he fled Jerusalem, he entered Samaria and carried out a prophetic ministry of proclaiming the gospel and doing signs and wonders.[137] The signs and wonders included exorcisms and healings, particularly healing of the lame, and demonstrated continuity with the ministry of Jesus and the apostles in the eschatological restoration of the people of God.[138] Luke records that as people "believed Philip as he preached good news about the Kingdom of God and the name of Jesus Christ, they were baptized, both men and women alike."[139]

The signs and wonders and their belief in Jesus all demonstrated that they were part of the people of God. When the community in Jerusalem heard that the Samaritans had accepted the word of the Lord, they sent Peter and John to validate it.[140] It was only when the apostles arrived and prayed that the Samaritans received the Spirit. There are two important reasons for this. At this point with few exceptions, the ministry of Jesus and the gift of the Spirit had only been given to the Jews. This was the first out-group that had been included in the people of God, and the delay of the Spirit until Peter and John's arrival legitimized the inclusion of the

134. Kuecker, *The Spirit and the 'Other,'* 154; Bock, *Acts*, 214.

135. Kuecker, *The Spirit and the 'Other,'* 154.

136. Kuecker, *The Spirit and the 'Other,'* 158.

137. There is an important subtext with Simon the magician. Simon in the story represents opposition to God's program. Philip's proclamation of the Kingdom of God confronts Satan's rule over humans in the form of Simon. The text indicates that Simon believed and became a part of the community. However, when Peter and John arrived, Simon wanted to buy the Spirit for himself, indicating egocentric values in opposition to the allocentric values of the community. Peter confronted this in his rebuke. This subtext reinforces that it is not ethnicity that excluded someone from the people of God, rather it was a rejection of core values of the community.

138. Johnson, *The Acts of the Apostles*, 146.

139. Acts 8:12.

140. Acts 8:14.

Samaritans in the people of God.[141] Kuecker also suggests a second reason: this is the first "out-group" that was included, and the apostles themselves had to have an identity transformation.[142] The people of God now included a different ethnic group and the structure/anti-structure identity overlap was challenged. Their acceptance that the Samaritans were now part of the anti-structural people of God was attested to by their ministry in Samaritan villages on their return.

The Marginalized

Luke continues to unfold God's plan of the restoration of the people of God in Acts by extending the gathering to the most extreme "other" in the ancient contexts, the Ethiopian. Luke describes the ethnic and social characteristics of the Ethiopian in great detail. He was a person of high status as an official of the queen.[143] He was also ethnically an Ethiopian, marking him as one of the most ethnically distinct people in the ancient world because oftentimes "black," constituting difference, was equated with being Ethiopian.[144] He also represents the most geographically distant of the exiles as Ethiopia represented the extreme limits of the known world.[145]

What is pointedly marked in Luke's description is the official's status as a eunuch and his exclusion from worship because of it. His status as a eunuch is mentioned five times within this pericope (Acts 8:27, 34, 36, 38, 39). Even as a part of Israel and a devout worshiper of the God of Israel, he was excluded from temple worship because of his physical disfigurement.[146] Johnson argues that the focus on his exclusion because of physical defect represented others with defects, placing continuity of the ministry to the Ethiopian with Jesus' ministry to those with physical defects who were at the margins of Israel's cultic community.[147] Kuecker observes that because

---

141. Kuecker, *The Spirit and the 'Other,'* 160.
142. Kuecker, *The Spirit and the 'Other,'* 160.
143. Kuecker, *The Spirit and the 'Other,'* 160; Acts 8:27.
144. Snowden, *Blacks in Antiquity*, 2.
145. Peterson, *The Acts of the Apostles*, 291. In Luke's narrative the religious identity of the Ethiopian is ambiguous. A long-held view is that he is a Gentile, based on his disfigurement. However, placement in the context of the previous narrative indicates he is a part of Israel. Based on the context of the Samaritan narrative, Pao argues that it must be read as part of the restoration of Israel (*Acts and the Isaianic New Exodus*, 140–41).
146. Johnson, *The Acts of the Apostles*, 155; Deuteronomy 23:1.
147. Johnson, *The Acts of the Apostles*, 116.

the Ethiopian was a eunuch, he would have been on the margins of both Israelite and Greco-Roman culture.[148]

Luke places special stress on God's engineering of the encounter between Philip and the Ethiopian and emphasized that the mission to this Ethiopian was not of human enterprise but of the Spirit.[149] Twice Philip was directed by the Spirit to reach the Ethiopian. First, Philip was directed to a geographic place, a remote road to Gaza. Then the Spirit directed him to the Ethiopian's chariot where he was reading from Isaiah. The passage the Ethiopian was reading was about the suffering servant; and he would have particularly noted the phrase "who will speak of his descendants."[150] Kuecker notes the significance of this passage to the eunuch who himself could not have descendants: "The text allows for a connection between the family-less Isaianic servant and the family-less eunuch."[151] Not only could he be included in the people of God, but he also could be a part of the household of God. Kuecker explains, "Just as Jesus' lack of 'descendants' did not prevent God from giving him a new and large family, the eunuch's lack of 'descendants' will not prohibit him from being incorporated into a new and large 'family.'"[152] The anticipation of Isaiah 56:3–8, in which eunuchs were included in God's in-gathering, reinforced the promise that inclusion in the people of God was based on a person's response to Jesus as the messiah, not on social, ethnic, or geographic identity. The eunuch believed and was incorporated into the people of God.

Summary

The groups discussed above demonstrate the incorporation of the "other" into the people of God. It was not by structural means, but anti-structural through obedience to the Davidic messiah. Second, people were incorporated into the people of God through the Spirit, which was the common identity marker for everyone in the people of God. However, people did not lose their structural identity markers but were incorporated into the people of God within their ethnolinguistic particularity. Now that those attached to Israel have been incorporated, Luke turns to the Gentiles.

---

148. Kuecker, *The Spirit and the 'Other,'* 167; see also Keener, *Acts: 3:1—13:28*, 1570–71.
149. Johnson, *The Acts of the Apostles*, 160.
150. Isaiah 53:7–8b.
151. Kuecker, *The Spirit and the 'Other,'* 167.
152. Kuecker, *The Spirit and the 'Other,'* 167.

Spirit-Marked Community—Gentiles

Up until this point, Luke's narrative has recorded the incorporation of those who identified with Israel into the people of God. They were in some way a part of ethnic Israel. The narrative has challenged the structural/anti-structural identity overlap but has not completely separated them. In Acts 9–15, the people of God confront the ethnic "other," the Gentile. The Jewish view of Gentiles varied widely from the more open position of the diaspora Jews to the hostile sectarian views. The suffering of the Israelites at the hand of Gentiles contributed to the mistrust of Gentiles and to open hostility.[153] There were also a variety of views regarding the fate of the Gentiles in the last days. Many texts reflected vindication of Israel over her enemies and God's judgment and condemnation of her enemies.[154] Others indicated an in-gathering of the nations to Israel and that Israel would be a light to the nations.[155]

Luke slowly and deliberately unfolds God's plan for the inclusion of the Gentiles in three separate but related accounts. Luke emphasizes three things in these accounts which highlight the Spirit's role in incorporating the Gentiles. First, each of these encounters starts with the Spirit's initiating or orchestrating the encounter with the "other." Second, Luke demonstrates the Spirit's role in the incorporation of the "other" into the people of God by providing a new identity that transcends ethnic identity but does not eliminate it. Finally, there is the acceptance by the church of what God is doing. Luke shows the transformation of the people of God as their understanding of the people aligns with God's deliberate action, climaxing in the council at Jerusalem. Throughout these accounts, Luke highlights that it is God who initiates and confirms the inclusion of the Gentiles through His Spirit, and then it is up to the church to accept what God is doing. The first of these accounts is Paul's calling as an apostle to the Gentiles.

Paul, Apostle to the Gentiles

Luke draws an extreme picture of Paul's opposition to the followers of Christ. He is the "other," not on the basis of ethnicity but by his opposition. At each point in the narrative, his opposition intensifies. In Acts 7:58 he is present at the stoning of Stephen. In Acts 8:1 he approves of Stephen's death. In Acts 8:3 he seeks out men and women followers of Christ and commits them to

---

153. Keener, *Acts 1:1—2:47*, 512.
154. Pao, *Acts and The Isaianic New Exodus*, 224.
155. Keener, *Acts 1:1—2:47*, 685; Isaiah 43:10–12; 49:6; 55:5.

prison.[156] When Luke opens his narrative in Acts 9:1–2, Paul (i.e., Saul) is pursuing them to Damascus. In Luke's narrative, Paul's extreme opposition is confronted with divine intervention, and Paul goes through a rite of passage to change his status from an enemy to a disciple of Christ.[157]

In Luke's account, two divine encounters are required for this transition to occur. The first is Paul's encounter with Jesus. In this encounter, Jesus reveals himself to Paul on his way to Damascus, which begins Paul's rite of passage. Kuecker notes that there is a central formula which is repeated verbatim in all retellings of the encounter (Acts 9:4–5, 22:7–8, 26:14–15).[158]

> Jesus: Saul, Saul, why are you persecuting me?
>
> Saul: Who are You, Lord?
>
> Jesus: I am Jesus whom you are persecuting.

According to Kuecker, the transformation for Paul came from the understanding that "the exalted Jesus identified himself with a particular group—the very group that Saul was persecuting."[159] Johnson summarizes, "For Saul, if the living and powerful Lord identifies himself with this community, then joining this community is the sign of obedience to his presence."[160] Paul went to Damascus and entered a period of liminality while God prepared the people of God for Paul. Not only must Paul identify with a new community, but the new community must also accept their former enemy.[161] For this, there was another divine intervention in the form of a vision to Ananias, one of the followers of Christ. This vision identified Paul as σκεῦος ἐκλογῆς ἐστίν μοι, "my chosen instrument," just as the apostles were μου μάρτυρες, "my witnesses."[162]

Ananias was obedient and went to his former enemy, calling him "Brother Saul" and identifying Paul as part of the people of God.[163] Paul regained his sight and received the Spirit as a sign of his incorporation and identity as a member of the reconstituted people of God.[164] Kuecker explains:

---

156. It is important to note that Luke mentions women in his narrative.
157. Kuecker, *The Spirit and the 'Other,'* 170.
158. Kuecker, *The Spirit and the 'Other,'* 170.
159. Kuecker, *The Spirit and the 'Other,'* 170.
160. Johnson, *The Acts of the Apostles*, 168.
161. Kuecker, *The Spirit and the 'Other,'* 171.
162. Acts 9:15.
163. Bruce, *The Book of Acts,* 310.
164. Bock, *The Book of Acts*, 262.

The inclusion into the community not only includes those who are socially and ethnically different but extends to those who are enemies. For the Spirit empowered community of Jesus-followers, peace does not come by removing or destroying enemies but by welcoming them into the in-group. Divine victory comes though the transformation of humans and their groups, resulting in the creation of a common identity that allows enemies to become brothers and sisters.[165]

Not only did Paul become a part of the very community he had been persecuting, but Luke also anticipates Paul's future ministry as God's chosen instrument to witness to the Gentiles and to Israel. This is the first explicit mention of the incorporation of the Gentiles into the people of God.[166] Paul is transformed from the enemy of the gospel to the messenger of the gospel to the Gentiles. However, Paul will only be reincorporated in this new role later in Acts 13 when God initiates mission to the Gentile world. But first, Luke provides the next step of the inclusion of the Gentiles with Peter's encounter with Cornelius.

Conversion of Cornelius

Luke is deliberate in detailing the narrative of Cornelius to emphasize God's divine direction and purpose. The inclusion of the Gentiles into the people of God includes eight references to the Spirit in Acts 10:1–11:18.[167] In Luke's narrative, the Spirit serves to overcome human hesitancy and resistance to inclusion of the "other" in the people of God. Acceptance of the Gentiles comes only after a demonstration of God's initiative.[168] As Kuecker points out, "This section in Acts most concerned with ethnic boundaries is also the section containing the densest cluster of Spirit-references."[169]

There are three parts to the narrative. In each part, Luke emphasizes the hand of God in the events that follow. This becomes a key apologetic for Peter when he explains his actions to the community: it is not his idea, but God's.

In the first part of the narrative, Luke brings Cornelius and Peter together through divine intervention. Cornelius is described as εὐσεβὴς

165. Kuecker, *The Spirit and the 'Other,'* 178.

166. Paul retells his encounter with Jesus two more times in Acts 22 and 26, each emphasizing his calling as a witness.

167. Kuecker, *The Spirit and the 'Other,'* 188.

168. Kuecker, *The Spirit and the 'Other,'* 188; Peterson, *The Acts of the Apostles,* 350; Johnson, *The Acts of the Apostles,* 186–87.

169. Kuecker, *The Spirit and the 'Other,'* 188.

καὶ φοβούμενος τὸν θεὸν σὺν παντὶ τῷ οἴκῳ αὐτοῦ, a Gentile who worships Israel's God and expresses his piety though the support of the synagogue and in continuous prayer.[170] In the first vision of the narrative, an agent of God appears to Cornelius and instructs him to send men to Joppa and bring back a man named Peter.[171] As they make their way to Joppa, Peter has his own vision.

Luke's narrative places Peter on the rooftop praying when he falls into a trance, and after seeing many different types of unclean animals, he is ordered to kill and eat. Peter rejects the order, believing that he is being faithful to God, and responds that he has never eaten anything unholy and unclean. Kuecker argues that food laws provide ethnic distinctiveness for Israel: "But we must go further and recognize that food laws were one of Israel's most prominent markers of ethnic distinction vis-à-vis the ethnos."[172] In many cultures, food and table fellowship are signs of social acceptance; purity distinctions and discrimination often mark the exclusion of the "other."[173] For first-century Jews, this was one of the clearest social markers of exclusion of the Gentiles.[174]

The answer to Peter's response is, "Do not call anything impure that God has made clean."[175] This vision occurs three times, but Peter is only given further insight when Cornelius' men arrive. Luke continues to emphasize God's direct intervention: "While Peter was reflecting on the visions, the Spirit said to him, 'Behold, three men are looking for you. Rise and go down and accompany them without hesitation for I have sent them.'"[176] Luke emphasizes that it is God who is directing Peter to meet the Gentiles. When Peter asks why the visitors are there, Luke again highlights God's intervention in their answer: "Cornelius, a centurion, an upright God-fearing man, who is well-spoken of

---

170. Polhill, *Acts*, 52; Johnson, *The Acts of the Apostles*, 183. Witherington provides an in-depth discussion on the use of the term φοβούμενος τὸν θεὸν, whether it is a technical term for a class of people or a term for a Gentile who worshiped the Israelite God. He notes that the term οι φοβούμενοι is used five times in the LXX, and each time it refers to Jews who are pious and righteous, though in the Psalms it could refer to Gentiles (2 Chronicles 5:6; Psalms of Solomon 115:15–9; 118:2–4; 135:19–20; Malachi 3:16). The term is generally used to describe those who frequented synagogues and tried to live as they could by the Torah. The term is also generally recognized to refer to Jewish sympathizers who may or may not have attended synagogue (Witherington, *The Acts of the Apostles*, 341–44).

171. Bock, *Acts*, 387.

172. Kuecker, *The Spirit and the 'Other,'* 190.

173. Bock, *Acts*, 390; Peterson, *The Acts of the Apostles*, 257.

174. Bock, *Acts*, 390.

175. Acts 10:15 (NIV).

176. Acts 10:19–20.

by the whole Jewish nation, was directed by a holy angel to send for you to come to his house and hear what you have to say."[177] In Luke's narrative, Peter invites the Gentiles to stay, demonstrating some understanding of the visions' implications about ethnicity. Kuecker notes, "Peter's extension of hospitality to the non-Israelites from Cornelius demonstrates that, given the Spirit's instruction, Luke's Peter thinks a certain level of social intercourse is now possible that previously was unlikely."[178]

Luke places the second part of the narrative at Cornelius' house. When Peter arrives at the house, he still does not know why he is there, only that God has directed him to go. Luke demonstrates that Peter's understanding at this point is that he can have some level of social intercourse with Gentiles: "You yourselves know how unlawful it is for a Jew to associate with or to visit with anyone from another nation, but God has shown me that I should not call any person common or unclean. So when I was sent for, I came without even raising any objections.[179] However, still not comprehending the purpose of his visit, he states, "I ask then what reason you have sent for me."[180] Cornelius then describes his vision to Peter. In Luke's narrative, Cornelius' vision is an indicator that Cornelius is an acceptable person to God.[181] It is at this point that Peter begins to understand that being a part of the people of God is not limited to membership in a particular nation or adherence to particular customs but obedience to God.[182]

The climax of the story is God's confirmation of his incorporation of the Gentiles into the people of God through the Spirit. As Peter preaches about Jesus, Luke writes that the Spirit is poured out on Cornelius and his household. Of the eight times the Spirit is mentioned in the Cornelius story, Luke mentions the Spirit three times in the four verses describing the Spirit coming upon the Gentiles. I have marked in italics the place in the text in which God's divine hand was emphasized in the narrative. First is the actual event in Acts 10:44, "While Peter was still saying these things, the *Holy Spirit fell upon all who heard the word.*" Then in Acts 10:45, Luke emphasizes it again by the reaction of the Jewish believers who had accompanied Peter: "All the believers from among the circumcised who had come with Peter were amazed, because the gift of the *Holy Spirit had been poured out even on the Gentiles.*" Finally it is emphasized in Acts 10:47,

---

177. Acts 10:22.
178. Kuecker, *The Spirit and the 'Other,'* 191.
179. Acts 10:28.
180. Acts 10:29.
181. Johnson, *The Acts of the Apostles*, 194.
182. Johnson, *The Acts of the Apostles*, 194.

when Peter states his understanding of the Spirit as the new identity marker for inclusion into the community: "Can anyone withhold water for baptizing these people *who have received the Holy Spirit just as we have?*" The emphasis of Luke's narrative is that it is the Spirit that incorporates the Gentiles into the people of God.

The third part of the narrative is the church's acceptance, which marks a turning point in the book of Acts. Again, Luke frames the narrative in such a way that the reader cannot mistake God's intervention. He once more demonstrates that the inclusion of the Gentiles is God's idea. The narrative opens when Peter returns to Jerusalem, and some of the Jewish followers of Jesus confront him for eating with Gentiles: "You went to uncircumcised men and ate with them."[183] In Luke's narrative, Peter makes it clear that God showed him a vision about not calling anything unclean that God has made clean. He clarifies that the Spirit told him to go to Caesarea with Cornelius' men and that it was God who had ordered Cornelius to send for Peter.[184]

Peter then describes the Spirit coming to the Gentiles in terms of the common gift between Jew and Gentile, but more importantly, he emphasizes the divine initiative in the process.[185] His argument is that God gave the same Spirit to the Gentiles as He gave to the Jews: "As I began to speak the *Holy Spirit* fell upon them *just as he did on us* at the beginning."[186] His conclusion is that if *God* gave them the same Spirit as He did the Jews, which incorporated them into the people of God, how could they exclude the Gentiles from the community? Peter concludes, "If then *God* gave the *same gift to them as he gave to us* when we believed in the Lord Jesus Christ, who was I that could stand in *God's way*?"[187] The implication of Peter's conclusion is that opposition to the acceptance of the Gentiles is opposition to God.[188] In Luke's narrative, the climax of the story comes when their understanding aligns with God's divine action: "Then to the Gentiles also *God* has granted repentance that leads to life."[189]

Luke's narrative highlights God's orchestration of events to bring Peter and Cornelius together. The Spirit coming upon the Gentiles in the same way that he did the Jews realigned how the Jewish members were to understand the people of God and who was a part of that restoration. As

---

183. Acts 11:2.
184. Acts 11:4–14.
185. Johnson, *The Acts of the Apostles,* 186; Bock, *Acts,* 403.
186. Acts 11:15.
187. Acts 11:17.
188. Polhill, *Acts,* 265.
189. Acts 11:18.

Turner notes, "Admission of Gentiles in principle redefines the people of God who are thereby no longer simply the Torah-centered Israel, but some transformation of Israel."[190]

First Missionary Journey

Luke's third narrative that is a part of this sequence of inclusion of the Gentiles in the people of God is the first missionary journey of Barnabas and Paul. This narrative illustrates the continued expansion of ministry to the Gentiles and becomes validating evidence of God's work among the Gentiles for the decision made in Acts 15. Luke provides similarities and continuities between the ministry of Paul and Barnabas among the Gentiles with the ministry of Jesus and the ministry of the apostles among the Jews.[191] This provides a direct progression from the ministry of Jesus, to the Apostles through the power of the Holy Spirit, and now to Paul and Barnabas among the Gentiles through the power of the Holy Spirit. Just as the Cornelius story illustrates that Gentiles can receive the Spirit like the Jewish followers of Jesus, now Luke demonstrates that Paul has the same kind of prophetic ministry among the Gentiles as the apostles and leaders of the Jerusalem church have among the Jews. In other words, Luke illustrates God's Spirit is working the same way among the Gentiles as He has among the Jews. What was initiated with Cornelius becomes programmatic in the first missionary journey.[192]

The setting for the beginning of the first missionary journey is at Antioch where Paul and Barnabas have been ministering to the Gentile believers.[193] Luke emphasizes the initiative for the mission trip is God's by repeating it twice. Acts 13:2–3 reads, "While they were worshiping the Lord and fasting, the Holy Spirit said, 'Set apart for me Barnabas and Saul for the work to which I have called them.'" This is reinforced in verse 4: "So being sent out by the Holy Spirit, they went down to Seleucia and from there they sailed to Cyprus." Luke is emphatic that the inaugural-planned evangelism to the Gentiles was initiated by God.[194]

Luke illustrates three different events that provide continuity of the prophetic ministry of Paul and Barnabas among the Gentiles to the ministry among the Jews. The first similarity is the confrontation of Paul and Barnabas

---

190. Turner, *Power from on High*, 378.
191. Johnson, *The Acts of the Apostles*, 207.
192. Johnson, *The Acts of the Apostles*, 244.
193. Acts 13:2.
194. Witherington, *The Acts of the Apostles*, 390.

with the magician Bar-Jesus, alluding back-to-back to the confrontation with Satan experienced by Jesus after his commissioning by the Holy Spirit and also Peter's confrontation with Ananias and Sapphira.[195]

The second event is the response to the word preached among the Gentiles. Paul goes into a synagogue to preach, and Luke highlights that Paul's audience includes Gentile God-fearers: "Men of Israel, and you who fear God, listen"[196] and "Brethren, sons of the family of Abraham, and those among you who fear God."[197] As Peter did in Jerusalem, Paul reviews salvation history and then demonstrates that Jesus is the promised Davidic messiah. For both Jew and Gentile, it is through obedience to the Davidic messiah that one becomes part of the people of God. The next Sabbath "unbelieving Jews," now defined as those who oppose God's plan, stir up the crowds. Paul and Barnabas respond to this increasing hostility by citing Isaiah 49:6 in their declaration to the Gentiles. This was a turning point in Acts, and mission to the Gentiles becomes the focus of Luke's narrative.[198] Luke makes it clear that the inclusion into the people of God is not by ethnic particularities but by response to the message of Jesus, crucified and raised as the promised messiah. Johnson summarizes:

> Luke must also make clear the basis for the inclusion of the Gentiles in the messianic movement. And by so doing, he begins the process of redefining for the reader the character of God's people. Luke now makes even more explicit the theme that has run through his entire work, that "faith saves." . . . Those who accept in faith become part of the authentic Israel in the Spirit. Those who do not still remain Jews according to the previous understanding of the identity, with the hearing and observance of Torah, but they refuse the invitation to share in this realization of the people: they are "disbelieving."[199]

The final similarity with the ministries of Jesus and the apostles is the healing of the lame man at Lystra.[200] Luke frames the healing so that there is little doubt in the similarity of the healing to that of Peter and John in Acts 3. In both cases, the man is lame from birth. In both cases, the apostle who heals him looks directly at him, and finally the man leaps up and begins to walk. The deliberate use of ἅλομαι alludes back to the healing in Acts 3:8

195. Johnson, *The Acts of the Apostles*, 226; Luke 4:1–13; Acts 5:1–11.
196. Acts 13:16.
197. Acts 13:26.
198. Acts 14:2.
199. Johnson, *The Acts of the Apostles*, 250.
200. Acts 14:8–10.

and is an indication that the eschatological blessings have arrived among the Gentiles just as they had among the Jews.[201]

When Paul and Barnabas return to Antioch, they related to the community all that God had done and how God "had opened a door of faith to the Gentiles."[202] Luke's narrative demonstrated that God was working in the same way among the Gentiles as he had among the Jews. Johnson notes, "Luke has shown that the conversion of the Gentiles, the door of faith opened to them, was not idiosyncratic or momentary."[203] God's work among the Gentiles in continuity with the apostles' ministry and validated by the Spirit becomes part of the evidence that is presented during the Jerusalem Council.

Jerusalem Council

Luke's three narratives have unfolded what he has framed as God's divine work and has led to this point, the council at Jerusalem. Luke used these narratives to demonstrate that God has included the Gentiles among the people of God, incorporating them through His Spirit just as He had for the Jews. The question that the council had to answer was this: Is the expression of the people of God through any one ethnic particularity? Which of the markers of identity, Spirit (anti-structural) or circumcision (structural), is the primary identity marker for the people of God?

There were three sets of evidence presented at the council. The first was Peter's recounting of Cornelius' conversion.[204] In his argument, Peter made it clear that the inclusion of the Gentiles was at God's initiative and was God's activity.[205] Peter argued that God gave the Gentiles the Spirit when they believed, and in doing so, God did not make a distinction between Jew and Gentile. The second set of evidence was the account of Barnabas and Paul. Luke highlights the "signs and wonders" as the activity of God.[206] Finally, the third piece of evidence was the reading of Amos 9:11–12. Kuecker notes that James' use of Amos 9:11–12 emphasized James' awareness that both Israelites and Gentiles share a common identity as one people

---

201. Witherington, *The Acts of the Apostles*, 423; Johnson, *The Acts of the Apostles*, 251.
202. Acts 14:27.
203. Johnson, *The Acts of the Apostles*, 257.
204. Acts 15:5–11.
205. Johnson, *The Acts of the Apostles*, 271.
206. Witherington, *The Acts of the Apostles*, 545.

of God.²⁰⁷ Kuecker observes that while many passages described nations joining the people of God, Amos 9:12 provides the only instance in which non-Israelites are called by God's name as God's possession: "James thus declares that non-Israelites belong to God as non-Israelites."²⁰⁸ The Gentiles were included in the people of God by obedience to Jesus and were incorporated into the community by the Spirit just as the Jews who had turned to Jesus as the messiah.²⁰⁹ There were "no Jews nor Gentiles" in the liminal people of God because their primary identity was the Spirit.²¹⁰ However, they lived this new identity within their ethnolinguistic particularity as Jews and Gentiles. In other words, their anti-structural identity was lived out in their respective structural, ethnolinguistic particularity.

At the end of the proceedings, James sent a letter requesting that Gentiles abstain from things polluted by idols, from sexual immorality, from what has been strangled, and from blood. There are several possible interpretations for this request.²¹¹ However, since the purpose was "not to trouble those of the Gentiles who are turning to God," then the injunctions must be interpreted in a way that the Gentiles were not required to follow Mosaic law or circumcision.²¹² The most plausible explanation is that the list was concerned with avoiding idolatry.²¹³ As Kuecker states, "The prohibitions of the decree were to communicate that the Gentiles should stay away from idol worship, a part of their culture that would be in direct conflict with the worship of the one true God."²¹⁴ It was not a change in ethnic

---

207. Kuecker, *The Spirit and the 'Other,'* 205; Acts 15:15–18a.
208. Kuecker, *The Spirit and the 'Other,'* 209.
209. Peterson, *The Acts of the Apostles,* 433.
210. Galatians 3:28.
211. Witherington notes there are three possible interpretations of these four injunctions. The first is that they are part of the Noahic covenant, applicable for all people. The second view is that the decrees reflect some of the prohibitions for resident aliens. Some see this view as something that God-fearers would already be following as part of their attachment to synagogues. The difficulty with this view is that not all of the prohibitions in Leviticus 17–18 are listed, and it is uncertain why James would list these four (*The Acts of the Apostles,* 460–467). Kuecker argues that this is not likely the reason because the imposition of these laws would indicate the primacy of ethnic Israel with those who are only resident aliens, making non-Israelites second-class citizens in the Spirit-enabled community (*The Spirit and the 'Other,'* 207–210). Witherington's third reason is the one that is used in my argument and seems the most likely in this narrative.
212. Acts 15:19.
213. Witherington, *The Acts of the Apostles,* 470.
214. Kuecker, *The Spirit and the 'Other,'* 209.

identity markers, but rather part of the change in allegiance required of all who chose to follow Christ.

Summary

Luke built a case for the inclusion of the Gentiles in the people of God through their obedience to the Davidic messiah. The inclusion of the Gentiles was not surprising since the eschatological promise to Israel included witnessing to the nations. What was surprising was that the Gentiles were to be included in the people of God while maintaining their ethnolinguistic particularity. For both Jew and Gentile, inclusion in the people of God was by an anti-structural criterion—obedience to the Davidic messiah. Both were incorporated into the liminal community by the Spirit, and their primary identity marker was the Spirit. This community was anti-structural; there was to be no difference between Jew and Gentile, reflecting what Paul writes in Galatians 3:28, "In Christ there is not Jew nor Gentile, male nor female, nor slave nor free." The Gentiles did not have to become Jews to be included in the people of God but became a part of the people of God as Gentiles. Kuecker summarizes:

> The transformation wrought by the Spirit in both persons and groups underscores the fact that, for Luke, the Spirit creates a new way of being human in community—especially as it relates to the "other." The Spirit molds followers of Jesus into Jesus' own allocentric image and forges an identity that transcends ethnicity, while refusing to eliminate all vestiges of "otherness."[215]

Conclusion

This chapter has demonstrated how in Luke's narrative the Spirit marked the people of God as a liminal community and incorporated people into this community. The chapter began by demonstrating the preparation of the community focused on the rite of passage that transformed the status of the disciples from followers of Christ to leaders of the restoration of the people of God. I then demonstrated that Pentecost both began the restoration of Israel and reincorporated the apostles as the leaders of the new community. Luke's narrative in Acts illustrated that entrance into the people of God was anti-structural; it was through people's response to Jesus as the exalted Messiah and their incorporation into the liminal community by the Holy Spirit.

---

215. Kuecker, *The Spirit and the 'Other,'* 221.

I also argued that in Luke's narrative, the people of God expanded to include people of different ethnolinguistic identities, and people were incorporated into the community within their particular ethnicity. They did not have to change their ethnic identity since the Spirit transcended ethnic identity, but they still maintained their ethnic particularity. Finally, I demonstrated that in Luke's narrative, the liminal community exhibited the characteristics of communitas: anti-structure and allocentricism. People did not change their status but lived anti-structurally within their structural statuses.

I propose that Luke's narrative of a community in liminality, in which people live anti-structurally within the structural statuses of society, provides an interpretive framework for the seemingly contradictory writings of Paul, in which he writes that in Christ there is neither male nor female, Greek nor Jew, nor slave nor free, but at times seems to reinforce structural hierarchical status arrangements. In the next chapter, I demonstrate that the framework of liminality, structure, and anti-structure provides a consistent interpretive framework between the narratives of Luke and Paul's letters to his communities.

Chapter 5

Liminality and Pauline Communities

THE NARRATIVE OF LUKE-ACTS discussed in previous chapters provided in narrative form the framework of liminality, structure, and anti-structure for in-Christ communities. Luke described the formation of communities who understood themselves to be living in temporal liminality. Membership and interpersonal relationships within these communities were based on anti-structural criteria, and in Acts, they were marked by a common identity marker, the Spirit. Rather than being separated from society, they were to live this life within the structures of their current society. The writings of Paul and those of his tradition articulate these concepts more fully, providing the theological foundations and descriptions of living anti-structurally within structure for specific in-Christ communities. The discontinuity that has been observed between the teachings of Paul and Jesus' traditions can be viewed in a fresh way within this framework. Both the teachings of Paul and the teachings of Jesus describe the formation of a community in liminality in which membership and interpersonal relationships are anti-structural.

In this chapter, I first discuss Pauline concepts of living betwixt and between the ages, specifically the three dimensions of his inaugurated eschatology.[1] Then I discuss the characteristics of the anti-structural in-Christ, Pauline communities. Finally I discuss Paul's instructions to these communities on how to live anti-structurally within their structural status in the hierarchical Greco-Roman Society.

---

1. My corpus of texts for Pauline communities include both the undisputed (Romans, 1 & 2 Corinthians, Galatians, Philippians, Philemon, 1 Thessalonians) and disputed (Colossians, Ephesians, 1 & 2 Timothy, Titus, 2 Thessalonians). Paul's ideal of living anti-structurally within structure reconciles some of the incongruences in the disputed texts.

Dimensions of Inaugurated Eschatology

The resurrection event both conditioned and determined Pauline tradition.[2] In Pauline theology, the cross marked the change of the eons and formed the basis of living in-Christ.[3] It marked the start of the new age in which God's rule had broken into the present age and the new creation had begun.[4] T. Ryan Jackson notes, "In contrast to the eschatology of Jewish traditions which influenced him, Paul shifts the eschatological focus from the strictly future to a view which has incorporated the past so that the Christ event becomes God's decisive incursion into the world."[5] There are three dimensions in Pauline inaugurated eschatology. First, there was the temporal dimension; the new age had dawned in the present age. Second, there was the embodied dimension; individuals who followed Christ embodied this liminality indwelt by the Spirit but still lived in their physical body. Finally, there was a social dimension; each individual follower of Christ was incorporated into a liminal community in which he or she related anti-structurally within the structures of society. I discuss each of these in the sections that follow.[6]

Temporal Dimension

Paul's understanding of the dawn of the new age was founded in the eschatological promises as depicted in the Old Testament in which two events accompanied the inauguration of the new age in Jewish eschatology: the arrival of the messiah and the outpouring of the Spirit.[7] In Pauline tradition, Jesus was understood as the messiah who inaugurated the new age. According to L. J. Kreitzer, Paul extensively uses messianic titles in describing Jesus, including the use of Son of God (16 times), Son of David (2 times), and Lord (275 times).[8] For Paul, the resurrection demonstrated that Jesus was the

2. Kreitzer, "Eschatology," 255.

3. Fee, *Paul, the Spirit, and the People of God*, 49–59; Jackson, *New Creation in Paul's Letters*, 91–113; Pate, *The End of the Age Has Come*, 44; Sampley, *Walking between the Times*, 7–24; Witherington, *Jesus, Paul, and the End of the World*, 23–35.

4. Strecker, *Die liminale Theologie des Paulus*, 222; Sampley, *Walking between the Times*, 247; Fee, *Paul, the Spirit, and the People of God*, 51; 1 Corinthians 5:17.

5. Jackson, *New Creation in Paul's Letters*, 99.

6. I discovered Strecker's *Die liminale Theologie des Paulus* as I was writing my own study. He has written extensively on liminality within Pauline theology, including a very important discussion on ritual and symbol. Because of the broad sweep of this study, I cannot go into depth for each of the topics in this section. Strecker provides detailed analysis for Paul's understanding of liminal time and life in liminality.

7. Ladd, *A Theology of the New Testament*, 402.

8. Kreitzer, "Eschatology," 256.

messiah and that the promised new age had begun. Kreitzer argues that this affected Paul's eschatology as follows:

> Yet it cannot be forgotten that the appearance of the Messiah was regarded within many writings of first-century Judaism above all as an eschatological event, an indisputable sign that the age to come had arrived. In a sense then, it is true to say that the linchpin of Paul's eschatology is the proclamation of Jesus of Nazareth as the Messiah. At the same time it also needs to be said the key event which guarantees, or authenticates that messiahship is the raising of Jesus from the dead, for it is that act of resurrection which demonstrates how the eschatological age has impinged upon the present.[9]

The second eschatological sign was the pouring out of the Spirit, indicating the renewed presence of God among people. According to Gordon Fee, there are three Old Testament antecedents for Paul's understanding of the relationship between the Spirit and the new age: (1) the association of the Spirit with the new covenant, (2) the language of "indwelling" or of receiving a new heart, and (3) the association of the Spirit with the imagery of the temple in which God is present among His people.[10] Fee notes, "By fulfilling both the new covenant and the renewed temple motifs, the Spirit became the way God himself is now present on the planet."[11] For Paul, the cross marked a change in dominion: God's rule had now begun in the present age.[12] The follower of Christ had been delivered from his past and was living in a new age while still in the present age.[13] Although God's rule had broken into the present and the new age had started, in Paul's understanding it was not to be completed until the parousia.[14] The new age overlapped the old.[15] The overlapping time in which the new age had been inaugurated into the present and the new dominion had begun but was not yet complete created a temporal liminality. In Pauline theology, the cross brought about

---

9. Kreitzer, "Eschatology," 256.

10. Fee, *Paul, the Spirit, and the People of God*, 15; Exodus 33:16; Isaiah 63:10; Jeremiah 31:31–33; Ezekiel 36:26–27; 37:14; Joel 2:28–30.

11. Fee, *Paul, the Spirit, and the People of God*, 15.

12. Strecker, *Die liminale Theologie des Paulus*, 234–35; Romans 6:19–23.

13. Ladd, *A Theology of the New Testament*, 597; Donfried, *Paul, Thessalonica, and Early Christianity*, 243; Pate, *The End of the Age Has Come*, 45; Fee, *Paul, the Spirit, and the People of God*, 49; 2 Corinthians 2:16; Galatians 6:8; Colossians 1:13; 1 Corinthians 15:50; Ephesians 2:5; Romans 6:41; Thessalonians 5:2; 2 Thessalonians 2:2; 1 Corinthians 1:8; 2 Corinthians 1:14; Philippians 1:6.

14. Donfried, *Paul, Thessalonica, and Early Christianity*, 234.

15. Lee, *The Cosmic Drama of Salvation*, 30.

an already/not yet experience that produced a tension of living in the new age while in the present age. This understanding of temporal liminality is found throughout Pauline writings (Figure 12).

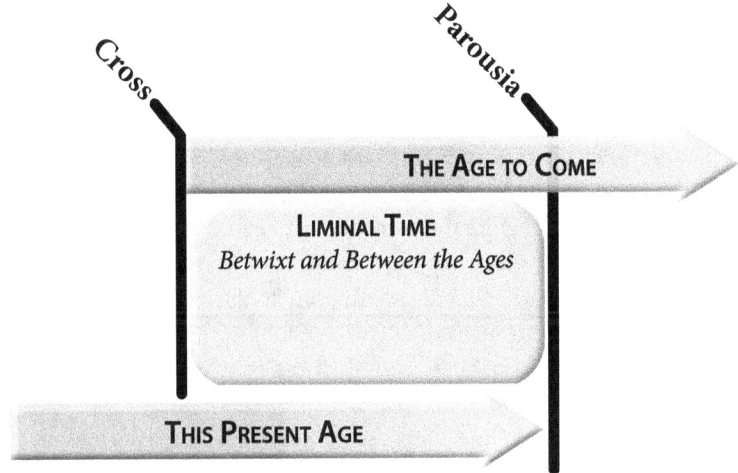

Figure 12. Temporal Liminality in Paul's Writings

Strecker highlights several images that Paul used to express the liminal quality of this inaugurated eschatology and the temporal liminality it created. The first was the metaphor of death, life, and birth pangs which represented the transitional period of the follower of Christ, who Paul saw as standing on the threshold between the resurrection of Jesus and the parousia.[16] Death had ultimately been defeated by Christ's death on the cross, but the Christ follower still lived within the domain of the old eon. Paul expressed that all of creation was in this liminal phase between the eons, so that the "whole creation has been groaning together in the pains for childbirth until now."[17] Creation itself was waiting for the final culmination of the last days: "The revealing of the sons of God."[18] Strecker notes that Paul was writing about procedural time, time that was heading toward an end point: the suffering of the present was not the end but rather the crossing. It was a liminal phase.[19]

Strecker also proposes that Paul's use of the images of night and day also indicated this liminal time. In Romans, Paul wrote that the day was at

16. Romans 8:18–25.
17. Romans 8:19–22.
18. Romans 8:19.
19. Strecker, *Die liminale Theologie des Paulus*, 243.

hand and that night had already gone.[20] Paul did not say that the day had come, speaking of culmination, but that the night had gone, indicating a new era had started. Members of the community were in the period of transition between day and night, like the dawn between night and day. Because night was gone, Paul told those who followed Christ to cast off all the works of the dark and put on the armor of the light.[21]

Finally, Strecker observes that in his letter to the Corinthians Paul compared the present life of temporal liminality to the wilderness wanderings of Israel after the exodus.[22] Paul writes that the Corinthian community was in the liminal time between Christ leading them out of the slavery of the old dominion and before the parousia, or general resurrection. Like the desert wandering of Israel, they were in a transitory state. Paul also compared the symbols of the in-Christ community to the wilderness experience of Israel. Israel passed through the Red Sea out of slavery just as the followers of Christ had been separated from their old state through baptism.[23] In the wilderness, Israel ate manna, just as in their liminality Christ followers eat the common meal of the Lord's supper.[24] According to Strecker, Paul also envisioned the liminal period in the wilderness as a time of suffering and testing.[25] The perils of the wilderness between Egypt and the promised land were now being experienced by Pauline communities who were living between the two ages—in the liminal state of already but not yet.[26] During this liminal period they experienced many afflictions and hardships, just as those going through rites of passage experience hardships and ordeals during liminality. The three analogies of temporal liminality that Strecker highlights can be diagramed as follows (Figure 13):

---

20. Romans 13:11.
21. Strecker, *Die liminale Theologie des Paulus*, 236–39.
22. 1 Corinthians 10:1–14.
23. 1 Corinthians 10:2.
24. 1 Corinthians 10:3.
25. 1 Corinthians 10:7–10.
26. Strecker, *Die liminale Theologie des Paulus*, 222–27.

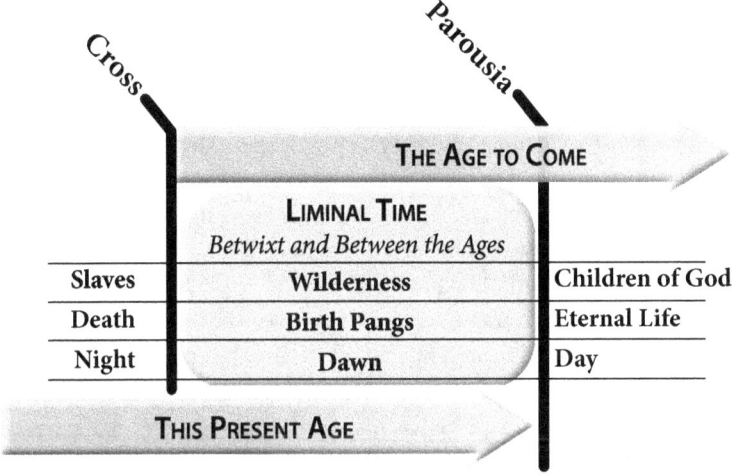

Figure 13. Analogies of Temporal Liminality

While Paul's antecedent for framing the Christ event was Jewish apocalyptic thinking, he radically transformed it by interpreting God's future action as something that had occurred already in the death and resurrection of Christ. Jackson concludes:

> The real distinction between Paul and the apocalyptic writings occurs in an area where there is clearly similarity—the division of time into two successive ages. The present age, a world hostile in manifold rebellion against God, will be overtaken by the new age of the Spirit when God will overcome all opposition to his rule (Ezra 4:26, 7:50). Whereas this intervention of God is viewed as a future event in the apocalyptic literature, Paul interpreted the Christ event as the pivotal crux of history which brought the old age to a close and initiated the subsequent and final age of God's reign. In this manner, Paul modified the Jewish thinking in which he had been steeped. He placed the time of God's most radical invasion of the world in the past in the events of the life, death and resurrection of Christ.[27]

Embodied Liminality

For Paul, the cross was the turning point of the ages and not only created a temporal liminality, but it also inaugurated an embodied liminality. The new

27. Jackson, *New Creation in Paul's Letters*, 102.

age commenced at the coming of the Spirit, who also indwelled those who were in-Christ. Individuals not only lived in liminal time but also embodied that liminality. For Paul, those who are in-Christ embodied the eschaton through the indwelling of the Spirit.[28] This embodiment was expressed in several ways in the Pauline traditions. First, when individuals were indwelt with the Spirit, their old life was put to death with Christ, and they experienced a new life in the Spirit. They were fully separated from their old life of sin and death and were transferred to a new domain.[29] They were under the law of sin and death, but in Christ they were placed under the law of Spirit and life. The flesh was alive to sin; however, the Spirit (liminality) was dead to sin.[30] Paul used several images to capture the essence of the changes that happened with the indwelling of the Spirit, including the Adam/Christ analogy, the extended image between old self/new self, outer self/inner self, and physical person/spiritual person.[31]

However, although the Spirit was embodied in the Christ followers, Paul also understood that they embodied the Spirit within their physical bodies and that they literally became liminal people. They embodied this already/not yet in the transition between a "fleshly body" and a spiritual/immortal body. They embodied liminality. Just as in the temporal aspects of liminality in which the new age had broken into the present age, Paul understood that Christ followers were still bound to the world through their physical body.[32] They were still part of the untransformed world, and the body was still subject to the attacks of the old power.[33] Paul emphasized that followers of Christ could not be saved apart from their bodies. However, they were to use their bodies in accordance with their new life in Christ. They were not to live as if they were still under the dominion of sin and death.[34] Paul sought for his communities to understand that although they were in a body of flesh, they had the capacity to live as children of God because of his Spirit in them. Therefore as liminal people, they were not to do the deeds of the flesh but to do the deeds of the Spirit.[35] They were to actively present their

---

28. Pate, *The End of the Age Has Come*, 153; Campbell, *Paul and Union with Christ*, 408.

29. Tannehill, *Dying and Rising with Christ*, 41.

30. Romans 8:2.

31. Kreitzer, "Eschatology," 257; Romans 5, 6:6, 7:22; 1 Corinthians 15; 2 Corinthians 2:14–16, 4:16; Ephesians 2:15, 3:15, 4:22–24; Colossians 3:9–10.

32. Tannehill, *Dying and Rising with Christ*, 79.

33. Gorman, *Cruciformity*, 56.

34. Russell, *The Flesh/Spirit Conflict in Galatians*, 2.

35. Galatians 5:15–16.

bodies for acts of righteousness, thus reflecting their change of allegiance to God and the new domain in which they lived.[36]

However, during this betwixt and between stage, they were in a state of transition and transformation. Paul expressed this transition as the outer nature, the physical body wasting away while the inner body was being renewed. Followers of Christ progressed in the renewing of the inner self by not conforming to the ideas and behaviors of the physical world but by each being transformed by the renewing of their mind toward the mind of Christ.[37] In Paul's writings, life in liminality was only temporary; life with Christ was eternal.[38] For Paul, participation in Christ's death and suffering assured future participation in the resurrection.[39]

The final part of the embodied liminality in Paul's writings was the reintegration to a new status—with Christ. Paul argued that the reintegration to this new status was at the death of the followers of Christ or at the return of Christ.[40] Paul used the hope of this reintegration to encourage followers of Christ to endure their "slight momentary affliction."[41] For Paul, present life was only temporary, a liminal phase prior to true life in Christ. Paul wrote, "But our citizenship is in heaven and from it we await a Savior, the Lord Jesus Christ, who will transform our lowly body to be like his glorious body, by the power that enables him even to subject all things to himself."[42] These three different stages—flesh, spirit/flesh, and spirit/new body—are reflected in Figure 14.

---

36. Ladd, *A Theology of the New Testament*, 528.
37. Romans 12:1; 2 Corinthians 4:16.
38. 2 Corinthians 2:18.
39. Sampley, *Walking between the Times*, 18.
40. 2 Corinthians 4:14.
41. 2 Corinthians 4:6.
42. Philippians 3:20–21.

	Separation Cross/Holy Spirit Baptism	Reintegration Parousia Death/Resurrection	
Old State **Flesh**	**Liminality** **Flesh/Spirit**	**New Status** **New body/spirit**
we were dead in our trespasses Ephesians 2:5	Dead to sin/Alive to God Romans 6:11	Glory revealed Romans 8:18
Slaves of sin Romans 6:6	Slaves of Righteousness Romans 6:18	Eternal weight of glory 2 Corinthians 4:6
Old self Romans 6:5	Crucified with Christ Romans 6:7	Eternal 2 Corinthians 2:18
Enemies of God Romans 5:10	Reconciled to God Romans 8:36	Be raised from the dead & present us in his presence 2 Corinthians 4:14
Law of sin and death Romans 7:23	Law of Spirit and Life Romans 8:2	Inheritance Colossians 3:24
Live according to the flesh Romans 8:5	Do not be conformed to the world Romans 12:2	But our citizenship is in heaven Philippians 3:20
Instruments of unrighteousness Romans 6:13	Put to death deeds of the flesh Romans 8:17	And we eagerly await a Savior from there, ...will transform our lowly bodies Philippians 3:20,21
Earthly bodies, perishable, mortal 1 Corinthians 13:3	First Fruits Romans 2:23	
	Sealed by the Holy Spirit Ephesians 4:30	
	Spirit of adoption Romans 8:16	
	Outer self wasting away 2 Corinthians 4:16	
	Fruit of the Spirit Galatians 5:15,16	
	Be transformed by the renewing of your mind Romans 12:1	
	Present sufferings Romans 8:18	

Figure 14. Rites of Passage and Embodied Liminality in Paul's Writings

For Paul, followers of Christ were already experiencing life in Christ. They embodied the "already" of life in Christ in the present age but expected to experience it fully at their reintegration. For Paul, death or the parousia accomplished the same thing—the reintegration into a new status as a citizen of heaven forever with Christ. Paul understood followers of Christ to already be living in eternal life through the Spirit while they participated in the structures of the world. Whether they lived until the parousia or died before Christ returned, for Paul it was the same result; they were with Christ. Paul wrote about the paradox of this embodied liminality in Philippians 1:21–26:

> For to me to live is Christ, and to die is gain. If I am to live in the flesh, that means fruitful labor for me. Yet which I shall choose I cannot tell. I am hard pressed between the two. My desire is to depart and be with Christ, for that is far better. But to remain in the flesh is more necessary on your account. Convinced of this, I know that I will remain and continue with you all, for your progress and joy in the faith, so that in me you may have ample cause to glory in Christ Jesus, because of my coming to you again.[43]

Social Dimension

Although many have written about the temporal and embodied liminality, less is written about the social dimension of inaugurated eschatology, the third and parallel dimension of inaugurated liminality. It is here that Turner's discussion of structure, anti-structure, and communitas provides terms in which to describe the Pauline teaching on the social body in liminality.

For Paul, there was a distinct transformation of social relationships for those who were followers of Christ. Pauline theology not only described the salvation of the individual, but it also described the new corporate community in which individuals became embedded when they became a follower of Jesus. In Paul's writings, the Spirit not only created liminal individuals, the Spirit also created a new community, the body of Christ. For Paul, the individual and community were vitally interconnected.[44] Volker Rabens states, "It is not difficult to demonstrate the centrality of relationships in the writings of Paul and the traditions on which he draws."[45]

---

43. Philippians 1:21–26.
44. Dunson, *Individual and Community*, 166.
45. Rabens, *The Holy Spirit and Ethics in Paul*, 133.

Paul's writings were permeated with ideas and concepts related to the community of Christ followers.[46] Paul made it clear that structural characteristics did not qualify someone to become a part of the community of Christ followers. Just as in the Jesus tradition, someone became a member of the community through the anti-structural criteria of obedience to Jesus.[47] Paul wrote, "For I am not ashamed of the gospel for it is the power of God for salvation to everyone who believes, to the Jew first and also to the Greek."[48] The difference was that in Paul's teaching, the gospel was the interpretation of the death, resurrection, and exaltation of Jesus as the Davidic king who had fulfilled the promises of God.[49] Jerry Sumney argues, "Our examination of allusions to the traditions Paul cites in his letters offers no evidence that there were branches of the church (or even of people favorably disposed to Jesus but outside the church) that did not give a central place to interpreting the death of Jesus as they defined their new identity."[50] In Pauline teaching, people not only experienced salvation as individuals, but they were also incorporated into a corporate liminal community of others "in-Christ" through the Spirit.

"In Christ" was used 164 times in writings to the Pauline communities, and there were several meanings for in-Christ in the context of Paul's letters, based on the context of their uses.[51] In Paul's teaching, to be "in-Christ" was to belong to, serve, and be ruled by Christ.[52] Although Paul applied the term to individual believers, he most consistently applied it to the corporate expression of Christ followers. William Barcley notes, "This would suggest that 'in Christ' should not be understood primarily as an expression of the individual believer's relationship with Christ, but rather as related to Paul's conception of the corporate nature of the life of faith."[53] The in-Christ life was fundamentally communal in character.[54]

Paul uses "in-Christ" to mark the identity of the individual as a member of the new community and also to articulate the expected actions of people within the new community.[55] In Paul's teaching, people in the community

46. Lohfink, *Jesus and Community*, 78.
47. Romans 4:13, 3:21–31; Galatians 2:15–21.
48. Romans 1:16.
49. Romans 1:1–6.
50. Sumney, "Christ Died for Us," 168.
51. Banks, *Paul's Idea of Community*, 38.
52. Barcley, "Christ in You," 110.
53. Barcley, "Christ in You," 112.
54. Banks, *Pauls' Idea of Community*, 17; 2 Thessalonians 2:13; Ephesians 1:4, 11.
55. Gorman, *Cruciformity*, 352.

were not differentiated by structural criteria, but all in the community had the same anti-structural status as being in-Christ. People "in-Christ" had the same identity that transcended ethnic, status, economic, and gender differences in the way that not only marked membership in the community but also defined the way they were to interact with one another.[56] I suggest that the baptismal statements in the Pauline corpus were not intended only to reflect an ontological equality in Christ but also to make apparent the anti-structural identity of people in the community of Christ followers.[57] This new anti-structural identity did not erase the status differences of people in the community, but people within their structural status were to relate to each other according to the same overarching status of "in Christ." I propose that this is the overarching hermeneutical framework for interpreting Paul's teaching concerning interpersonal relationships within the community.

As in Luke's narrative of Acts, the Spirit was the common identity marker of Christ followers in the Pauline communities. Paul wrote, "You however are not in the flesh but in the Spirit, if in fact the Spirit of God dwells in you. Anyone who does not have the Spirit of Christ does not belong to Him."[58] The Spirit was the common possession of all Christ followers and was the common identity marker for the new community in which social, gender, and ethnic barriers were eliminated.[59] According to Paul, people were "baptized by one Spirit into one body."[60] Lohfink notes, "Only in the Spirit is it possible to dismantle national and social barriers, group interests, caste systems and domination of one sex over another . . . The people of God, the church as a Body of Christ, is a social reality."[61] Paul used several analogies based on their common anti-structural identity of being in-Christ and being marked by the Holy Spirit to demonstrate the unity and solidarity that transcended, but he did not eliminate ethnic, social, economic, and gender differences.[62]

The first metaphor was the body. Body imagery was commonly used in antiquity to describe political and social entities.[63] Paul described all in-Christ believers together as the body of Christ, particularly when defining the unity of the corporate nature of the believers and their particular

---

56. Hansen, *All of You Are One*, 6.
57. Galatians 3:28; 1 Corinthians 12:13; Colossians 3:11.
58. Romans 8:9.
59. Lohfink, *Jesus and Community*, 88.
60. 1 Corinthians 12:13.
61. Lohfink, *Jesus and Community*, 93.
62. Pate, *The End of the Age Has Come*, 170; Fee, *God's Empowering Presence*, 874.
63. Gorman, *Cruciformity*, 360.

expression of being in-Christ. He wrote, "And he put all things under his feet and gave him as head over all things to the church which is his body, the fullness of him who fills all things."[64] Paul also described how the anti-structural incorporation by the Spirit did not erase structural status differences, but unity resulted nonetheless as this new identity was lived out in their relationships with one another. He wrote, "For just as the body is one and has many members and all are members of the body, though many are one body, so it is with Christ. For in one Spirit we were all baptized into one body—Jews or Greeks, slaves or free—and all were made to drink from one Spirit."[65] Fee states, "God by His Spirit had formed into one body a radical eschatological fellowship that transcended ethnic (Jew and Gentile) as well as socioeconomic (slave and free) statuses."[66] All who were in-Christ were united with Christ and were members of the body of Christ.[67] Paul also emphasized the unity of the body that was created through the Spirit. Fee notes, "The community of God's people owe their life together as a body to the common lavish experience of the Spirit."[68]

The body image allowed Paul to affirm diversity within the community and at the same time emphasize the unity of being in-Christ. Being of one body was foundational for the unity within the community. People were not to relate to each other based on structural statuses nor did they gain special status within the corporate expression of being in-Christ through the gifts of the Spirit.[69] Unity was found in this diversity of gifts: "For as in one body we have many members, and the members do not all have the same function, so we, though many, are one body in Christ and individually members one of another."[70] Every member was indispensable because each one had a different gift from God.[71] The body not only expressed unity in diversity but also reflected how an individual's actions or actions against other members affected the corporate whole.[72] Paul explains, "If one person suffers, all suffer together."[73] As a body, the communities were to foster allegiance to Christ

---

64. Ephesians 1:22–23; see also Ephesians 4:15–16; Colossians 1:18, 24; 3:15.
65. 1 Corinthians 12:12–13.
66. Fee, *Paul, the Spirit, and the People of God*, 70.
67. Dunson, *Individual and Community in Paul's Letter to the Romans*, 166.
68. Fee, *Paul, the Spirit, and the People of God*, 66.
69. Kim, *Christ's Body in Corinth*, 31.
70. Romans 12:4–5.
71. Gorman, *Cruciformity*, 166.
72. Banks, *Paul's Idea of Community*, 65.
73. 1 Corinthians 12:26.

and the values of the cruciform faith: love, humility, and hope.[74] As Yung Suk Kim observes, "This notion of the body of Christ envisions a community that negates hegemony and affirms diversity."[75]

The second metaphor Paul used to describe the corporate nature of those in-Christ was family and household.[76] In Pauline tradition, followers of Christ were understood to be children adopted into the family of God, and the Spirit that dwelt in the believer was the witness that they were God's children.[77] Paul emphasized that it was the common Spirit that demonstrated their adoption as children of God and heirs with Christ.[78] Through the Spirit they were now related to God as true heirs and could call God "Abba! Father!"[79] The metaphor of adoption became central to their understanding of their relationships to others in the community. Their common adoption imagery linked sonship to behavior toward others in the community.[80] Behavior of those in the same family honored or dishonored their father and their new family's reputation.[81] It also defined a common metaphor for the anti-structural relationships within the community.

In Paul's teaching, the new anti-structural family had only one father, God.[82] Paul wrote, "Yet for us there is one God, the Father, from whom are all things and for whom we exist, and one Lord, Jesus Christ, through whom are all things and through whom we exist."[83] In his use of sibling terminology, Paul sought to bring an end to hostilities and divisions between people of different ethnic, social, and economic standing.[84] Sibling language was used to underscore the solidarity and unity that was expected of those in the family of God.[85] Trevor Burke notes that Paul's use of sibling terminology "helps bind together a community of people who had not had a previous connection, commitment or social involvement with one another."[86] There were no fathers

---

74. Colossians 3:15.

75. Kim, *Christ's Body in Corinth*, 31.

76. Hellerman, *The Ancient Church as Family*, 92–126.

77. Romans 8:16.

78. Fee, *God's Empowering Presence*, 873.

79. Romans 8:14–17; also Galatians 4:6.

80. Fee, *God's Empowering Presence*, 560–70; Rabens, *The Holy Spirit and Ethics of Paul*, 209–37.

81. Burke, *Family Matters*, 164, 201, 222.

82. Bartchy, *Call No Man Father*, 9–10.

83. 1 Corinthians 8:6.

84. Burke, *Family Matters*, 166, 248.

85. Burke, *Family Matters*, 173.

86. Burke, *Family Matters*, 174.

in the community; rather they were all brothers and sisters under their father, God.[87] Being brothers and sisters became one of the ways anti-structure was expressed in communitas, which I discuss below.

Finally, Paul used the metaphor of a temple of God to promote correct behavior and a positive identity in the community of Christ followers in Corinth.[88] Paul made it clear that the community was founded on their in-Christ identity. Christ was the "cornerstone in whom the whole structure, being joined together, grows into a holy temple in the Lord."[89] The in-Christ identity brought together people from a variety of social, economic, and ethnic backgrounds; and in Corinth, this led to factions and conflict within the community. The disunity of the Corinthians seriously threatened their in-Christ identity. Kar Yong Lim states, "Instead of building up the temple of God that would have defined their identity in Christ, they were going in the opposite direction by destroying the temple."[90] Paul appealed to the temple imagery to promote unity within the community.

Not only did Paul use temple imagery to symbolize the unity and identity of the Christ community, but he also used it as the image of the presence of God among the community. In using the temple image, Paul compared the Spirit's presence among the community to the Old Testament understanding of God dwelling among his people.[91] God's temple was a sign of God's presence.[92] Moral behavior was to reflect the community's new in-Christ status by consistently presenting itself as God's dwelling place.[93] The community as the temple of God was to be a powerful, attractive icon in which the values of unity and holiness of the community were on display.[94] Lim explains, "In the use of temple imagery, Paul is differentiating his audience from the surrounding society by promoting positive group identity and moral standards that are compatible with their new status in-Christ."[95]

Paul's use of these three images reflected the anti-structural character of the corporate community of Christ followers. Although they came from different backgrounds, they had the same common identity in-Christ and

---

87. Bartchy, *Call No Man Father*, 18.

88. Lim, "Paul's Use of Temple Imagery in the Corinthian Correspondence," 189–208.

89. Ephesians 2:20–22.

90. Lim, "Paul's Use of Temple Imagery in the Corinthian Correspondence," 200.

91. Lim, "Paul's Use of Temple Imagery in the Corinthian Correspondence," 193.

92. Fee, *Paul, the Spirit, and the People of God*, 19.

93. Lim, "Paul's Use of Temple Imagery in the Corinthian Correspondence," 194.

94. Lim, "Paul's Use of Temple Imagery in the Corinthian Correspondence," 200.

95. Lim, "Paul's Use of Temple Imagery in the Corinthian Correspondence," 204.

were indwelt by the Spirit. Like other communities in liminality, these images reflected the unity of people from different ethnic, social, economic, and gender statuses into a common identity. Unlike other liminal communities which separate themselves from structure or erase social distinctions, the in-Christ identity marked by the Spirit transcended but did not erase these social differentiations. Despite social differences, interpersonal relationships within the community were to be characterized by communitas, reflecting their transcendent anti-structural identity. The three dimensions of inaugurated eschatology are diagramed in Figure 15.

Dimension	Old State	Transition	Liminality	Transition	New State
Temporal	Old Age	Separation / Cross / Holy Spirit/Baptism	New Age in Old Age	Reintegration / Death or Parousia / Resurrection	New Age
Embodied	Flesh		Spirit in the Old Body		Spirit in a New Body
Social	Status (Structure)		In-Christ in Status (Anti-Structure in Old Structure)		In-Christ (Anti-Structure in New Structure)

Figure 15. Rites of Passage and Three Dimensions of Inaugurated Eschatology

Characteristics of Relationships of In-Christ Communities

Just as in other communities in liminality, interpersonal relationships in the in-Christ communities were to be characterized by communitas. However, unlike other communities in communitas, the characteristics of these relationships were to be extended beyond their own group to those outside their community. Pauline writings not only redefined relationships between members of the communities, they also redefined leadership and authority within the community as well as relationships with those outside the community. These new types of relationships marked by humility, love, and mutuality were distinctive characteristics of the early Christian communities.

Relationships Within the Community: Siblings in-Christ

First and foremost, the relationship between members of the communities was one of family. One of the most pervasive metaphors that Paul used to describe the interpersonal relationships between members of the in-Christ community was sibling language. Hellerman notes that sibling terminology occurs 118 times in the broader Pauline corpus.[96] He states, "The idea of the church as family is ubiquitous in Paul's writing and is, therefore, central to Paul's understanding of the manner in which interpersonal relationships are to function in the communities to which he writes."[97] However, as with any metaphor, there are multiple and complex meanings that can be attached to it. There are three primary ways in which sibling terminology defined the nature of interpersonal relationships in Pauline communities.

First, sibling terminology highlighted the primary identity of in-Christ community members as the basis of their relationships. Lohfink states, "The brotherhood and sisterhood of the early Christian communities were based on the eschatological outpouring of the Spirit."[98] The primary identity of community members was as siblings under the authority of God the Father. The in-group was no longer defined by bloodlines but by the Spirit of Christ.

Second, Paul's use of siblingship reflected the anti-structural nature of interpersonal relationships that were lived out within structural roles. There were differences in status among members of Pauline communities. Interpersonal relationships between community members were not based on these statuses but on their common identity as siblings in Christ. They were, as Bartchy describes, non-patriarchal without being egalitarian.[99] Paul's use of sibling terminology was to project relationships of mutual responsibility and sharing within the community. The early community was not homogenous, but rather the sibling terminology allowed the community to "embody differences and asymmetrical relationships among members for reciprocal collective actions."[100]

Third, Paul's use of sibling terminology not only redefined the structure of social relationships in the community but behavior within these social relationships. Hellerman suggests that of the total repertoire of relationships in the ancient world, Paul used the sibling relationship because it most closely provided the model for the quality of interpersonal relationships in the community.[101] Through the use of sibling terminology, Paul reinforced behavior characterized by mutuality and solidarity.

96. Hellerman, *The Ancient Church as Family*, 92.
97. Hellerman, *The Ancient Church as Family*, 92.
98. Lohfink, *Jesus and Community*, 108.
99. Bartchy, *Call No Man Father*, 37. There are various viewpoints on whether the use of sibling terminology reflects or undermines patriarchal household structure. Bartchy, Lohfink, and Hellerman argue that sibling relationships undermined patriarchy. Sandnes sees egalitarian structures emerging in patriarchy. Aasgaard argues for a metaphorical use which shaped relationships.
100. Brawley, "From Reflex to Reflections," 128–46.
101. Aasgaard, *My Beloved Brothers and Sisters!*, 312.

Several expectations concerning behavior of siblings in the ancient world were reflected in Paul's writings. First, there was the expectation of generalized reciprocity in both meals and resources.[102] Second, there was to be an affection for one another that was lived out in respect, honor, and caring for one another.[103] Siblings were also to protect each other from adversaries as well as provide correction in behavior when necessary.[104] Finally, ideal sibling relationships were characterized by harmony and peace.[105] All of these reflected the mutual love and affection that Paul expected of interpersonal relationships within the in-Christ communities. This ideal for interpersonal relationships was reflected in Paul's rhetorical strategy, particularly when addressing his fellow Christians. Paul employed the sibling metaphor so that members of the community would relate to each other in the manner expected of those in the same consanguineal family. Reider Aasgaard summarizes Paul's use of sibling terminology:

> It had high and positive expectations attached to it. Ideally, sibling relationships were conceived to be fairly unproblematic. They also left room for differences as regards to status, disposition, age, and gender, but without sanctioning hierarchy. No other social relationships could offer comparable benefits, whether the parent/child relation, the friendship relation, or the patron/client relation. Thus, it is very likely that the sibling role was the social role that best suited Paul's general understanding of what Christian community should be like (ecclesiology), of what it implied to belong to such a community (ethics), and of what their relationships vis-à-vis the outside world were to be, especially in relation to the households they met.[106]

Three prominent characteristics of sibling relationships were reflected in Paul's writings: mutuality, humility, and love. Mutuality was expressed in Paul's extensive use of the reciprocal pronoun ἀλλήλων, "one another," in his exhortations to the in-Christ communities. This reflected a mutual kind of relationship that displayed communal solidarity and a transcendence over status boundary markers in interpersonal relationships in the community.[107] For Paul, these mutual relationships were only possible through the

---

102. Hellerman, *The Ancient Church as Family*, 113.
103. DeSilva, *Honor, Patronage, Kinship, Purity*, 165–69.
104. DeSilva, *Honor, Patronage, Kinship, Purity*, 165–69.
105. Burke, *Family Matters*, 167.
106. Aasgaard, *My Beloved Brothers and Sisters!*, 312.
107. Dunson, *Individual and Community in Paul's Letter to the Romans*, 171.

mutual indwelling of the Spirit and the mutuality of the cruciform life.[108] As members of the same body, they were to be committed to and engaged with each other in mutual exhortation, care, and harmony.[109] Rabens asserts, "This is even intensified by the fact that Paul longs for mutual participation in each other's spiritual life, which results in both parties being encouraged."[110] Lohfink provides the following as some of Paul's use of the reciprocal pronoun ἀλλήλων:[111]

- Outdo one another in showing honor (Romans 12:10)
- Live in harmony with one another (Romans 12:16)
- Welcome one another (Romans 15:7)
- Admonish one another (Romans 15:4)
- Greet one another with a holy kiss (Romans 16:16)
- Wait for one another (1 Corinthians 11:33)
- Have the same care for one another (1 Corinthians 12:25)
- Be servants of one another (Galatians 5:13)
- Bear one another's burdens (Galatians 6:2)
- Comfort one another (1 Thessalonians 5:11)
- Build one another up (1 Thessalonians 5:11)
- Be at peace with one another (1 Thessalonians 5:13)
- Do good to one another (1 Thessalonians 5:15)
- Bear with one another lovingly (Ephesians 4:2)
- Be kind and compassionate with one another (Ephesians 4:32)
- Be subject to one another (Ephesians 5:21)
- Forgive one another (Colossians 3:13)

The mutuality expressed in these commands reflected the anti-structural characteristic of communitas. Members of the in-Christ community were no longer to relate to one another on the basis of structural statuses but as fellow members of the same body through the Spirit. They were to "one another" each other on the basis of their common identity in-Christ. This did not mean an erasure of these statuses; they continued to have different social statuses. Nor did it mean that all in the community had the same capabilities, since people had different spiritual gifts. However, their social statuses and spiritual gifts were to be used for the benefit of one another.[112] Mark Strom comments, "The members met to use their personal

---

108. Gorman, *Cruciformity*, 55.
109. Rabens, *The Holy Spirit and Ethics in Paul*, 136.
110. Rabens, *The Holy Spirit and Ethics in Paul*, 238.
111. Lohfink, *Jesus and Community*, 99.
112. Dunson, *Individual and Community in Paul's Letters to the Romans*, 129.

endowments from the Spirit for common good."[113] In Pauline writings, empowerment for individuals to live the cruciform life came from the mutual expression of gifts used for the common good. These commands to mutuality expressed a commitment to other members of the community and deep involvement in their lives. The corporate community of Christ followers expressed their unity and solidarity by acts of "one anothering." Rabens notes, "Paul is thus aware that the empowerment and building up of a people is the result of the Spirit's work in the dynamics of interpersonal relationships."[114] "One anothering" each other was an expression of communitas.

Another characteristic of the in-Christ sibling relationships was humility. Humility was antithetical to the Greco-Roman value of keeping or increasing one's status at the expense of others.[115] Humility in Pauline writings was not a servile attitude of submission under the domain of others, but it was a recognition of the value, dignity, and worth of each member of the community regardless of social status.[116] The life of humility was choosing a life in mutual submission and of honoring one another that reflected both the anti-structural and allocentric characteristics of communitas in the in-Christ communities.[117]

Paul expressed this call to humility in several ways. One was that people were not to consider themselves in a higher status position than others or base their interactions on status differences. As Michael Gorman explains, they were to be humble in regards to others and regard others as better than themselves.[118] They were not to separate themselves based on their statuses. Paul encouraged those who had higher status not to be haughty but to associate with the lowly.[119] People were also not to humiliate others because of their low structural status, such as was happening in the Corinthian church at meals.[120] Nor were they to compare themselves with others. They were not to judge others nor elevate themselves

---

113. Strom, *Reframing Paul*, 174.

114. Rabens, *The Holy Spirit and Ethics in Paul*, 239.

115. Theissen, *The Religion of the Earliest Churches*, 72.

116. Heen, "Phil 2:6–11 and Resistance to Local Timocratic Rule," 129.

117. Heen, "Phil 2:6–11 and Resistance to Local Timocratic Rule," 150; Ephesians 5:21.

118. Gorman, *Cruciformity*, 257; Philippians 2:34.

119. Romans 12:16.

120. 1 Corinthians 11:22.

by boasting or becoming conceited.[121] They were not to envy those whose status might be higher.[122]

Another way humility was expressed is that they were not to use their status for their own gain. They were not to be involved in rivalries or competitions for honor, and they were to relinquish claims of recognition and offer recognition to others.[123] They were not to use their prerogative of status to elevate their own interests but were to consider others and others' interests as more important than their own.[124] They were not to be self-seeking nor to do anything from rivalry or conceit.[125] They were to rejoice in another's honor rather than promote their own.[126] Those who became humble renounced their rights to use status, knowledge, or freedom for themselves.[127]

The exhortation to humility and considering others was both a recognition of status differences within the community and at the same time a way of overcoming status differences by redefining what was honorable within the community.[128] Paul did not reject the notion of honor but redefined what was honorable in the in-Christ community. Social capital or status was not something to be exploited for oneself but rather something that was to be used for others. Honor was ascribed to those who used their status to serve others and build up the community.[129] Those who were stronger were under obligation to help the weaker members and not do anything that would harm them. People in the community were expected to bear one another's burdens and to seek to please their neighbor. As Gorman notes, all relationships were to be built on interest in the needs of the other.[130] This redefinition of honor—from using status for self-gain to using status for the benefit of others—promoted and maintained unity in the community. Acting humbly reflected the anti-structural and allocentric characteristics of communitas.

Paul illustrated this willingness to give up honor and status sacrificially for the benefit of others with Christ's example. Christ was the exemplar of humility and sacrifice for the community. Paul used the highest status

121. Romans 14:10; 1 Corinthians 3:21, 15:6; Galatians 5:26.
122. Galatians 5:26; Colossians 3:8; 1 Corinthians 3:18.
123. DeSilva, *Honor, Patronage, Kinship & Purity*, 77.
124. Romans 12:16; Ephesians 4:2.
125. Philippians 2:3; Romans 2:8.
126. DeSilva, *Honor, Patronage, Kinship & Purity*, 77.
127. Gorman, *Cruciformity*, 233.
128. Hellerman, *Reconstructing Honor in Roman Philippi*, 165.
129. Banks, *Paul's Idea of Community*, 166; 1 Corinthians 13:5.
130. Gorman, *Cruciformity*, 231; Theissen, *The Religion of the Earliest Churches*, 77.

position to provide an example of the attitude that those with high status should have. Philippians 2:5–11 states:

> Have this mind among yourselves, which is yours in Christ Jesus, who, though he was in the form of God, did not count equality with God a thing to be grasped, but emptied himself, by taking the form of a servant, being born in the likeness of men. And being found in human form, he humbled himself by becoming obedient to the point of death, even death on a cross. Therefore God has highly exalted him and bestowed on him the name that is above every name, so that at the name of Jesus every knee should bow, in heaven and on earth and under the earth, and every tongue confess that Jesus Christ is Lord, to the glory of God the Father.

The greatest reversal of status was exemplified by Christ Jesus who could claim equality with God but did not. Instead he humbled himself and endured the most dishonorable death, a death that was meant to profoundly shame him. Yet because of his humility, having experienced the most shameful death according to man's standard, he was exalted and honored by God. In Pauline communities, people were not to exalt themselves by seeking after honor, status, and position but were to serve with humility, obedience, and in solidarity. God would then honor them. Through Christ's example, Paul provided an example of the redefinition of honor in the community of Christ followers.[131]

While mutuality and humility were important for overcoming status differences, for Paul, love was a central characteristic of communitas in the liminal community. Love transcended the limitations of economic, ethnic, gender, and insider/outsider boundaries. It was the primary action for all who were in-Christ. Fee argues that in the in-Christ community, love had to have absolute supremacy if one was to be a Christian in any sense.[132] In Pauline tradition, love was the outworking of the new life through obedience to Christ and the indwelling of the Spirit.[133]

Love was at the heart of interpersonal relationships within Pauline communities. The love Paul intended was ἀγάπη.[134] This is the word he used to describe how God acted on behalf of those who were alienated from him through the life and death of Christ.[135] Thus, the cross was central to Paul's

---

131. Hellerman, *The Ancient Church as Family*, 165.

132. Fee, *God's Empowering Presence*, 203.

133. Romans 5:5; Galatians 4:6–7; Philippians 1:8.

134. Witherington, *Conflict and Community in Corinth*, 269.

135. Witherington, *Conflict and Community in Corinth*, 269; Fee, *God's Empowering Presence*, 201; Romans 5:6–8.

concept of love. Fee contends that for Paul, "To have love means to be toward others the way God in Christ has been toward us."[136] Paul exhorted people to "be imitators of God."[137] Members were to look to Christ's example for their understanding of what it meant to love others in the in-Christ community. They were to "walk in love as Christ loved us and gave himself up for us."[138] For Paul, love was action that was directed towards others and sought the best for them.[139] Love was allocentric and the core expression of the communitas of the in-Christ community. Love was to be a way of life.[140]

Love encompassed the other characteristics of the liminal community.[141] Paul's exhortation about relationships within the community taught ways in which love was expressed and what it meant to be other-centered: to "one another," to have humility, and to treat each other as brothers and sisters. Many times in his exhortations, Paul did not list specific actions but rather allowed individuals to be guided by love and to do what was best for the other in a particular situation.[142] For instance, rather than telling Philemon what to do about his runaway slave Onesimus, Paul instead appealed to Philemon to do the right thing, trusting a decision based on love.[143] In Paul's treatise on love in 1 Corinthians 13, he appealed to the Corinthians to use gifts not for themselves but to use them according to agape love so that they served others.[144] As Michelle Lee notes, "Only when they are used in love do they become useful in building up the church."[145] Conversely, when gifts were not used in love, Paul considered them useless because they divided the community.[146] For Paul, love was the basis for unity; actions based on self-interest divided the church.[147] Love was what gave the community unity.[148] Roy Ciampa and Brian Rosner state about

---

136. Fee, *God's Empowering Presence*, 201.
137. Ephesians 5:1.
138. Ephesians 5:2.
139. Lee, *Paul, the Stoics, and the Body of Christ*, 184.
140. Witherington, *Conflict and Community in Corinth*, 266.
141. Banks, *Paul's Idea of Community*, 54.
142. Fee, *God's Empowering Presence*, 201.
143. Philemon 8–17.
144. 1 Corinthians 13.
145. Lee, *Paul, the Stoics, and the Body of Christ*, 183.
146. 1 Corinthians 12–14.
147. Ephesians 4:2; Galatians 5:16–26.
148. Verses for unity: Romans 12:10, 16, 18; 14:1, 19; 15:5–6; 1 Corinthians 1:10; 10:16–17; 2 Corinthians 13:11; Galatians 3:27–28; 5:22–23; 6:2; Ephesians 4:1–6; Philippians 1:27; 2:1–4; 4:2; Colossians 2:2, 19; 3:12–14; 1 Thessalonians 5:13–14. Verses for disunity: Romans 12:16; 14:1–23; 16:17; 1 Corinthians 3:3–4; 4:6; 11:18–22; Galatians 5:15, 19–21; Ephesians 4:25, 31; Philippians 2:3–4; Colossians 3:8–9.

1 Corinthians 13: "Paul's comments about love are not based on some abstract, context-free meditation on the subject, but on providing a stinging contrast to the behavior of some members of the Corinthian community."[149] Love was the foundation for communitas. Allocentric and anti-structural actions defined love in Pauline tradition.

Love in the Pauline community was expressed in concrete ways, specifically in guiding the community members' attitudes toward possessions. In the Greco-Roman world, people could gain honor by using their wealth for the common good, which generally entailed building public buildings and monuments. In doing so, they were acting in their own self-interest, maintaining or increasing their honor in society. However, in Pauline communities, possessions were not a means to gain status and honor for oneself but a means to express allocentric behavior towards others. Pauline communities were exhorted to give generously, not only to their own group but also to the broader community of believers.[150] These same allocentric, anti-structural characteristics were also practiced by those in leadership.

Communitas and Authority

Mutuality, humility, and love were also to be characteristics of authority within the in-Christ communities. The membership within the church was never homogenous, but rather members had a common identity in-Christ and were incorporated into the community by the Spirit.[151] It is important to distinguish the differences between asymmetry of people in leadership in the community and the exercise of the authority within the community. From the beginning of the in-Christ community, there was a degree of asymmetry in relationships between recognized leaders and the rest of the community: the apostles of Jesus in Jerusalem, choosing of the deacons to help in service, the prominence of James, and the appointing of elders in the churches on the early missions of Barnabas and Paul.

The development of hierarchical or differentiated roles in the community is often interpreted in terms of the institutional exercise of authority through chains of command. There is the tendency to assume that when there are named positions of leadership, leaders have authority based on that position and exercise institutional or positional authority.[152] Robert Banks asserts, "We are fascinated with the issues of leadership, with

---

149. Ciampa and Rosner, *The First Letter to the Corinthians*, 640.
150. 2 Corinthians 9:2.
151. Harland, "Connections with Elites in the World of Early Christians," 385–408.
152. Banks. "Church Order and Government," 132.

chains of command, lines of authority and so forth. As a result we are in constant danger of reading the priority we accord these matters into Paul's ideas about the church."[153] However, in the in-Christ community, the exercise of authority was not to dominate.[154] For Paul and leaders of the early communities, legitimacy and the exercise of authority was not based on position (structure) but rather on the embodiment of the values of the community and service to the community (anti-structure). The same characteristics of authority that are found in the ritual leaders of communitas—embodiment of values of the community and exercise of authority for the good of the community—were characteristics of the leadership of the Pauline communities. Paul's claims for the legitimacy of his authority and how he exercised authority and instructed others to exercise authority in the community were anti-structure vis-à-vis the structural expectations of teachers and leaders in the Greco-Roman world.

Teachers and leaders in Greco-Roman culture used domination of their pupils to gain and maintain honor for themselves. There was competition among students to follow great teachers, and the competency of the teacher was determined by the number of students he had acquired.[155] However, in the in-Christ community, authority was legitimized by experiential authority; leaders demonstrated their authority to speak to the community by their life and their actions. Legitimate authority for Paul came from embodiment of the values of the community and a relationship of trust through service to others.[156] In Pauline writings, this was demonstrated in three ways.

First, he was exemplary in the ministry that God had given him on behalf of others, "For our boast is this, the testimony of our conscience, that we behaved in the world with simplicity and godly sincerity not by earthly wisdom but by the grace of God, and supremely so toward you."[157] In writing to the Thessalonians, Paul remarked that he worked day and night and that his conduct was blameless.[158] He claimed that his authority was based on the

---

153. Banks, "Church Order and Government," 131–37.

154. Ehrensperger, *Paul and the Dynamics of Power*, 173.

155. *Libanius: Autobiography and Selected Letters*, 51. Although later in the fourth century, the autobiography of Libanius is informative. He tells of beating out rivals for students and gaining fame for the number of students he has. In addition, Libanius gains fame through the adulation of his audience and by the status of those in his audience. The "frequent declamations and excited applause at each of them, throngs of students and their progress, study by night and the sweat of my labors by day, honor, kindness and affection" are the objects of Libanius' success.

156. Ehrensperger, *Paul and the Dynamics of Power*, 184–85.

157. 2 Corinthians 1:12.

158. 1 Thessalonians 2:9–10.

results of his work. He did not need recommendations from other people to legitimize his authority; rather his work and its results were his letter of commendation.[159] He states, "You yourselves are our letter of recommendation, written on our hearts, to be known and read by all."[160]

Second, the legitimacy of Paul's authority was demonstrated through the presence of the power of God in his life, both in word and deed. Paul declared to the Corinthians, "My speech and my message were not in plausible words of wisdom but in demonstration of the Spirit and of power so that your faith might not rest in the wisdom of men but in the power of God."[161] Legitimization by the Spirit was also claimed through signs and wonders he performed: "The signs of a true apostle were performed among you with utmost patience, with signs and wonders and mighty works."[162] Finally, the legitimacy for Paul's authority came from his endurance through suffering, affliction, and sacrifice.[163] He embodied the cruciform life that he taught.[164]

The third way Paul claimed legitimacy and credibility for his authority was his own embodiment of the values of the community. Paul's use of authority was directed toward empowering the communities to live their lives according to the gospel; therefore, his life needed to reflect those values.[165] Paul encouraged people to be imitators of him because he desired them to embrace the cruciform life that he had embraced.[166] He stated, "What you have learned and received and heard and seen in me—practice these things and the God of peace will be with you."[167] In cases in which Paul encouraged the community to imitate him, there were specific values which Paul desired the communities to imitate in specific circumstances.[168] In three of the six instances where Paul called upon people to imitate him, he contrasted his behavior to the behavior of those who were claiming authority over the community.

One example is when he wrote in the context of various factions that were created by comparisons and rivalries among leaders in Corinth.[169] The

---

159. Agosto, "Patronage and Commendation, Imperial and Anti-Imperial," 103–25.
160. 2 Corinthians 3:1–3.
161. 1 Corinthians 2:4–5.
162. 2 Corinthians 12:12; see also Romans 15:19; Galatians 3:5; 1 Thessalonians 1:5.
163. 1 Corinthians 4:8–13; 2 Corinthians 4:4–18; 2 Corinthians 11:22–33.
164. Ehrensperger, *Paul and the Dynamics of Power*, 105.
165. Ehrensperger, *Paul and the Dynamics of Power*, 62.
166. Landolt, "Be Imitators of Me, Brothers and Sisters," 285.
167. Philippians 4:9.
168. Ehrensperger, *Paul and the Dynamics of Power*, 294.
169. 1 Corinthians 4:16.

Corinthians thrived on the displays of power of word and deed and were inclined to submit to dominance by those who claimed authority.[170] Paul, however, demonstrated from his life that true authority came from embodying the way of the cross through self-sacrifice for others.[171] In the context of divisions based on meats offered to idols, Paul asked them not to seek their own good, but the good of others: "Give no offense to Jews or to Greeks or to the church of God, just as I try to please everyone in everything I do, not seeking my own advantage but that of many, that they may be saved."[172] In writing to the Philippians he called upon them to imitate his example in humility in which there was nothing in and of himself about which he desired to boast, except Christ.[173] In the other three passages, Paul provided his own example of how to live betwixt and between. In 1 Thessalonians 1:6 and 2:14, they were to imitate his faithfulness in suffering and distress, the embodiment of the way of the cross.[174] And finally, 2 Thessalonians 3:7–9 reflected living anti-structurally while in structure. Like Paul, they were to continue supporting themselves through work.

The same kind of legitimacy through the embodiment and practice of community values was reflected when Paul recommended co-workers or addressed the qualifications for leadership.[175] Neither Paul's co-workers nor those who were appointed to leadership positions had privileged status because of their association with Paul. People were leaders in the community because their lives reflected the values of the communitas community: hard work, service, and concern for others.[176] For instance, Paul commended Timothy to the Philippians because Timothy was genuinely concerned for their welfare, and he had served with Paul in presenting the gospel.[177] He instructed the Corinthians to be subject to Stephanas because Stephanas' household had devoted themselves to the service of the community. He instructed them to obey others who reflected the same kind of commitment.[178] The two pastoral letters addressed to Timothy provide a list of requirements for both ἐπίσκοπος and διακόνος that reflect both the embodiment of the

---

170. Witherington, *Conflict and Community in Corinth*, 138.
171. Witherington, *Conflict and Community in Corinth*, 146.
172. 1 Corinthians 10:32–33.
173. Philippians 3:17.
174. Agosto, "Patronage and Commendation, Imperial and Anti-Imperial," 105.
175. Lohfink, *Jesus and Community*, 119.
176. Agosto, "Patronage and Commendation, Imperial and Anti-Imperial," 162.
177. Philippians. 2:19–24.
178. 1 Corinthians 16:15–6.

values of the community and authority through experience in ministry.[179] Although these letters reflect the organization of positions of leadership, legitimacy of authority was based on anti-structural criteria, not on noble birth, riches, or military success.

Finally, the exercise of authority within the community was redefined. It was not to be characterized by domination, self-serving, or self-aggrandizing but through service, love, and building up the community in humility.[180] Pauline writings reflect the redefinition of honor and expectations of teachers and leaders in Greco-Roman society (structure). In Greco-Roman society, leaders gained their position through patrons and benefactors and kept their position and gained new positions by becoming a patron and acquiring clients. A patron's honor was reflected in the number of clients he could claim.[181] The patron provided services for his clients in exchange for the honor and loyalty that the clients would provide.[182] In structure, leaders sought to gain honor for themselves. Therefore, they sought to please and impress people with their appearance and their words. To keep their positions, they had to have the power and means to compete and dominate others.[183]

However, leadership and authority were redefined for leaders in Pauline communities and reflected the anti-structural characteristics of communitas. Leaders were to serve and nurture the communities as parents.[184] Authority was not exercised for domination and power but rather sacrifice and servanthood. The exercise of power within the community was to empower the community to live the cruciform life.[185] Paul very rarely used commands to demand communities do what he thought was important. Rather he appealed, παρακαλέω,[186] or requested, ἐρωτάω,[187] that they do

---

179. 1 Timothy 3:1–13.

180. Ehrensperger, *Paul and the Dynamics of Power*, 177; Philippians 3:17; 4:9; 1 Corinthians 16:15.

181. DeSilva, "Patronage," 766–71.

182. DeSilva, "Patronage," 766.

183. Ehrensperger, *Paul and the Dynamics of Power*, 103.

184. 1 Thessalonians 2:1–7.

185. Ehrensperger, *Paul and the Dynamics of Power*, 184.

186. Romans 12:1; 16:7; 1 Corinthians 1:10; 4:13, 16; 16:15; 2 Corinthians 2:8; 6:1; 10:1; 12:18; Ephesians 4:1; Philippians 4:2; 1 Thessalonians. 4:1, 10, 5:14; 1 Timothy 2:1; Philemon 9, 10.

187. Philippians 4:3; 1 Thessalonians 4:1; 5:12; 2 Thessalonians 2:1.

what was right. He spoke to them as fellow workers, συνεργοί,[188] who mutually encouraged each other in the faith.[189]

Authority in the community was not to be exercised for self-gain but to honor God and for the benefit of others. The exercise of authority within the community was to serve the community, and many times Paul referred to himself as a servant.[190] The exercise of authority was allocentric rather than self-focused. Allocentric concern rather than selfish ambition was the motive for those who taught in Pauline communities.[191] Teachers were not to use smooth talk, flattery, or deceit, nor were they to seek to please others; they were only to speak in a way that pleased God.[192] The goal of ministry was not to gain followers but to empower others to follow Christ. As Paul states, "I have become all things to all people, that by all means I might save some."[193] The exhortations and the exercise of authority were to benefit the community in order to bring unity and empower people to live a cruciform life: "Though I am absent in body, yet I am with you in spirit, rejoicing to see your good order and the firmness of your faith in Christ."[194] Leaders in the Pauline communities were to use authority in a way that reflected the anti-structural and allocentric characteristics of communitas.

Relationships Outside Community—
Do Not Be Conformed

One of the unique features of the early Christian community is that though they were a liminal community with a distinct eschatological orientation, their interaction with structure was different from many liminal communities: they neither withdrew from society, nor did they seek revolt against structure.[195] Not only were they not to withdraw from society, they were to live exemplary lives in structure and extend their communitas relationships and values to those in structure outside their group. Rather than strengthening insider/

---

188. It is used 34 times in Pauline communities: Colossians 4:7; 1 Thessalonians 3:2; 2 Corinthians 6:1; Philippians 2:25; 1 Corinthians 3:9; 2 Corinthians 8:32.

189. Romans 1:2.

190. Romans 1:1–2; 1 Corinthians 4:57.

191. Philippians 2:5.

192. 1 Thessalonians 2:1–8.

193. 1 Corinthians 9:22.

194. Colossians 2:5.

195. This was in stark contrast to those such as Essenes, sectarian groups, or millenarian groups.

outsider boundaries as many sectarian groups did, they were to welcome all and transcend in-group/out-group boundaries.

As in the Jesus tradition, love was not limited to the people in a particular in-group. Structural in-group boundaries no longer existed in the liminal community of Christ followers. Paul exhorted community members to extend hospitality to strangers.[196] Corneliu Constantineanu states, "In expounding genuine love, Paul emphasizes its implications for everyday life by highlighting that it brings about a specific conduct towards all people."[197] In contrast to sectarian communities with strong in-group/out-group boundaries, Pauline communities extended communitas to all. They were to love their neighbors and provide real care and concern for them.[198] However, this extension of communitas was not just to their neighbors but to their enemies as well. If their enemy was hungry they were to feed him.[199] They were not to take revenge but were to bless those who cursed them and not repay evil with evil.[200] Love rather than self-interest was to mark all relationships of followers of Christ. Paul appealed to believers to pursue behaviors that would have a positive impact for all people.[201] It was through positive, allocentric actions that communitas was extended to those outside the community.[202]

Pauline writings also reflect several aspects of the Christ-follower's life within the structures of society. First, Paul seemed to affirm the Roman imperial order and the rights of the authorities. He did not deny their right to rule nor their ordination from God, nor did he provide a systematic or comprehensive critique on the emperor or the empire.[203] Paul did not call for insurgence, resistance, or revolt.[204] Rather, he advocated for compliance to both the Roman imperial government and local authorities.[205] The responsibility of people in-Christ extended to living responsibly as citizens in the society at large.[206] People in Christ communities were to respect those

---

196. Romans 12:13.
197. Constantineanu, *The Social Significance of Reconciliation in Paul's Theology*, 159.
198. Constantineanu, *The Social Significance of Reconciliation in Paul's Theology*, 160.
199. Romans 12:20.
200. Romans 12:14.
201. Constantineanu, *The Social Significance of Reconciliation in Paul's Theology*, 160.
202. Galatians 6:10.
203. Stegemann, "Coexistence and Transformation," 3–23.
204. Stegemann, "Coexistence and Transformation," 9.
205. Stegemann, "Coexistence and Transformation," 9.
206. Constantineanu, *The Social Significance of Reconciliation in Paul's Theology*, 165.

to whom respect was due and to give honor to whom honor was due.[207] In other words, they were to relate in appropriate ways to the leaders of their structural community, including those who were benefactors or other high-status persons. They were to pay what was owed to the appropriate people: revenue to whom revenue was due and taxes to whom taxes were due. They were to be exemplary citizens because, according to Pauline thought, even those rulers were there by God's divine authority.[208]

However, the rulers of the imperial government belonged to the "present age," and Paul anticipated an imminent regime change. According to Ekkehard Stegemann, "Paul and his audience believed that Christ would soon bring an end to all powers, authorities, and rulers—Caesar included."[209] Stegemann argues that obedience to the Roman Imperial powers and obedience of faith in Jesus could coexist without contradiction. The early Christian community, as a liminal anti-structural community, was expected to live anti-structural lives as the in-Christ community while at the same time participating in the Roman imperial structures. However, they were not to be conformed to these structures; rather they were to transform them by extending the communitas relationships to those outside the community.

Paul rejected any kind of anarchy or withdrawal from the concrete conditions of everyday life in society.[210] He made it very clear that they were to participate fully in the structures of society and behave in a manner toward outsiders that provided a positive impression upon outsiders. Constantineanu observes, "For Paul, love as a practice of reconciliation, is not limited to the community of believers but extends also to 'the other'—who might be the enemy or the governing authorities."[211] Those in Pauline communities were not to return evil for evil, rather they were to love their enemies. They were to do good to those they called their enemy, to give them something to eat when they were hungry or something to drink when they were thirsty.[212] They were not to speak evil of anyone; they were to avoid quarreling and to

207. Romans 13:7.
208. Romans 13:1–7; Titus 3.
209. Stegemann, "Coexistence and Transformation," 14.
210. Constantineanu, *The Social Significance of Reconciliation in Paul's Theology*, 165. Because of the eschatological focus on the parousia and the emphasis on communitas living, there may have been those in the Pauline communities who understood that their lives were to be lived apart from structure as in other communities in liminality. In other words, because the end was near or because they were a new community, there may have been those who considered themselves a protest community or a millenarian group which withdrew from participation in the social structures of their communities. Paul corrected these ideas in his writings.
211. Constantineanu, *The Social Significance of Reconciliation in Paul's Theology*, 171.
212. Romans 12:18–21.

show courtesy to all people.[213] They were to walk in wisdom toward outsiders and be gracious in answering each person.[214] Leaders of the community were to be respected by outsiders.[215] Their consistent anti-structural behavior of love, mutuality, and humility was an immense challenge to the values of the Greco-Roman world, both to those who dominated and those who were under subjection.[216] Kathy Ehrensperger asserts, "Thus in relation to the competitive dimension of Greco-Roman culture, and in relation to the perception and evaluation of the diversity of peoples, the Pauline letters witness to a strong, even passionate challenge to the dominating cultural, political, social and religious values of the empire."[217] Paul was convinced that he and other in-Christ believers were living between the times in liminal time. Therefore, followers of Christ were to live in a way that reflected their values and way of life in the new age as they waited for the final days of the present age. They were to be a contrast society while living within society.[218] They were to do more than just live according to the structural values of their society; they were to live out the values of the in-Christ community within the social structures of society.

Summary

This section has examined the interpersonal relationships of the Pauline communities. Members of the communities were defined by anti-structural characteristics; they were in-Christ and marked by the Holy Spirit. The in-Christ, Spirit-marked identity was an identity that transcended other identities marked by economic, ethnic, social, and gender status differences. Their corporate identity was compared to a body, a temple, and a family. Like other communities in liminality, their relationships were characterized as communitas: allocentric and anti-structural. These characteristics were highlighted in exhortations to mutuality, siblinghood, humility, and love. Finally, the authority in communitas was not based on structural authority but was legitimized by embodying the values and service to the community. The exercise of authority was not to gain dominance but to serve and build up the body of Christ.

---

213. Titus 3:1.
214. Colossians 4:4.
215. 1 Timothy 3:7.
216. Ehrensperger, *Paul and the Dynamics of Power*, 193.
217. Ehrensperger, *Paul and the Dynamics of Power*, 193.
218. Lohfink, *Jesus and Community*, 122.

Although the early in-Christ communities were liminal, they were unique from other communities in liminality in that they were not separated from society. They were to extend communitas to those outside their community. They also did not erase their social distinctions but were to live out communitas relationships within the structures of their society. They were to live anti-structural lives in the structures of their society. This dialectic between structure and anti-structure is discussed in the next section.

Anti-Structure in Structure— In the World but Not of the World

The anti-structural community reflected the salient social identity of being in-Christ.[219] As described above, Paul used several metaphors—temple, family, and body—to strengthen and reinforce the value of unity in the diversity of the early Christian communities. The anti-structural characteristics of mutuality, siblinghood, humility, and love reinforced the equality of all "in-Christ." However, their in-Christ identity, their liminal identity, did not erase social distinctions nor was the liminal identity just an ontological spiritual reality as some have suggested.[220] Paul's exhortations make it clear that the in-Christ community's behavior and interpersonal interactions were characterized by communitas. However, these interactions were lived out in their statuses in a society in which hierarchy and power were the norm.[221] They had to live in family-like unity within their distinct structural statuses.[222] For instance, within the Corinthian community, Paul elaborated how he envisioned that social distinctions of sexuality, gender, slave/free, Jews/Gentile, food-related practices, and economic differences could be lived out in solidarity and mutuality within the in-Christ community.[223] Paul did not ignore these distinctions nor reject them, but he provided guidelines on how to live out their in-Christ identity within these social distinctions.

However, some writings in the Pauline tradition seem to reinforce structural values, particularly in the case of the household code. I propose that Paul's vision of the in-Christ community stated in Galatians 3:28—"There is neither Jew nor Gentile, there is neither slave nor free, there is no male and female, for you are all one in Christ Jesus" (NIV)—is not just an ontological

---

219. Tucker, *Remain in Your Calling*, 49.

220. Hogan, "No Longer Male and Female," 7.

221. Tucker, *Remain in Your Calling*, 59.

222. Hansen, *All of You Are One*, 86; 1 Corinthians 5–7; 1 Corinthians 8–10; 1 Corinthians 7:18–19, 21–23; 9:19; 11:17–34.

223. Hansen, *All of You Are One*, 156.

spiritual reality nor an attempt to define a utopian ideal. Rather, I suggest that Galatians 3:28 represented the anti-structural, in-Christ identity that was to be lived out within these structural statuses and, in doing so, transform them. This provides the interpretive framework for understanding the relationship between the mutuality in the community and the hierarchy within structural statuses of the society in which they are embedded. Within the community, they were to transcend the hierarchical and other structural statuses of Roman society and live in love and mutual submission within these statuses, thus transforming the fabric of Greco-Roman society. I address each of these as ordered in Galatians 3:28.

Neither Jew nor Gentile

Luke's narrative in Acts discussed in the last chapter demonstrated that people who had different ethnic identities were incorporated in-Christ and marked by the Spirit with a common identity. However, they were to live out their new in-Christ identities within their ethnic particularities. Bruce Hansen argues that in Pauline writings becoming a part of the in-Christ community did not fundamentally change people's ethnic categories, but the in-Christ communities were free of cultural domination.[224] Jews were not forced to become Gentiles, nor were Gentiles forced to become Jews.[225] Within Paul's writings, although Jews and Gentiles are one in Christ, they still retained their ethnolinguistic distinctions.[226] Paul did not ignore ethnic differences; however, they were to live as one within their ethnic particularity.[227] Paul recognized and supported diversity in the community, and although Jew and Gentile were equal, they were not the same.[228]

Paul writes 1 Corinthians 12:13 in a Roman context: "For we were all baptized by one Spirit so as to form one body—whether Jews or Gentiles, slaves or free—and we were all given the one Spirit" (NIV). In the Greco-Roman culture, ethnic differences were also a part of the discourse of hierarchy and domination. Ehrensperger observes, "To be a member of a people other than Greeks or Romans, and to adhere to another culture and value system meant to be despised as uncivilized, barbaric, even born to be slaves."[229] To become a member of the dominant culture, people

---

224. Hansen, *All of You Are One*, 104.
225. Campbell, *Paul and the Creation of Christian Identity*, 10; 1 Corinthians 7:18.
226. Hansen, *All of You Are One*, 104.
227. Tucker, "Baths, Baptism, and Patronage," 177.
228. Campbell, *Paul and the Creation of Christian Identity*, 166.
229. Ehrensperger, *Paul and the Dynamics of Power*, 192.

had to become Romanized or Hellenized and lose the distinction of their ethnolinguistic particularity. There was no equality for people of a different ethnic background. The hierarchy of peoples was absolutely clear in Greco-Roman culture, and it justified domination of others.[230] The mutuality and solidarity between people of different ethnicities in-Christ challenged the hierarchical Greco-Roman world filled with the dominating and dominated. In both these cases, the Jewish exclusion of Gentiles and the Roman domination of others, the common in-Christ identity challenged both exclusion and domination based on ethnolinguistic identity. They were not to change their condition or become the same, but they were to be united in their diversity. They were to express their anti-structural identity in-Christ within their ethnolinguistic particularity.

Neither Slave nor Free

Just as Paul did not encourage Jews and Gentiles to change their ethnicity, neither did he encourage slaves to change their condition. However, what Paul advocated was the inclusion and equality of all statuses in-Christ, just as he did for economic status, marital status, and gender. Paul welcomed slaves into the community as equals within the body of Christ, and they shared in the common identity of in-Christ. According to Bartchy, Paul saw religious, social, or legal status as neither a hindrance nor an advantage with respect to living according to their calling.[231] God had not called them out of their previous statuses but into Christ.[232] For Paul, the status of slave and free were meaningless for those in-Christ. Obedience to Christ's commands, in other words living anti-structural lives within the structures of their society, was what mattered.[233] However, this did not mean God was prohibiting them from changing their status.[234]

Although Paul did not directly challenge the institutions of slavery, he did change the perception of the slave. Within the in-Christ community, the slave was no longer a thing, but rather a person, a fellow brother or sister in Christ.[235] In his letter to Philemon, Paul acknowledged the institution of slavery and the right of Philemon to own Onesimus. Although Paul would have liked to have kept Onesimus with him, he left the decision to Philemon.

230. Ehrensperger, *Paul and the Dynamics of Power*, 192.
231. Bartchy, *Mallon Chresai*, 151.
232. Bartchy, *Mallon Chresai*, 151.
233. 1 Corinthians 7:18.
234. Bartchy, *Mallon Chresai*, 153.
235. Ehrensperger, *Paul and the Dynamics of Power*, 195.

He wrote, "I preferred to do nothing without your consent."[236] Although there was implicit acknowledgement of the slave/master relationship, Paul appealed more strongly to the new anti-structural relationship of mutual membership in the body of Christ. Paul wrote to Philemon that he returned Onesimus to him no longer a slave but more than a slave—as a dear brother, a member of the in-Christ community.[237] Finally, Paul asked that Philemon welcome Onesimus as he would Paul himself, reflecting that in Christ there was no difference between free and slave.[238] What is interesting is that Paul did not demand that Philemon free Onesimus but rather that he encouraged him to treat Onesimus as he would any member in the body of Christ, even while he remained a slave. However, implied in Paul's letter is the desire that Onesimus would become socially what he was in-Christ.[239]

Male nor Female

Having established the hermeneutical framework of the Pauline tradition of living anti-structurally in-Christ while in structure, I apply this same framework to statements in Pauline tradition on gender roles, particularly in marriage.[240] Using a consistent framework for my interpretation of gender relationships as for other statuses, I propose that these statements redefined how men and women, particularly husband and wives, were to live as brothers and sisters within their culturally defined roles.[241] The in-Christ identity and mutual submissions relativized the hierarchical arrangement of statuses in marriage. I examine two distinct passages about the relationships of husbands and wives to illustrate how they are consistent with other Pauline instructions of living anti-structurally within structural status.

In 1 Corinthians 7, Paul wrote extensively about issues of marriage, sexuality, and divorce, addressing both men and women in a balanced way. There were three distinct aspects of marriage that Paul addressed. Within marital rights, the structural expectations of marriage were that women belonged to their husbands.[242] It was the structural role of a wife to fulfill

236. Philemon 14.
237. Philemon 16.
238. Hogan, "No Longer Male and Female," 32; Philemon 17.
239. Hogan, "No Longer Male and Female," 32.
240. I realize that this is a very broad subject with many diverse opinions and is a hotly contested area. It is not my intent to address the history of the variety of opinions on this issue. An overview of the scholarly discussion can be found in Pierce, "Contemporary Evangelicals for Gender Equality," 58–78.
241. Hansen, *All of You Are One*, 135.
242. 1 Corinthians 7:1–7.

her duty to her husband because her body did not belong to her, but to her husband.[243] However, in the new community (the body of Christ), mutuality was expressed within these structural roles. Not only were women to fulfill their duties to their husband, but husbands were also mutually responsible for fulfilling their duties to their wives because their bodies belonged to their wives.[244] The mutual responsibilities—the "one anothering" of the in-Christ community—was demonstrated in marital relationships between husband and wives.

The second way that Paul demonstrates this same kind of mutuality within marriage was in the marital responsibility and choice within mixed marriages: marriages in which one spouse was a follower of Christ and the other was not.[245] In these passages, Paul spoke about divorce, particularly about divorce and choice in mixed marriages. A wife who had an unbelieving husband was instructed not to divorce her husband because she might save him. In the same way, men were not to force their wives to stay married or convert to Christianity. Once again, Paul expressed the mutuality of the in-Christ community by making the same demands on men as on women. Men were not to divorce their wives, and they are instructed to stay married to unbelievers should the unbelieving spouse desire it. Both men and women had the same obligation to their marital partners. This evenhanded mutuality stood in contrast to what might have been expected from other first-century authors.[246]

Finally, Paul addressed marital choices and service to the Lord.[247] Both men and women were given the choice whether to marry or remain single in their service to Christ. As with ethnicity and slavery, they were to pursue living the cruciform life in the context of their present status.[248] Once again, in a society that gave men the choice in regard to marriage or celibacy, in the in-Christ community there was no difference in choices given to men and women. Both were allowed to determine what was best for them in regard to marriage and service to Christ. As Gilbert Bilezikian notes, "This text indicates that the early church did not perpetuate in its life the functional differentiations between male and female that were

---

243. Hogan, "No Longer Male and Female," 38; Witherington, *Conflict and Community in Corinth*, 175.

244. Hogan, "No Longer Male and Female," 32; Paget, *As Christ Submits to the Church*, 69.

245. 1Corinthians 7:8–16.

246. Ciampa and Rosner, *The First Letter to the Corinthians*, 296.

247. 1 Corinthians 7:25–35.

248. Hansen, *All of You Are One*, 138.

prevalent in its ambient patriarchal society. Men and women were treated as equals in their service in the church."[249]

The final passage that I examine is the description of a new way of living as husband and wife within the household code.[250] Some argue that in these passages, the writer is reinforcing the hierarchy and domination of the *pater* over the household.[251] However, this passage must be interpreted using the same hermeneutical framework of living anti-structurally (in-Christ) within the structures of society. In this passage, the author addressed the mutual submission of in-Christ people in three different role relationships within the social body: husband-wife, father-child, and master-slave. The structural obligations within the Greco-Roman society were for wives to submit to their husbands, children to obey their fathers, and slaves to obey their masters. In writing about the household code, the author supported the foundational structure of Greco-Roman society. However, he wrote about how in-Christ members were to live anti-structural, exemplary lives within that structure. The writer made two fundamental changes to the expectations of the traditional household code for husbands and wives.

First, he provided a new motivation for societal expectations. Wives were not to submit to husbands because of societal expectations and obligations, but rather submission was based on mutual submission and respect for members in the in-Christ body.[252] For a wife who was a Christ follower, especially if married to someone who was not, this provided a way for her to please Christ within the structural obligations of her household. As a member of the in-Christ community, her conduct toward her husband, whether Christian or non-Christian, was to be Christ-like. Second, the writer outlined reciprocal submission for the man in his structural role as husband. The author does not deny that hierarchy exists but reinforces the in-Christ community expectations that those in the superordinate position were to serve and use their status for the benefit of others.[253] As a Christ follower, the man was to express those relationships not in power and authority but

---

249. Bilezikian, *Beyond Sex Roles*, 134.

250. Ephesians 5:22—6:9.

251. O'Brian, *The Letter to the Ephesians,* 409–38. O'Brian argues that Paul is reinforcing the natural order of subordination of wife, children, and slave. Some form of this argument is used by those who argue that Paul or the writer of Ephesians is reverting back to more conservative views of gender relationships within the household. See also Hoehner, *Ephesians: An Exegetical Commentary*, 720–84; Arnold, *Ephesians: Exegetical Commentary on the New Testament*, 363–410.

252. Keener, *Paul, Women, and Wives*, 185.

253. Fee, "Hermeneutics and the Gender Debate," 364–81.

in love and service.²⁵⁴ Mutual love and submission were actions expected of every in-Christ member, even for husbands and wives in their patriarchal context.²⁵⁵ The actions of husbands and wives toward each other were to reflect the mutuality of members of the in-Christ community and in doing so relativized the hierarchical structural role relationships between husband and wife. Sandnes argues that it is within the context of household that a new reality emerged.²⁵⁶ The siblinghood of fellowship was thus embedded in the household structures and transformed them. Within the structural arrangements of the hierarchy, the relationship between husband and wife was to reflect the anti-structural characteristics of communitas. They were to live anti-structurally within structure.

Summary

The uniqueness of the Pauline communities was not that its members were in liminality. Many communities experience this phenomenon. The unique aspect of the liminality of the in-Christ communities was that it did not eliminate the structures of society, but it redefined how people related to one another within those structures. In the Pauline communities, followers of Christ did not step out of nor renounce their statuses; rather they were to live and to relate to one another as if there were no status differences. The hermeneutical framework of living anti-structurally within the structures of society allows a consistent interpretation of what Paul meant in Galatians 3:28 and how it was lived out in Pauline communities. People did not stop being women or men. It did not change their status as Jew or non-Jew, slave or free, nor did it disengage them from the hierarchical structures of the Greco-Roman society. However, it redefined how people were to relate to one another. They were to relate to one another in love rather than in power and hierarchy. Bartchy concludes, "The person who had been called was no longer defined as a Jew or Greek, as a male or female, as a slave or a freeman, but as a saint; this 'holiness of Christ' was not a status but a new way of existing in the world under the grace and the command of God."²⁵⁷ They were to live anti-structural lives within structure.

---

254. Fee, "Hermeneutics and the Gender Debate," 379.
255. Ephesians 5:21.
256. Sandnes, "Equality Within Patriarchal Structures," 157.
257. Bartchy, *Mallon Chresai*, 153.

Conclusion

This chapter has demonstrated that Paul understood himself and his communities to be living in liminality. Liminality was expressed as living in the overlap of the ages: the new age had begun within the present age. Liminality was also embodied within individuals. They were indwelt by the Holy Spirit but still lived out their in-Christ lives in their physical bodies. Finally, individuals were incorporated into the people of God who had a common identity in-Christ and were marked by the Holy Spirit. This in-Christ community was liminal and was marked by interpersonal relationships that were characterized by communitas: anti-structural and allocentric. Just as in any liminal community, there was a dialectic between structure and anti-structure. The in-Christ community was expressed as living anti-structurally in structure.

In Turner's understanding of the dialectic of structure and anti-structure, anti-structure typically reinforces the structures of society. Power, authority, status, and roles are strengthened through their relationship to anti-structure. However, in Pauline communities the anti-structural relationships lived within structure served to critique and transform the structure itself. In the next chapter, I explore how these same characteristics continue to be exhibited by the in-Christ members in post-Pauline communities.

Chapter 6

Liminality in Transition: Post-Pauline Communities

THE PERIOD AFTER THE apostolic age and before the conversion of Constantine was one of change, transition, and development for the early church.[1] The transition occurred as the communities sought to respond to the growing challenges they faced. Some of those challenges came from within the communities as a variety of divergent beliefs, leaders, and groups developed within them as a result of porous boundaries and evangelistic inclusiveness. The second- and third-century communities of Christ followers began to organize themselves around a centralized leadership structure in response to these challenges. Unity in the community and uniformity of belief were central themes for many of the writers during this period. The communities sought to establish their continuity with apostolic tradition by defining authoritative beliefs, writings, and leadership.

The post-Pauline communities were also experiencing growing challenges as they sought to define themselves and their place vis-à-vis Roman society. Because early Christians did not participate in the polytheistic pagan rites, their relationship with the broader Greco-Roman social and political world was conflicted. In some cases, their stances on pagan worship antagonized Greco-Roman leaders and led to persecution, and at the same time, they engaged in society and sought to lead exemplary lives. Apologists took up the challenge to defend and explain Christianity to audiences within the broader structures of society in the second and third centuries.

---

1. What literature actually begins this period depends on the dating of the pastoral epistles. Most scholars agree that there is not a clear-cut boundary between the literature of the apostolic and post-apostolic periods. They note the continuity between the pastoral epistles and Ignatius, Polycarp, and Clement. See Aageson, *Paul, the Pastoral Epistles, and the Early Church*, 122–56, for a discussion on the placement of the pastoral epistles.

The combination of these challenges, both internal and external, and the church's responses to them creates a multifaceted, diverse, and imprecise understanding of the post-Pauline Christian communities during this period.[2] As Walter H. Wagner describes it, this period was "messy."[3] For the purpose of this discussion, I am focusing on the internal life of the church with only a brief mention of its response to persecution and the pagan culture in which it was embedded. The first question I seek to answer in this chapter is whether the interpersonal relationships within the communities still reflected the characteristics of communitas within the developing organizational structure. And secondly, did people in these communities still seek to live anti-structurally within the structures of society? In other words, were they still living "in the world but not of the world"? In order to answer these questions, I first examine the responses of the post-Pauline communities of Christ followers to the internal challenges the members faced. I then explore how the communities expressed temporal and embodied liminality as well as the liminality of the social body. Finally, I examine the relationship of the anti-structural communities and the structures of society.[4]

Challenge and Change

Many scholars have argued that the organizational changes in the post-Pauline communities developed out of response to different schisms and sects that began to threaten the unity of the communities.[5] During this period of time, the communities began to address the disunity created from different schisms and heresies by articulating the continuity of apostolic authority in leadership and belief. There were three primary questions that internal challenges required the community to address. First, what were the defining beliefs in apostolic tradition? In other words, what was considered orthodoxy? Second, who had authority to determine those beliefs and what did they base it on? Third, what writings carried apostolic authority and what differentiated these writings from others? These three questions led to the

2. MacMullen, *Christianizing the Roman Empire A.D. 100–400*, vi.

3. Wagner, *After the Apostles*, viii.

4. In order to explore these themes, I selected writings that reflected a broad spectrum of genre as well as geographic locations. I sought to explore the earliest writings after the pastorals through as late as AD 258 with the writings of Cyprian. The writers and writings include: 1 Clement, Didache, Letters of Ignatius, Polycarp, Letter to Diognetus, Justin Martyr, Athenagoras, Irenaeus, Tertullian, Origen, and Cyprian. They represent Western, West African, and Alexandrian Christianity.

5. Aageson, *Paul, the Pastoral Epistles, and the Early Church*, 122–72. For shifts in use of Pauline interpretation see Chadwick, *The Early Church*, 32–41; Frend, *The Rise of Christianity*, 193–228; McKechnie, *The First Christian Centuries*, 151–89.

development of a centralized leadership organization in the communities, an articulation of foundational apostolic traditions, and the development of a set of writings that were considered authoritative. In this section, I describe the main challenges to the post-Pauline communities of Christ followers and how they were addressed.

Challenges to the Post-Pauline Communities of Christ Followers

The post-Pauline communities of Christ followers encountered numerous schisms and a variety of beliefs as they dispersed from Jerusalem to the far reaches of the empire.[6] However, there was continuity between the Pauline tradition and the practice of the post-Pauline communities in the second century. These formed the basis for normative beliefs and practices that would later become the foundation of orthodoxy. Formalized orthodoxy developed in response to the challenges from diverse teaching by Marcion, Montanus, and various gnostic teachers.[7] Here, the term "heresy" denotes a choice or opinion of a religious group, philosophy, or a common way of thinking. It is only as orthodox beliefs were formalized that such opinions were labeled as divergent or false doctrines.[8] These new and different divisions within the early church created a situation in which a majority opinion had to be articulated, and the one with authority to articulate it needed to be defined. William H. C. Frend notes, "Through most of the second century orthodoxy stood on the defensive representing tradition against innovation."[9] Each of these major challenges to church unity is described briefly below.

The first of these challenges came from Gnosticism. The term gnosticism is derived from the Greek term *gnosis* meaning "knowledge" and is used to cover a broad range of beliefs.[10] Gnosticism is also a generic term that has been used to refer to theosophical adaptations of Christianity propagated by several dozen rival sects in early Christianity between AD 80–150.[11] Irenaeus attributed the origins of Gnosticism to Simon Magus, whose work

---

6. Hultgren, *The Rise of Normative Christianity*, 84. He notes that Eusebius already had a list of various sects (*Ecclesiastical History* 4.22).

7. Hall, *Doctrine and Practice in the Early Church*, 36.

8. Hall, *Doctrine and Practice in the Early Church*, 36.

9. Frend, *The Rise of Christianity*, 195.

10. Davidson, *The Birth of the Church*, 163–64; Hall, *Doctrine and Practice in the Early Church*, 35.

11. Chadwick, *The Early Church*, 34.

was continued by his disciple Menander (flor. 60–100) in Antioch and later into the second century by Saturninus (flor. 100–120).[12] Frend speculates that the teaching of the docetic nature of Christ, which angered Ignatius, might have been part of this sectarian movement.[13] Another proponent of the docetic concept of Christ was Basilides, whose teachings were also challenged by Irenaeus. Another major branch of Gnosticism that was heavily influenced by Platonism was taught by Valentinus in approximately AD 130–160. This version of Gnosticism dominated intellectual life at Alexandria and spread throughout Italy and Asia Minor.[14]

There was not a uniform corpus of gnostic beliefs. Most scholars use Gnosticism as an umbrella term that designated religious systems or attitudes that had a common view of the world, its origin, and the "the ultimate destiny of the spiritual nature of human beings."[15] There were some elements that were common to most gnostic groups. They are as follows:

1. The original divine element produced other spiritual creatures, but a fault occurred in the spiritual world. As a result, matter came into existence. The material world is evil and not the creation of a supreme being.[16]

2. All humans have body and soul, but a few have a "divine spark" that is a remnant of the spiritual world.

3. Redemption comes from the knowledge of the origin of the world and of the supreme god. Salvation is the assent to a new spiritual realty and obtaining the full spiritual reality.

4. A redeemer figure is to reveal the divine spark in people. Gnostics deny the reality of the death of Christ and his incarnation into a human body.[17] Salvation involved freeing the spirit from matter.[18]

Although there are many versions of the gnostic myth, they all presented a challenge to some of the fundamental beliefs of the early Christian communities.[19] First, they denied the goodness of the created order and the

---

12. Grant, *Augustus to Constantine*, 122–23.
13. Frend, *The Rise of Christianity*, 196.
14. Frend, *The Rise of Christianity*, 196.
15. Ferguson, *Church History*, 89.
16. Ferguson, *Church History*, 93.
17. Johnson, *The Evolution of Christianity*, 26.
18. Latourette, *A History of Christianity*, 338–56.
19. Pagels, *The Gnostic Gospels*, 28–47.

identity of the creator.[20] In doing so, they separated creation from redemption. Second, they denied the full incarnation of Christ as well as his death and resurrection.[21] Not only did this promote doceticism, but it also created a faith that had no bearing on what people did in the material world. Because they believed that the material world was evil, it led followers into either denial of the physical through asceticism or indulgence of the physical.[22]

A second challenge to the post-Pauline communities came from Marcion and the Marcionites. The Marcion controversy started around AD 140 when the son of a wealthy ship owner from Sinope developed his own distinctive theology.[23] Marcion's own system had the same dialectical opposition of spirit and matter that was in common with Gnosticism. However, his theological system contrasted Judaism and Christianity. Marcion believed that Jesus' apostles had obscured the true message of the gospel by tying it too closely with Judaism.[24] Marcion contrasted the creator God depicted in the Hebrew Bible and the savior God Jesus. The former he called demiurge[25] and described it as the evil creator of the evil material world. In Marcion's teachings, this god was a vindictive and vengeful being; law and judgment belonged to him. However, redemption, grace, and salvation belonged to an unknown God who was revealed in Christ.[26] This God is a God of goodness and love. Like many Gnostics, Marcion promoted asceticism and condemned marriage.[27]

One of the lasting impacts Marcion had on the direction of the post-Pauline communities was that he developed his own canon of authoritative writings. He rejected the Old Testament as authoritative for the church and created a canon that consisted of a shorter version of Luke, which was edited to fit his theology, and the Apostles as well as ten letters attributed to Paul, which included Romans, 1–2 Corinthians, Galatians, Ephesians (Laodiceans), Philippians, Colossians, 1–2 Thessalonians, and Philemon.

20. Wagner, *After the Apostles*, 77.
21. Wagner, *After the Apostles*, 91.
22. Wagner, *After the Apostles*, 125.
23. Davidson, *The Birth of the Church*, 170.
24. Latourette, *A History of Christianity*, 126; Hall, *Doctrine and Practice in the Early Church*, 36.
25. The demiurge was a Platonic term that was also employed by the Gnostics, who believed that the demiurge created the evil material world. Like the Gnostics, Marcion believed that the demiurge created man's body and soul, but in contrast to the Gnostics, Marcion believed that the demiurge also created the spirit. However, Marcion saw a contrast between the spirit and flesh. See Latourette, *A History of Christianity*, 126.
26. Hall, *Doctrine and Practice in the Early Church*, 38.
27. Johnson, *The Evolution of Christianity*, 31.

Marcion's attempt to identify some writings as authoritative has been seen as the impetus for the post-Pauline communities to move toward identifying writings that had apostolic authority.[28]

Another early schism was the rise of Montanism. Montanism was practiced around AD 170 and responded as a protest sect against the developing centralized church.[29] Unlike Gnosticism and Marcion that challenged the fundamental doctrines of the early church, Montanism challenged the authority of the church leaders and the lifestyle of the church. Montanism is perhaps the most anti-structural internal challenge to the growing organization of the church. It sought to return the church to its early roots with reliance on the Spirit, the egalitarian exercising of spiritual gifts, the inclusion of women and their leadership, and a return to the spontaneity of the Spirit.[30] Many viewed Montanism as a renewal movement within the early church that brought a revival of charismatic practices and an expectation of the imminent end of the world.[31] People were attracted to its emphasis on personal morality and piety that included observing stricter fasts, prohibiting second marriages, and stricter discipline in life as well as an expectation of martyrdom.[32] Many joined the movement because they were concerned about the growing worldliness of the church, including its most famous adherent, Tertullian.

Response of the Post-Pauline Communities

During the late first century and early second century, writings of the church began to address the growing challenge of diverse beliefs and schisms among various Christian communities. Cyril Richardson notes, "The unity of the church around its leaders and the preservation of faith from perversion are the dominant themes."[33] There were three developments that defined the unity, authority, and structure of the early church in the late first century and the early second century.[34] They were the development of an authoritative leadership of the church, the development of authoritative beliefs in the form

---

28. Johnson, *The Evolution of Christianity*, 57.
29. Hall, *Doctrine and Practice in the Early Church*, 46.
30. Hall, *Doctrine and Practice in the Early Church*, 47.
31. Johnson, *The Evolution of Christianity*, 24.
32. Johnson, *The Evolution of Christianity*, 24; Hall, *Doctrine and Practice in the Early Church,* 46; Richardson, "Introduction to Early Christian Literature," 25.
33. Richardson, "Introduction to Early Christian Literature," 17.
34. Richardson, "Introduction to Early Christian Literature," 17.

of a set of rules of faith, and finally, the defining and compiling of authoritative writings of the church. I discuss each below.

There is considerable debate about the development of leadership and the rise of a monoepiscopacy within post-Pauline communities. Claudia Rapp maintains that the earliest communities were led by a group of elders, some of which were headed by a bishop, and there was no clear distinction between elders and bishops in the early writings.[35] The Didache reflected a transitional point in the church in which teachers and prophets still had authority, but it also mentions elders, deacons, and a bishop.[36] Ferguson notes that there is evidence of a particular church order in the late first-century and early second-century writings found over a widespread area that included a plurality of elders or bishops who were assisted by deacons. These included the following (Table 3):[37]

Table 3. Passages That Reflect Development of Church Leadership

Jerusalem and Judea	Acts 11:30, 15:6; James 5:14
Syria	Didache 15:1
Galatia	Acts 14:23
Asia Minor	1 Peter 5:1–4
Ephesus	Acts 20:17, 28; 1 Tim. 3:1–13
Philippi	Philippians 1:1; Polycarp; Philippians 6
Corinth	1 Clement 42:4, 44:3–6
Rome	1 Clement 42, 44; Hermas, Vision 3.5.1
Crete	Titus 1:5–7

How or why the early Christian communities made a transition from a plurality of elders to a single authority is not clear, nor is it clear what authority was held by the single leader of the community. Ignatius writes of a monoepiscopacy in which a single bishop had authority over a community. Whether that was the norm or he was trying to promote this innovative form of leadership is unclear, but references to a bishop and calls for submission are pervasive in his writings.[38] For Ignatius, unity and assurance of

---

35. Rapp, *Holy Bishops in Late Antiquity*, 26.
36. Rapp, *Holy Bishops in Late Antiquity*, 26.
37. Ferguson, *Church History*, 107.
38. Wagner, *After the Apostles*, 152.

faithfulness to correct teaching came through submission to a bishop.[39] The development of authority based on apostolic succession is reflected in the letter of Clement to the community at Corinth in the early second century.[40] In this situation, there was a younger generation of Christ followers who were trying to oust the current leaders. However, Clement argued in his letter that the apostles appointed the leaders as bishops and deacons of believers. These leaders then appointed other men who were approved to take over leadership of the church.[41] It was because of this succession of authority in leadership that he urged the community to submit to their appointed leaders. Later in the century, Irenaeus also argued that unity in the community came through the submission to bishops who were in the line of succession from the apostles; therefore, they embodied apostolic authority.[42]

Although a monoepiscopate developed later, it is not clear what kind of authority was held by the bishop. Rapp contends that during the apostolic age, bishops were nothing more than administrators of the church. However, she argues that the bishop had developed into a hybridization of an administrator and a spiritual leader by the second century.[43] A stronger picture of the authority of the bishop is in Ignatius' writings. He insisted that the unity of the church was based on submission to the local bishop and the council of presbyters.[44] In Ignatius' writings, the bishops were the "guarantors of unity and judges of false teaching."[45] However, James Aageson raises the question of whether Ignatius understood the bishop's power in terms of institutional or charismatic power. He argues that on the one hand, Ignatius understood that unifying, disciplining, and having liturgical responsibilities were in the hand of the bishop. However, he contends that Ignatius does not seem to have moved his view of the bishop from the person to the office.[46]

For Irenaeus writing later in the second century, theological unity and ecclesiastic unity were intertwined; theological and doctrinal unity were centered in a unified church. This unity was derived from the continuity of the succession of authority from the apostles, which had been transmitted through a succession of bishops. It was through this line of succession that

---

39. Wagner, *After the Apostles*, 152.
40. Wagner, *After the Apostles*, 151.
41. *1 Clement* 42.1–5.
42. Aageson, *Paul, the Pastoral Epistles, and the Early Church*, 136; Irenaeus, *Against Heresies*, 3.3.1–3.
43. Rapp, *Holy Bishops in Late Antiquity*, 24.
44. Grant, *Augustus to Constantine*, 148.
45. Davidson, *The Birth of the Church*, 182.
46. Aageson, *Paul, the Pastoral Epistles, and the Early Church*, 136.

the church preserved correct doctrine because it suppressed innovation.[47] Irenaeus argued that any secret knowledge that the apostles imparted would have been given to those they confidently appointed as leaders of their flock, which prevented individuals from claiming special knowledge.[48]

Authoritative Beliefs—Rules of Faith

The need to distinguish false teachers from true teachers and orthodoxy from heterodoxy led to the development of a common set of central beliefs or "rules of faith" in the second century.[49] These rules of faith provided a basis to unite the churches and differentiate teachings of apostolic authority from other teachings.[50] The rules of faith were understood to contain core beliefs that were handed down from the apostolic tradition.[51] Although rules of faith differed in phrasing and order, they contained fundamental truths of the faith handed down by the apostles.[52] Commonly, the rules of faith asserted the oneness of God as the creator; the birth, death, and resurrection of Jesus; the Holy Spirit; and future judgment.[53] The most primitive rules of faith are found in Irenaeus toward the end of the second century.[54] The rules were intended to provide unity for the church through the affirmation of unity of doctrine. At the same time, they provided a means through which teaching could be assessed against central beliefs of the church and a framework for the interpretation of Scripture.[55]

The rules of faith were formalized into a creedal form that was used in the second century as an interrogative at baptism and later developed into the Roman Symbol which underwent various revisions until the seventh century when it became known as the Apostles' Creed.[56] Irenaeus' prologue to his rules of faith demonstrated an attempt to define apostolic tradition in

---

47. Aageson, *Paul, the Pastoral Epistles, and the Early Church*, 162; Irenaeus, *Against Heresies*, 3.3.1–3.

48. Ferguson, *The History of Christianity*, 108; Irenaeus, *Against Heresies*, 3.3.1.

49. Nystrom and Nystrom, *The History of Christianity*, 87.

50. Ferguson, *Church History*, 110.

51. Ferguson, *Church History*, 110–11.

52. Nystrom and Nystrom, *The History of Christianity*, 87.

53. Guy, *Introducing Early Christianity*, 256; Hall, *Doctrine and Practice in the Early Church*, 61.

54. Richardson, "Introduction to Early Christian Literature," 22; Irenaeus, *Against Heresies*, 1.10.

55. Nystrom and Nystrom, *The History of Christianity*, 87.

56. Richardson, "Introduction to Early Christian Literature," 22.

a way that refuted many of the beliefs of the early schisms. The following is one such example:

> Now the church, although scattered over the whole civilized world to the end of the earth received from the apostles its faith in one God, the Father Almighty, who made the heaven and the earth and the seas and all that is in them, and in one Christ Jesus, the Son of God, who was made flesh in our salvation, and in the Holy Spirit, who through the prophets proclaimed the dispensations of God—the comings, the birth of a virgin, the suffering, the resurrection from the dead, and the bodily reception into the heavens of the believed, Christ Jesus our Lord, and his coming from the heavens in glory of the Father to restore all things, and to raise up all flesh, that is the whole human race, so that every knee may bow, of things in heaven and on earth and under the earth, to Christ Jesus our Lord and God and Savior and King, according to the pleasure of the invisible Father and every tongue may confess him, and that he may execute righteous judgment on all.[57]

The rules of faith clearly refuted gnostic tendencies in several ways. First, they declared that there is only one God who was both the creator God and the God of the New Testament. The rules of faith also refuted docetic tendencies by declaring that Jesus was made flesh and also by declaring the death and resurrection of Jesus as well as the resurrection of the body of believers in Christ. It also solidly affirmed the incarnation of Christ as well as the divinity of Christ as God's son. These rules of faith were not necessarily designed to become a ritual but to reaffirm the apostolic authority in certain teachings that defined followers of Christ. They also set a boundary of acceptable beliefs that were considered a part of the apostolic tradition. In the same manner, the church began to determine which writings carried apostolic authority.

Authoritative Writings

The first attempt to define a collection of authoritative writings was made by Marcion in the second century. Whether Marcion's development of a fixed set of authoritative writings prompted the post-Pauline communities to respond or whether it just reinforced a process that was already happening is debated.[58] It did, however, bring into focus the question of which

---

57. Irenaeus, *Against Heresies*, 1.10.1.
58. Johnson, *The Evolution of Christianity*, 32.

writings were authoritative for teaching within the church and what made them authoritative.[59] The question the post-Pauline communities had to ask was: "If Marcion is wrong, on what points was he wrong? On what grounds were some writings to be afforded normative status while others received some other ranking?"[60] In other words, why were some writings held as authoritative and others not?

The post-Pauline communities already considered the Hebrew Bible as authoritative, and its basic canon was generally shaped to include the Law, Prophets, and Writings.[61] The process of the development of the New Testament canon was much more fluid and went through several stages. The first stage was the transition from oral tradition to written tradition. Many of the post-Pauline writers quoted extensively from apostolic writing, particularly Pauline tradition, to support their arguments against the various sects and to support their teachings.

The second stage was determining which writings were authoritative. The key question was apostolic authority: "Did the writing reflect apostolic teachings?"[62] There were four criteria that determined which were to be included. The first was apostolic authority: was it considered to be written by one of the apostles? The second was orthodoxy: did it conform to the apostolic teachings? The third was recognition: was it widely recognized as authoritative? The fourth criterion was antiquity: was it written during the apostolic period?[63] By the fourth century, the Christian communities had developed a general agreement on several books to be included in a canon.

Summary

The post-Pauline communities of Christ followers were in a time of transition. They were in the process of defining which teachings were authoritative, what way of life reflected apostolic teaching, and who had the authority to make those decisions. While the post-Pauline communities seemed to have begun to develop some structural elements in the form of an organized leadership, authoritative writings, and rules of faith, these developments were a result of internal challenges to the unity of the community. These developments ensured continuity with apostolic teachings that focused on

---

59. Nystrom and Nystrom, *The History of Christianity*, 86.

60. Davidson, *The Birth of the Church*, 174.

61. Ferguson, *Church History*, 112. Ferguson, however, notes the exact books included in the Writings was fluid.

62. Davidson, *The Birth of the Church*, 176–77.

63. Nystrom and Nystrom, *The History of Christianity*, 87.

living liminally in structure. The communities of Christ followers of the second and third centuries rejected teachings that denied the physical reality of the world or encouraged believers to withdraw from the world, which were found in gnostic teaching and the teachings of Marcion. They also rejected the extreme eschatological position of Montanus. The teachings of the apostles did not encourage followers of Christ to withdraw from society; they encouraged them to live liminally within the structures of society. Despite the organization of church leadership and the centralization of authority, the developments of the post-Pauline communities contributed to the preservation of anti-structural living within structure against the challenges of Gnosticism, Marcion, and Montanus. In the next section, I demonstrate that second- and third-century writers still reflect the Pauline tradition of understanding the life of the Christ follower in living in a temporal liminality and that they embody this liminality in their individual lives.

Betwixt and Between— Temporal and Embodied Liminality

Although the communities of Christ followers in the second and third centuries were found over broad geographic situational contexts, there is evidence in the writings from this period that there was a consistent belief that they were living betwixt and between in temporal and embodied liminality. Following Pauline tradition, the writings of this period reflected the understanding that through the death and resurrection of Christ, the new age had broken into the present. The cross marked the change of the eons, and the Spirit had been given as a sign of the in-breaking of the ages. The writings of this period also reflected the understanding that they embodied this new age through the indwelling of the Spirit in their physical bodies. However, just as in Pauline tradition, these writings reflect an understanding that they were living in overlapping ages. They understood that they were already experiencing the blessings of the new age through the Spirit of God who dwelt in them, while at the same time they remained in the flesh and in the world. Their hope was that they would fully experience the Kingdom and be with Christ once a bodily resurrection took place, either at his return or following their death. In this section, I examine the writings of the communities that reflect both this temporal liminality and the embodied liminality of individuals.

Temporal Liminality

The writers in post-Pauline communities expressed that they understood themselves to be living in liminal time in continuity with Pauline tradition. For the post-Pauline communities, salvation was a present reality. They were living in a new age and were experiencing life between the ages, the time between an inaugurated eschatology and the hope of the parousia.[64] Throughout this period of time, there was a distinct understanding that through the cross, the new age had begun. The "last days" anticipated in the Old Testament had broken into the present. Ignatius declared, "The last days are here."[65] It was through the Christ event that the new age had begun: "Ignorance was done away with, and the ancient kingdom was utterly destroyed, for God was revealing himself as a man, to bring newness of eternal life."[66] Eternal life for Ignatius was already beginning with the death and resurrection of Jesus Christ. Writers in the mid-second century also understood that the Christ follower was already living in a new age between the two advents of Christ. Living between two ages, the age between the cross and the parousia, was a central tenant of the early Christian communities' self-understanding. Justin Martyr in his first apology articulated this tenant in this way:

> Since we have shown that all these things that have already happened were proclaimed in advance through the prophets before they happened, it must similarly be believed that those things which were similarly prophesied and are yet to happen will take place . . . For the prophets foretold of two comings of Christ—one, which has already happened, as that of a dishonored and passible man, and the second, when as has been foretold he will come from heaven in glory with his angelic host, when he will raise the bodies of all the men who have ever lived.[67]

Irenaeus also included the two advents in what is considered his rules of faith, which were central to the understanding of life and teaching in the early church.[68] Later into the third century, inaugurated eschatology continued to be a central feature of post-Pauline teaching and life. Tertullian argued that the outpouring of the Spirit marked the last days and was

---

64. Davies, *The Early Christian Church*, 98–99.
65. Ignatius, *Letters: Ephesians*, 11.
66. Ignatius, *Letters: Ephesians*, 19.
67. Martyr, "First Apology," 52.
68. Irenaeus, *Against Heresies*, 1.10.1.

the sign demonstrating that Jesus is the Christ.[69] Origen, in his apologetic against Celsus, referred to the outpouring of the Spirit in Joel as marking an inaugurated eschatology "in these last days."[70] He continued, "Each one of us, then, is come 'in these last days,' when one Jesus has visited us, to the 'visible mountain of the Lord,' the Word that is above every word, and to the 'house of God,' which is 'the church of the living God, the pillar and ground of the truth.'"[71] This Spirit was poured upon believers.[72]

The post-Pauline communities understood themselves to be living in the new age that had broken into the present. The inaugurated eschatology was foundational for the self-understanding and behavior of post-Pauline communities. They referred to themselves as aliens and foreigners in the world.[73] The second-century author of 2 Clement emphasized that life in the world and the flesh was temporary, but those in Christ should live as though the new age had come. He stated, "What, then, must we do to get these things, except lead a holy and upright life and to regard the things of the world as alien to use and not desire them?"[74] Brian Daley notes that Ignatius' call for radical behavioral choices was based on the assertion that the "last days were here."[75] It was because they lived in this new age that they were to live life according to this newness of life: "Since then, we are a holy portion, we should do everything that makes for holiness."[76]

Third-century writings also reflected the understanding of living in a new age as motivation for a new way of living. Tertullian quoted extensively from Paul's letter to the Romans as motivation for new behavior. Following Pauline tradition, Tertullian understood that it was through Christ's work that the early Christ followers had died to sin and rose to a newness of life: "Buried with him, then, we have been through the baptism into the death, in order that as Christ hath risen again from the dead, so we too may walk in the newness of life."[77] He also argued from Romans that those who had died to sin were no longer to present their bodies for acts of unrighteousness but for righteousness.[78] Cyprian used Paul's allusions of day and night

---

69. Tertullian, *The Passion of the Holy Martyrs Perpetua and Felicitas*, 699–706.
70. Origen, *De Principiis* 2.7.2.
71. Origen, *Against Celsus* 5.33.
72. Origen, *De Principiis* 2.7.3.
73. *Diognetus* 5.5.
74. *2 Clement* 5.6.
75. Daley, *The Hope of the Early Church*, 12.
76. *2 Clement* 30.1.
77. Tertullian, *On Modesty*, 17.
78. Tertullian, *On the Resurrection of the Flesh*, 47.

to illustrate the temporal liminality in which Christ followers lived and exhorted them to right behavior. Cyprian understood early Christ followers to be living in the light while still living in a world of darkness. He contended, "The night has passed over, and the day is approaching, let us therefore cast away the works of darkness and let us put upon us the armor of light."[79] The exhortation to right behavior that followed in his writing was based on the understanding that the new age had arrived.[80] For Cyprian, like Paul, there had been a change in time: the night had left, the day was approaching; but at the present, early Christ followers lived in the liminal time between day and night.[81] Also in the third century, Origen used the metaphor of "ambassador" to describe the Christian's life in the world. They were ambassadors for Christ and were to live a life that reflected their true citizenship (in heaven), but they did it while living in the world.[82] They could not bow to any other ruler, because they were under the rule of God alone, and their ruler was Christ.[83]

While they believed that the new age had begun, it was the hope of experiencing it fully that provided early Christ followers not only the motivation to live in a new way but also the courage to die for it as well. For early Christ followers, whether the parousia came while they lived or if they died first, both resulted in the same end: they would be reunited with Christ. Ignatius demonstrated that for early Christ followers both life and the willingness to die were motivated by the understanding that they presently lived in union with Christ. Ignatius stated, "Each bears its own stamp, unbelievers that of this world; believers, who are spurred by love, the stamp of God the Father through Jesus Christ. And if we do not willingly die in union with his Passion, we do not have his life in us."[84] For Ignatius, death was not the end, but for the ancient follower of Christ, it meant gaining life with Christ. Because of this hope, he wrote to the Romans pleading with them not to rescue him: "But if I suffer I shall be emancipated by Jesus Christ; and united with him, I shall rise to freedom."[85] He urged them, "Only let me get to Jesus Christ."[86] Throughout the literature of the second century, the suffering that Christ followers faced in the world was compared to the glory that

---

79. Cyprian, *The Treatises* 10.10.
80. Cyprian, *The Treatises* 10.11–12.
81. Cyprian, *The Treatises* 10.10.
82. Origen, *Against Celsus* 8.1.
83. Origen, *Against Celsus* 8:6, 11.
84. Ignatius, *Letters: Magnesians* 5.0.
85. Ignatius, *Letters: Romans* 4.3.
86. Ignatius, *Letters: Romans* 5:3.

they would receive when they finally reigned with Christ at the resurrection, whether by death or at the parousia: "For we think, that even if we lose our lives, we shall suffer no evil compared to the reward we shall receive from the great Judge for a gentle, generous, and modest life."[87] There was a consistent hope throughout post-Pauline writings that when the parousia came, they would live with Christ. The character of the post-Pauline communities was based on their understanding that they were already experiencing the last days but that they would experience them even more fully with their death or the return of Christ. Daley notes:

> But eschatology is secondary, in Jewish and Christian faith at least, because it is the hope that grows from faith and leads to love: a projection onto an unknown future of the understanding of God and God's workings with which believers presently live, a drawing into final convergence of the incomplete acts presently described by their doctrine of God, their understanding of God's saving activity, their conception of the human person and the faithful community.[88]

Although there was a steadfastness in the idea of inaugurated eschatology, the formulations of the final consummation at Christ's return were diverse in post-Pauline writings. There were some writers who emphasized a spiritual, individual consummation of being with Christ in the resurrection. Other writers in the second and third centuries began to develop a millennial view with a physical reign of Christ on earth.[89] However, as Daley notes, reconceptualization of the final hope might have changed as the return was delayed, but this did not cause a change in the overall orientation on the part of the post-Pauline communities of Christ followers. Their belief in inaugurated eschatology remained steadfast while there was increased speculation of the parousia. Daley summarizes this belief:

> The first Christians believed the end was near, almost certainly, and they hoped for a radically better life for themselves, because they believed Jesus had risen from the dead, and because they were convinced that the community's new experience of the charisma of the Spirit was a first taste of the Kingdom of

---

87. Athenagoras, *A Plea Regarding Christians*, 12.
88. Daley, *The Hope of the Early Church*, 2.
89. Hill, in his book *Regnum Caelorum*, traces patterns of both non-chiliastic and chiliastic views of the culmination of the last days in the early church. Although this is an important debate, what is consistent is that the early church believed they were living in inaugurated eschatology which would have a final culmination; they were living between the times.

God. The fulfillment of their early hopes was surely delayed, and the delay required just as surely a constant reconception and reexpression of the community's conviction that it was called to share in the divine life and power that had been bestowed on the risen Lord. But this reorientation of the timeline of its eschatological hope, if we are to trust the evidence at hand, seems to have caused no more of an upheaval for the Christians of the first and second centuries than it does for the modern believers . . . and the disappointment of this hope, in a temporal sense, seems to have strikingly little effect on the overall character and content of faith.[90]

Embodied Liminality

Not only did post-Pauline tradition reflect a belief in inaugurated liminality, but it also reflects an understanding of embodied liminality. Congruent with Pauline tradition, writers in the second and third centuries understood that the Spirit not only marked the last days but was given to those who believed in Christ. The Spirit was a foretaste and a promise of the final hope of being with Christ, whether it was preceded by a millennial earthly reign of Christ or not. Although much writing in the third century focused on the character of the Spirit in relationship to God, the Spirit was still fundamental for their understanding of living in the last days. As in Pauline tradition, writers during the second and third centuries understood that each individual was made new through the indwelling of the Spirit but embodied this new life within their physical bodies. They embodied the inaugurated liminality. The Holy Spirit during this period was still "a primary fact of Christian experience, rather than a subject for investigation and exact definition."[91]

Although there is variation in emphasis among writers during this period, there is still a common understanding that everyone who followed Jesus had the Spirit.[92] The Spirit was the identity marker of all believers, irrespective of their status or position. The Didache stated, "For when he comes to call us, he will not respect our station, but will call those whom the Spirit has made ready."[93] The writer of the *Shepherd of Hermas* clearly affirmed the Holy Spirit as dwelling in the early followers of Christ: "For the Spirit of God which has been granted to us to dwell in this body does not endure

---

90. Daley, *The Hope of the Early Church*, 3.
91. Swete, *The Holy Spirit in the Ancient Church*, 16.
92. Morgan-Wynne, *Holy Spirit and Religious Experience*, 273–74.
93. *Didache* 4.10.

grief nor distress."[94] The writer also declared, "For if you be patient, the Holy Spirit that dwells in you will be pure."[95] Irenaeus provided a summary of the threads of early writers about the Spirit:

> Since the Lord redeemed us by his own blood, and gave his soul for our souls, and his flesh for our bodies, and poured out the Spirit of the Father to bring about the union and communion of God and man—bringing God down to men by [the working of] the Spirit, and again raising man to God by his incarnation—and by his coming firmly and truly giving us incorruption, by our own communion with God, all the teachings of heretics are destroyed.[96]

According to the view common to many writers of this period, the Spirit was what renews human beings and made them a new creation, one that was different from the old. Speaking of the Holy Spirit, Irenaeus acknowledged, "This earnest, therefore, thus dwelling in us, renders us spiritual even now, and the mortal is swallowed up by immortality."[97] The writers of the third century also viewed the Spirit as both an identity marker and an indication of the last days. Tertullian argued that the promises in Isaiah were fulfilled in the pouring out of the Spirit upon all people as a mark of the new age: "Now was absolutely fulfilled that promise of the Spirit which was given by the word of Joel 'In the last days will I pour out of my Spirit upon all flesh, and their sons and their daughters shall prophesy; and upon my servants and upon my handmaids will I pour out my Spirit.'"[98] He also followed Pauline tradition in understanding that the Spirit gave different gifts and was the guarantee of the hope that ancient followers of Christ had in Christ. He believed that "the earnest of His Spirit" provided the hope of the early Christ follower so that they would be present with the Lord in death.[99] They believed it was through the Spirit that people embodied liminality: "If any man is in Christ he is a new creature, old things have passed away; behold all things are become new" (2 Corinthians 5:17) in fulfillment of the prophecy in Isaiah.[100] Tertullian affirmed that all early Christ followers were "sealed with his Holy Spirit of promise."[101]

94. Shepherd of Hemas, *Commandments* 2.10.2.
95. Shepherd of Hemas, *Commandments* 2.5.1.
96. Irenaeus, *Against Heresies* 5.1.1.
97. Irenaeus, *Against Heresies* 5.8.1.
98. Tertullian, *Against Marcion* 5.8.
99. Tertullian, *Against Marcion* 5.12.
100. Tertullian, *Against Marcion* 5.12.
101. Tertullian, *Against Marcion* 5.17.

These writers also followed Pauline tradition in their understanding that the life in the Spirit was lived in the flesh in embodied liminality. The writer of 2 Clement stated, "In what state were you saved? In what state did you regain your sight, was it not while you were in the flesh?"[102] As in Pauline tradition, the Spirit gave life within the mortal body. The writer of 2 Clement remarked, "This flesh is able to share in so great a life and immortality, because the Holy Spirit cleaves to it."[103] Polycarp echoed Paul in his description of the conflict of the flesh and the Spirit: "It is a fine thing to cut off oneself from the lusts that are in the world for every passion of the flesh wages war against the Spirit."[104] Ignatius also wrote of the conflict between spirit and flesh: "Carnal people cannot act spiritually, or spiritual people cannot act carnally, just as faith cannot act like unfaith, or unbelief like faith. But even what you do in the flesh you do spiritually."[105] In the third century, Tertullian's discourse on the resurrection sought to refute the idea that the Spirit could not dwell in the flesh. Following Pauline tradition, he argued that the Spirit was poured out upon the flesh, and it was in the flesh that the Spirit dwells. He argued that it was through the Spirit that the early Christ followers lived in Christ. Since they lived in Christ, "they should set their affections on things above."[106] Although in-Christ they were flesh/Spirit, they were to live their lives according to the Spirit: "Whereas they pleased God, who although existing in the flesh were yet walking in the Spirit."[107]

Also in the third century, Origen wrote about the Spirit's relationship to the Christ follower, noting that the Spirit was given to all who followed Christ.[108] Origen also continued the Pauline tradition when commenting on the embodiment of liminality in the flesh/Spirit dichotomy, using Romans 8:9 in his argument as he explained the meaning of "But ye are not in the flesh, but in the Spirit if the Spirit of God dwells in you."[109] Also, concerning the new man in the Spirit he argued, "If ye live after the flesh, ye shall die; but if ye by the Spirit do mortify the deeds of the body, ye shall live."[110]

Cyprian, in the mid-third century, also wrote about the role of the Spirit in the life of the early Christ follower, particularly his own life. He

---

102. *2 Clement* 9.3.
103. *2 Clement* 14.5.
104. Polycarp, *Letter to the Philippians* 5.3.
105. Ignatius, *Letters: Ephesians* 8.2.
106. Tertullian, *On the Resurrection of the Flesh* 23.
107. Tertullian, *On the Resurrection of the Flesh* 46.
108. Origen, *De Principiis* 4.2.
109. Origen, *Against Celsus* 7:45.
110. Origen, *Against Celsus* 7.52.

explained that it was the Spirit which was the agent of his second birth. In speaking of his own conversion he wrote, "But after that, by the help of the water of new birth, the stain of former years had been washed away and a light from above, serene and pure, had been infused into my reconciled heart, after that by the agency of the Spirit breathed from heaven a second birth had restored me to a new man."[111] He acknowledged the embodied liminality of this state: "Being born of the flesh, had been living in the practice of sin, was of earth, earthly, but had now begun to be of God, and was animated by the Spirit of holiness."[112] He also reflected Pauline teaching of the common Spirit as the basis for unity and morality. He wrote of both obedience to Christ and being in Christ as the motivation to love and live in love for the others: "Know ye not that you are the temple of God and the Spirit of God dwelleth in you—even although love urged us less to bring help to the brethren, yet in this place we must have considered it that it was the temples of God which were taken captive and that we ought not by long inactivity and neglect of their suffering to allow the temples of God to be long captive . . ."[113] He also followed Pauline teaching on the contrast of the flesh and Spirit: "The flesh lusteth against the Spirit and the Spirit against the flesh, for these are contrary the one to the other, that ye cannot do even those things which ye wish."[114]

The writers in the post-Pauline period, like those of the Pauline tradition, understood that their stay in the world was short; and although they were in the world, they were waiting for a time when they would reign with Christ in an incorruptible body. The writers of the second and third centuries also understood that the final stage of reintegration was the bodily resurrection of the Christ follower or with the return of Christ. Tertullian, arguing against Marcion, made it clear that resurrection involved a new "spiritual body." The physical body which is natural "will become spiritual since it raises through the Spirit to an eternal life."[115] The resurrection will be bodily but not with a body that is corruptible: "But those shall be raised incorruptible, because they shall regain their body—and that a renewed one, from which shall come their incorruptibility."[116] In arguing against Celsus, Origen also reflected this same understanding of a bodily resurrection. He stated, "And therefore those who expect the resurrection of the dead, we

111. Cyprian, *The Epistles* 1.4.
112. Cyprian, *The Epistles* 1.4.
113. Cyprian, *The Epistles* 59.2.
114. Cyprian, *The Treatises* 4.16.
115. Tertullian, *Against Marcion* 5.10.
116. Tertullian, *Against Marcion* 5.12.

assert that the qualities which are in bodies undergo change: since some bodies, which are sown in corruption, are raised in incorruption . . . And those which are sown natural bodies are raised as spiritual."[117] He later expands this and relates the necessity of the corruptible and mortal tabernacle to put on that which is incorruptible and immortal.[118]

Summary

The post-Pauline communities were aligned with Pauline traditions in their understanding of both temporal and embodied liminality. They believed that the last days had been inaugurated by the cross of Christ and were marked by the Spirit. They also believed that Christ would return and that they were living in the overlap of the two ages. The new age had broken into the present. They embodied that liminality as well. They had received the Spirit but lived the new life in the body of flesh. They believed that when they died they would be resurrected into a new incorruptible body and live fully with Christ.

The writings of this period, as in the earlier Pauline tradition, provided evidence that their understanding of the Spirit reflected the same kind of rite of passage that framed Pauline tradition. They understood themselves to be separated from the domain of the old age through the indwelling of the Spirit. They were experiencing a new life, a life of the spirit, but they lived that life in the flesh. They embodied liminality. They would be reincorporated to a new status in a new body in which they would fully experience this new life "with Christ." They understood their reincorporation would take place in death or with the coming of Christ. For the post-Pauline followers of Christ, death or the return of Christ meant the same thing: they would live forever with him. The belief that they were living in the new age provided the motivation to live in a new way. The belief that they only experienced it partially gave them the hope and courage to face death. A third aspect of this liminal life was the social body in which they lived out liminal life in relationships marked by communitas.

Social Dimension of Inaugurated Liminality

Just as post-Pauline writers reflect Paul's writing on the temporal and embodied dimensions of inaugurated liminality, they also reflect Paul's writing on the social dimension of inaugurated eschatology. Criteria for

117. Origen, *Against Celsus* 4.57.
118. Origen, *Against Celsus* 5.19.

membership within the post-Pauline community, as in Pauline tradition, was anti-structural; it was not based on status, ethnicity, occupation, or gender. The post-Pauline communities drew their membership from both the lowest ranks of society and high-status people.[119] As with communities in the Pauline traditions, all members were marked by a common identity through the indwelling of the Holy Spirit. Post-Pauline Christ followers believed that they became members of a liminal community through the belief in Christ and that they were marked by the Spirit. As part of a new liminal community that lived between the times, they were to reflect the characteristics of communitas in their interpersonal relationships within the community. This section examines the identification of the corporate community, the characteristics of the interpersonal relationships within the community, and the authority within the community.

Entering Communitas

As with Pauline communities, the inclusion into the post-Pauline communities was through anti-structural criteria, based on a belief in Christ and incorporation thought the Holy Spirit. The Spirit was the common identity marker for members in the post-Pauline communities. For instance, in the beginning of the letter of Clement of Rome to the church in Corinth, he assumed that the community was made up of those "who are called and sanctified by God's will through our Lord Jesus Christ."[120] He reminded them that they were incorporated into the body through the Spirit: "The Holy Spirit was poured out on all of you."[121] It was from this dual identity, in-Christ and indwelt by the Spirit, that he considered them members of the same corporate community and by which he admonished them to practice unity and moral behavior. He reminded them that Christ's sacrifice is the motivation for moral behavior: "This is the way, dear friends, in which we found out salvation, Jesus Christ, the high priest of our offerings, the protector and helper in our weakness."[122] It was because of this common identity that they sought to live a different way of life: "Whoever has Christian love must keep Christ's commands."[123] Ignatius' letters also reflected identity in Christ as the motivation for living like Christ. In his letter to the Ephesians, he mentioned their "upright nature, marked by faith in Jesus Christ, our Savior, and by

---

119. Origen, *Against Celsus* 3.9.
120. *1 Clement* 1.0.
121. *1 Clement* 2.2.
122. *1 Clement* 36.1.
123. *1 Clement* 49.1.

love of him."¹²⁴ He also noted their "genuine life in Christ" and their "union with Christ."¹²⁵ This common identity in Christ was to be the basis of their actions towards each other and toward others: "Similarly, those who profess to be Christ's will be recognized by their actions."¹²⁶ In his letter to the Magnesians, Ignatius stated, "We have not only to be called Christians, but to be Christians."¹²⁷ According to Ignatius it was by their actions in love that each person bears their own stamp of Christ.¹²⁸ Their common identity motivated obedience and a common life together.

Post-Pauline writers understood that those who were part of the community had a single identity; it was inclusive of ethnicity, status, and gender. Ignatius wrote that it was faith in Christ that united all who professed him: "Every one of you, meeting together under the influence of the grace that we owe to the Name, in one faith and in union with Christ."¹²⁹ This included Jew and Gentile; they were all one in Christ. He wrote, "And thus by his resurrection, he raised a standard to rally his saints and faithful forever, whether Jew or Gentile, in one body of his church."¹³⁰ Those in-Christ also included slaves. He exhorted members not to treat slaves with contempt, nor were slaves to grow insolent.¹³¹

Irenaeus also provided a description of the common identity of those who are in-Christ as well as the diversity of people who were included. Their common faith in Christ who suffered, rose from the dead, and was exalted provided membership in the community of those who were "scattered over the whole civilized world to the end of the earth."¹³² Those who embraced these beliefs "remain in his love, some from the beginning and some since their repentance, he will by his grace give life incorrupt, and will clothe them with eternal glory."¹³³ Irenaeus wrote of the corporate nature of the community as a single unity: "She has one heart, and one soul, and preaches them harmoniously, teaches them, and hands them down, as if she had one mouth."¹³⁴ He also noted the inclusion of the "other" marked by the same

---

124. Ignatius, *Letters: Ephesians* 1.1.
125. Ignatius, *Letters: Ephesians* 11.1.
126. Ignatius, *Letters: Ephesians* 14.2.
127. Ignatius, *Letters: Magnesians* 4.1.
128. Ignatius, *Letters: Magnesians* 5.1.
129. Ignatius, *Letters: Ephesians* 20.2.
130. Ignatius, *Letters: Smyrnaeans* 1.2.; also Ignatius, *Letters: Magnesians* 10.3.
131. Ignatius, *Letters: Polycarp* 4:3.
132. Irenaeus, *Against Heresies* 1.10.1.
133. Irenaeus, *Against Heresies* 1.10.1.
134. Irenaeus, *Against Heresies* 1.10.2.

marker of identity—the Spirit: "Many barbarian peoples who believe in Christ follow this rule having salvation written in their hearts by the Spirit without paper and ink."[135] The inclusiveness of the early communities of Christ followers is also highlighted in his statement of Jesus' purpose: "He appeared in these last times and gathered and united into one those who were far off and those who were near."[136] They understood that the Spirit was the identity marker given to all without regard to status. The Spirit was "poured out on the human race according to the Father's decree."[137] In the late second century, Clement of Alexandria quoted the baptismal formula from Galatians 3 to emphasize the common identity of the post-Pauline Christ followers: "For ye are all the children of God through faith in Jesus Christ."[138] He then argued that this was free of all partiality: "There is neither Jew nor Greek, there is neither bond nor free, there is neither male nor female: for you are one in Christ."[139]

Later in the third century, Cyprian also acknowledged the corporate character of those in Christ, calling them "flocks of Christ" and "members of Christ."[140] Those who belonged to this corporate identity were "confessors of Christ."[141] According to Cyprian, people became part of this corporate community through Jesus. Quoting extensively from the Gospels, Cyprian insisted on anti-structural criteria for membership in the community. The post-Pauline community was inclusive of all types of people who were marked by the Holy Spirit in equal measure: "Repent and be baptized every one of you in the name of the Lord Jesus Christ for the remission of sins, and you shall receive the gift of the Holy Spirit."[142] Cyprian understood that all early Christ followers were given the Spirit and that it was poured upon all people in equal measure. He explains, "Nay verily the Spirit is not given by measure, but is poured out altogether on the believer."[143] He compared the giving of the Spirit to God giving manna in the exodus: "For there without distinction either of sex or of age, an omer was collected equally by each one. Whence it appeared that the mercy of Christ, and the heavenly grace that would subsequently follow was equally divided among all—without

135. Irenaeus, *Against Heresies* 3.4.2.
136. Irenaeus, *Against Heresies* 3.5.3.
137. Irenaeus, *Against Heresies* 3.11.9.
138. Galatians 3:26; Clement of Alexandria, *The Instructor* 1.6.
139. Galatians 3:28; Clement of Alexandria, *The Instructor* 1.6.
140. Cyprian, *The Epistles* 6.1; 5.3.
141. Cyprian, *The Epistles* 8.1.
142. Acts 2:38; Cyprian, *The Epistles* 72.17.
143. Cyprian, *The Epistles* 75.14.

difference of sex, without distinction of years, without accepting of persons—upon all the people of God the spiritual grace was shed."[144]

There were several images that post-Pauline writers used to demonstrate the corporate nature of the community of believers. Several writers in the post-Pauline period used the analogy of the temple to describe the corporate nature of Christ followers. Ignatius' writing to the community at Ephesus about their resistance to false teachers compared them to stones that were being lifted up by Christ and tied together by the Holy Spirit into God's temple.[145] They were encouraged to remain unified in Christ in their resistance to the false teaching. Clement of Alexandria, quoting 1 Peter 2:5, also wrote of Christ followers as the true temple built by Jesus: "Ye also as living stones are built up, a spiritual house, a holy temple, to offer spiritual sacrifices, acceptable to God by Jesus Christ."[146] In his defense against Celsus, Origen wrote of individual Christ followers as temples as well as being individual stones in the corporate temple of God: "Each of those who are led by the word of God, to strive together in the duties of piety, will be a precious stone in the one great temple of God."[147]

The metaphor most commonly used to identify the unity and diversity of the post-Pauline community of believers was the body of Christ. In some cases, it was closely tied to the assembly as a whole, and sometimes it was used to illustrate individual members as part of a corporate entity. In arguing for unity of the post-Pauline communities, Clement of Rome in writing to the Corinthians, appealed to the fact that all of the people in the body were needed; each had their own rank as in an army, and the great could not exist without the small. Using the example of the physical body, he argued that all parts are important. Then he made the comparison to the early Christian community: "Following this out, we must preserve our Christian body too in its entirety."[148] Ignatius implied the body metaphor when he stated that the early Christ followers would be recognized as "members of his Son" by good deeds.[149]

Writers in the third century continued the use of the body analogy for the corporate nature of the community of Christ followers. Tertullian also illustrated the diversity in the united body, also quoting from 1 Corinthians

---

144. Cyprian, *The Epistles* 75.14.
145. Ignatius, *Letters: Ephesians* 9.1.
146. Clement, *Fragments* 3.
147. Origen, *Against Celsus* 8.19.
148. *1 Clement* 38.1.
149. Ignatius, *Letters: Ephesians* 4.2.

as well as writing about "our bodies as members of Christ."[150] Cyprian alluded to the body image when he wrote about being members of one another: "Whether one member suffer, all members suffer with it; or one member rejoice, all the members rejoice with it."[151] In defending the higher virtue from the word of God on which Christ followers based their actions, Origen demonstrated it through the analogy of the body:

> We say that the holy Scriptures declare the body of Christ, animated by the Son of God, to be the whole Church of God, and the members of this body—considered as a whole—to consist of those who are believers, which of itself has not the natural power of motion like a living being, so the Word, arousing and moving the whole body, the Church to befitting action, awakens, moreover, each individual member belonging to the church, so that they do nothing apart from the word.[152]

Writers in the post-Pauline tradition indicated that it was understood that individuals enter the community of post-Pauline Christ followers through anti-structural criteria based on obedience to Christ. They understood that Christ followers were marked without differentiation by the Spirit while at the same time kept their structural statuses. However, there was a common identity in-Christ that was marked by the Spirit. Two metaphors accentuated the diversity within the community, first that individuals were stones that build a single Temple of God and secondly that they were members of one body. They understood that it did not mean that everyone was the same within the communities. There were, as discussed below, different functions within the church, particularly as it related to leadership and authority. The writings also reflected the anti-structural, allocentric commitments of interpersonal relationships, particularly so that these relationships strengthened and maintained unity, which I examine below.

Communitas—Anti-Structural, Allocentric

The foundation of interpersonal relationships among members within the post-Pauline in-Christ community was their common identity in the Spirit. Writing about early Christian communities, Helen Rhee notes, "Eschatology in the pre-Constantine period carried significant social and moral implications for the corporate lives."[153] As in early Pauline communities,

150. Tertullian, *Against Marcion* 5.7.
151. Cyprian, *The Epistles* 59.1.
152. Origen, *Against Celsus* 6.48.
153. Rhee, *Loving the Poor, Saving the Rich*, 51.

the post-Pauline communities understood themselves to be in liminality; they were between the times, already experiencing the Spirit but also waiting for the culmination which would come with the parousia or their deaths. This was the basis of their ethical behavior within and outside of the community.[154] Within the community, their relationships were to be marked by the anti-structural, allocentric characteristics of communitas: mutuality, siblinghood, humility, and love.

Mutuality was a hallmark of Pauline communities, demonstrated in the use of the reciprocal pronoun ἀλλήλων. The commitment of mutual responsibility for each other reflected the anti-structural nature of interpersonal relationships and the involvement within the lives of other members in the community. Many of the early writings of the post-Pauline communities were written in crisis, particularly to address dissention within the community, divergent teachings, and attacks from outside the community. There was an urgent admonition to unity in many of the writings of this period. Exhortations for "one anothering" were often negative ones directed toward behaviors that caused dissention and disunity within the community. However, there was still evidence of the positive commitment and mutual responsibility. The writer of 1 Clement exhorted the Corinthians to "be kind to one another" and to "be subject to his neighbor, according to his gifts."[155] The strong were exhorted to take care of the weak and the rich to take care of the poor. These statements expressed the concern they were to have for one another and at the same time acknowledged differences in statuses. As with earlier Pauline communities, their interpersonal relationships were characterized by anti-structural values.

Anti-structural relationships within structure are also evident in Ignatius' letters. Ignatius was concerned for the unity of the community, and he addressed issues to restore unity, particularly addressing submission to leaders in the community. They were to "defer to the bishop, but also to defer to one another as well."[156] While they were to submit to leadership, they were also in the same way to submit to one another, expressing the mutuality of communitas. He also admonished them to "respect one another" and to "love one another."[157] They were to stay united and to make it a priority: "Stay united and pray for one another."[158] They were to "love

---

154. Rhee, *Loving the Poor, Saving the Rich*, 72.
155. *1 Clement* 38.1.
156. Ignatius, *Letters: Magnesians* 13.2.
157. Ignatius, *Letters: Magnesians* 6.2.
158. Ignatius, *Letters: Trallians* 12.2.

one another with an undivided heart."[159] For Ignatius, mutuality promoted unity in ancient communities of Christ followers.

Later in the second century, Clement of Alexandria, writing about life as the "chosen people," highlighted the mutual aspects of their relationships with one another, drawing on Pauline tradition. He reminded the community that they were members of one body as the foundation for their interpersonal relationships. He reminded them that they must be committed to one another and therefore must speak truth to one another and not allow any bitterness, wrath, or evil to come between them. They were to be kind to one another, tender-hearted, and forgiving of one another.[160] They were also to love one another and bear one another's burdens.[161] He also repeated the Pauline tradition of mutual submission within the hierarchy of the household code.[162] This mutuality within the community was highlighted by the Pauline epistle material that Clement quotes. Pauline Hogan argues that in Clement's selection of Pauline material she sees the early Christian community united through the equality of mutual relationships.[163] Hogan notes, "It is clear that Clement understands Christian equality in terms of social relationships within the church, and not solely in terms of individual growth or spiritual status before God."[164]

Finally, there were similar commands in the third-century writings of Cyprian. Cyprian was also concerned about unity within the community, and his admonitions of mutuality were often negative commands against actions that brought disunity. For instance, he exhorted the community members, "There ought to be no contentions and emulations among you," and also, "If you bite and find fault with one another, take heed that ye are not consumed one of another."[165] He then provided positive commands that reinforced unity. They were to love one another and encourage one another by mutual exhortations. By doing so, Cyprian believed that they would be empowered to "go more and more forward in the Lord."[166] They were also to sustain one another, "Bearing with one another in love, endeavoring to keep the unity of the Spirit in the bond of peace."[167] Mutuality was stressed

159. Ignatius, *Letters: Trallians* 13.2.
160. Clement of Alexander, *The Instructor* 3.12.
161. Clement of Alexander, *The Instructor* 3.12.
162. Clement of Alexander, *The Instructor* 3.12.
163. Hogan, *No Longer Male and Female*, 105.
164. Hogan, *No Longer Male and Female*, 107.
165. Cyprian, *The Epistles* 6.5.
166. Cyprian, *The Epistles* 6.6.
167. Cyprian, *The Epistles* 51.24.

as a way of maintaining unity within the third-century community, and these mutual behaviors marked those who belonged to the community.[168] Throughout the writings of the post-Pauline communities, there was a commitment to one another. They continued the Pauline tradition of unity through acting mutually in positive ways toward one another. They were not to treat each other based on status differences but on their common identity of being one in the Spirit.

Another demonstration of anti-structure was the continued use of sibling terminology to refer to those in post-Pauline communities. Lohfink notes that the notion of siblinghood continued to be an important aspect of post-Pauline communities. He argues that the responsibilities that these communities had as siblings not only included members of their own communities but other communities as well as noted by the Roman community's concern for the community at Corinth, expressed by Clement in his letter to the Corinthians.[169] Hellerman has done an extensive study of the use of sibling terminology among post-Pauline writers, reflecting both continuity and innovation through the use of the terminology. He notes that in Clement's first letter to the church at Rome, there is frequent use of kinship terminology.[170] He observes that Clement's use of sibling terminology reinforced the solidarity in the community and is in continuity with Pauline usage of the terminology. He also observes that Clement's exhortations to mutual sharing is congruent with the reciprocal sharing expected of ancient Mediterranean families.[171] However, he argues that Clement's appeals of submission to recognizable leaders within the community was an innovation because it appealed to a "recognized hierarchy of ecclesiastical authority."[172] He suggests that this demonstrates that the early community of Christ followers in Corinth was following a typical pattern of institutionalization of dynamic organisms.

However, in the previous chapter, I argued that there was a variety of organizational structures in the Pauline communities. The authority exercised by leaders was not positional authority but rather personal or skill authority. Authority was not used to dominate members but was exercised for the common good. Rather than interpreting Clement's call to submission as discontinuity with Pauline tradition, I argue that Clement is following Pauline tradition. Clement was addressing those who by their rebellion were

168. Cyprian, *The Epistles* 51.24; 6.3.
169. Lohfink, *Jesus and Community*, 154–57.
170. Hellerman, *The Ancient Church as Family*, 130.
171. Hellerman, *The Ancient Church as Family*, 130.
172. Hellerman, *The Ancient Church as Family*, 30, 134.

destroying the communitas of the community. Submission to their leaders promoted good community: unity and solidarity.

Hellerman finds the same kind of tension in the letters of Ignatius. Ignatius himself embodied the tension between mutuality and authority. Ignatius employed sibling terminology frequently and affectionately towards the post-Pauline community, yet addressed the community with authority. Hellerman also notes that Ignatius used sibling-related concepts to reinforce unity among the members of the community. In particular, he notes Ignatius' use of non-retaliatory action among members of the post-Pauline community that extends beyond community members.[173] Hellerman also examines the writings of Irenaeus, Justin Martyr, and Clement of Alexandria and finds numerous examples of sibling terminology and the characteristics of family in the actions of the community in the second and third centuries. Despite the increasing hierarchy within the community, sibling metaphors continued to reflect the mutuality within the communities in continuity with Pauline tradition. He concludes, "Nevertheless, much remains the same, particularly regarding interpersonal relationships. Clement of Rome, Ignatius, Justin Martyr, Clement of Alexandria, and Irenaeus all attest to a relational solidarity in their local communities, which finds its primary explanation and legitimation in the family model."[174] His detailed analysis of North African churches also demonstrates the continued use of sibling terminology to both manifest and reinforce solidarity in interpersonal relationships of the communities well into the third century.[175]

Humility, submission, and redefinition of honor also continued to be important characteristics of liminality in post-Pauline Christianity. The opposite of these characteristics—seeking one's own benefit, striving for honor, and envy—are frequently mentioned by writers of this period as antithetical to the characteristics of community. Clement of Rome urged the Corinthians to submit to their leaders as an act of obedience and humility to restore the unity of the community. For Clement, humility was the means to solve the current crisis.[176] In addressing the post-Pauline community, he first reminded them of their contributions to community life: they labored for the whole community, they wept for the faults of their neighbors, they humbly dealt with their own faults, and they did good deeds.[177] Clement defined humility as seeking the good of the community, and then he

---

173. Hellerman, *The Ancient Church as Family*, 143.
174. Hellerman, *The Ancient Church as Family*, 167.
175. Hellerman, *The Ancient Church as Family*, 212.
176. Bakke, *Concord and Peace*, 126.
177. *1 Clement* 1.3—2.8.

contrasted it with the self-serving of their current condition: "From this there arose rivalry and envy, strife and sedition, persecution and anarchy, war and captivity."[178] Then he described a reversal of an already reversed of status: "The dishonored rose up against those who were held in honor," those of no reputation against the notable, the stupid against the wise, the young against the elders.[179] In a different context, this might be counter-intuitive of mutuality and the opposite of status reversal by supporting the strong over the weak as Hellerman suggests.[180] However, I argue that there were two discrete differences. What was presently happening in the community was an overthrow of those whom God had honored by those whom God had not honored.[181] The second difference was that this reversal was not from God. The low in status rising up against the high in status was by human initiative, not God's. By reversing the topos of reversal, Clement demonstrated the grievous nature of the schism by the sedition. Rather than living anti-structurally, the perpetrators were acting according to structural rules of conduct, not anti-structural: "For this reason righteousness and peace are far from you, since each has abandoned the fear of God and grown blind in his faith and ceased to walk by the rules of his precepts or to behave in a way worthy of Christ."[182]

Clement's solution was exhortation to accept the diversity of members in the post-Pauline community and to be willing to be subject to one's neighbor according to their gifts. Clement stressed that no part of the body was more or less important, but each had to act in obedience for the body to function. They needed to be willing to act according to the gifts God had given.[183] What was needed for unity to return to the community was submission; as Christ submitted to the Father, so they were to submit to leadership.

Ignatius also wrote against disunity from schisms and likewise urged the communities to submit to the leadership of the bishops in their community. Particularly in his letter to the community at Magnesia, he stressed that they needed to be united in their submission to the bishop and the elders.[184] Despite the youthfulness of their bishop, he commends the presbyters'

---

178. *1 Clement* 3.2.

179. *1 Clement* 4.3.

180. Hellerman, *The Ancient Church as Family*, 135.

181. *1 Clement* 3.2–3. The first reversal was God honoring those who were humble, those now in the position of leadership.

182. *1 Clement* 3.4.

183. *1 Clement* 41.

184. Ignatius, *Letters: Magnesians* 2.1—3.2.

deference to their bishop, noting they do so out of deference to God.[185] They were to show humility by "deferring to the bishop and to each other as Jesus did to the Father in the days of his flesh."[186] Ignatius' comparison of their imitation of Christ's submission to the Father is reminiscent of Philippians 2 in the Pauline tradition.

Humility, submission, and seeking the interest of others permeated the writings of the early Christ communities and was a distinguishing feature of the behavior of members in the communities. Polycarp exhorted the community at Philippi to follow the example of Christ, "Preferring one another and despising no one."[187] They were to "submit themselves to one another."[188] The letter to Diognetus in the second century contrasted people in the broader society who promoted self-interests with Christ followers who imitated Christ through loving one another. Rather than seeking to dominate or gain an advantage over weaker people, a person who imitated Christ "takes up his neighbor's burden on himself, and is willing to help his inferior."[189] In other words, a distinguishing characteristic of early Christ followers in which honor was redefined was that they looked out for another's interests, the allocentric characteristic of communitas.

Cyprian continued the discussion of humility into the third century. Post-Pauline followers of Christ were not to be haughty but were to humbly follow the Lord.[190] They were to imitate Christ's example of serving others, such as when he washed his disciples' feet.[191] For Cyprian, humility was necessary for unity. He also cautioned those who acted in pride or sowed seeds of discord to remember that those who humbled themselves were the ones who would be exalted.[192] Members were not to fight or find fault with each other.[193] In Cyprian's writings, humility, tranquility, and peace were the characteristics that exemplified the Christian life.[194]

As in the Pauline tradition, there was a redefinition of honor as a part of the rhetoric of humility in the post-Pauline writing, both in second- and third-century writers. Christians were not to seek honor according to the

---

185. Ignatius, *Letters: Magnesians* 3.2.
186. Ignatius, *Letters: Magnesians* 13.2.
187. Polycarp, *Letter to the Philippians* 10.1.
188. Polycarp, *Letter to the Philippians* 10.2.
189. *Diognetus* 10.6.
190. Cyprian, *The Epistles* 5.2–3.
191. Cyprian, *The Epistles* 5.2.
192. Cyprian, *The Epistles* 5.3.
193. Cyprian, *The Epistles* 6.5.
194. Cyprian, *The Epistles* 6.3.

standards of the broader Greco-Roman society. First, they were to avoid the outward trappings of honor, or "human glory," as defined by the Greco-Roman society.[195] They were not to attend spectacles and feasts, and women were not to wear jewelry or dye their hair.[196] Their speech was to be simple and straightforward.[197] Their example was Jesus, who did not come in pomp and pride but in humility.[198] Second, honor came from seeking first the Kingdom and doing good works for the good of the community.[199] They were to feed the poor rather than seek wealth.[200] They were not to promote themselves or create monuments to themselves but rather foster obedience to God.[201] Honor for the early Christian was not in comeliness and glory but in toil, affliction, and being mocked and despised.[202] Honor was given for a life of virtue and faith, including death.[203]

Love was another expression of the allocentric nature of communitas in the post-Pauline communities. Like Pauline communities, this was the central value and characteristic of the communities and was expressed throughout second- and third-century writings. Throughout the writings of this period, love not only demonstrated the quality of relationships within the community; it was a part of the apologetic to those outside the community. In a culture where self-interest, competition, and domination ruled, love for one another marked the communities as "contrast-societies."[204]

Clement of Rome appealed to love to resolve the conflict within the early community at Corinth. He reminded them that love was the central quality of the Christian life: "Without love nothing can please God."[205] For him, it was through God's great love that followers of Christ reflected that love to others.[206] He alluded to Paul's great treatise on love in his exhortations for unity: "Love puts up with everything and is always patient. There is nothing vulgar about love. Love knows nothing about schism or revolt.

---

195. Origen, *Against Celsus* 7.24.
196. Cyprian, *The Treatises* 2.21.
197. Cyprian, *The Epistles* 1.2.
198. *1 Clement* 16.2.
199. Cyprian, *The Epistles* 1.2–5.
200. Cyprian, *The Treatises* 8.7, 13–14.
201. Cyprian, *The Epistles* 18.13–15.
202. *1 Clement* 16.3–4.
203. Cyprian, *The Epistles* 34, 36.
204. Lohfink, *Jesus and Community*, 211.
205. *1 Clement* 49.5.
206. *1 Clement* 49.1–6.

Love does everything in harmony."[207] Ignatius also remarked that love was the identifying marker of the early follower of Christ: "Each bears its own stamp—unbelievers of the world; believers, who are spurred by love, the stamp of God the Father through Jesus Christ."[208] Followers of Christ were to "love what he loved."[209]

Post-Pauline followers of Christ were not only to love those within the community of faith, but they were also to love their neighbors and their enemies. The extraordinary behavior of second- and third-century followers of Christ was often cited in apologetic writing as evidence of the veracity of their beliefs.[210] Tertullian's well-known quote demonstrates that this was noticeable to outsiders: "But it is mainly the deeds of love so noble that lead many to put a brand upon us, *See,* they say, *how they love one another.*"[211] However, the converse was also true as stated in 2 Clement: "But when they see that we fail to love not only those who hate us, but even those who love us, then they mock at us and scoff at the Name."[212] Rhee argues that caring and sharing possessions (acts of love) were what distinguished orthodox Christians from heretical so-called Christians. In his letter to the Smyrnaens addressing docetism, Ignatius pointed to the actions of the leaders of the schisms as evidence of their wrong beliefs: "They care nothing about love: they have no concern for widows or orphans, for the oppressed, for those in prison or released, for the hungry or the thirsty."[213] As Rhee notes, "Christian identity is predicated upon these acts of orthopraxis as much as their orthodoxy."[214]

In post-Pauline communities, loving one's neighbor was expressed in tangible ways—or as Tertullian noted, "deeds of love"—both to those inside and outside the community. There were several ways in which the love of the community was expressed. First was the community chest in which those who had money were able to give to the church, which provided for the needs of the poor, widows, and orphans. Rhee notes that despite the conflicts and social distinctions within the community, giving to support others reflected a concrete way in which Christian ideals were expressed and understood by

---

207. *1 Clement* 49.4–5.
208. Ignatius, *Letters: Magnesians* 5.
209. Polycarp, *Letter to the Philippians* 2.2.
210. Justin, *First Apology* 9–17; Athenagoras, *A Plea Regarding Christians* 11–12; Tertullian, *Against Marcion* 4.16; Origen, *Against Celsus* 1.67.
211. Tertullian, *Apology* 39.
212. *2 Clement* 13.4.
213. Ignatius, *Letters: Smyrnaeans* 6:2.
214. Rhee, *Loving the Poor, Saving the Rich*, 173.

their surrounding communities.[215] The purpose of the common treasury was to provide for all who had needs, including widows, orphans, the sick, those in prison, and sojourners who were strangers.[216]

The feeding of the poor and needy was a regular part of the expression of love, both corporately and individually in sources throughout second- and third-century literature.[217] Common meals were one way in which the mutuality of the community across social distinctions was maintained. Clement of Alexandria argued that the meal was not just for the purpose of charity but was an expression of love: "But the supper is made of love but the supper is not love (agape); only a proof of mutual and reciprocal kindly feeling."[218] Love was also expressed in hospitality to strangers, to the sick, and the imprisoned within their communities. Strangers who came into their midst may have been members from other communities scattered by persecution or traveling missionaries or prophets. Members of the church were charged with responsibility for providing hospitality to visitors from a common fund.[219] The Didache provides extensive guidelines concerning hospitality to traveling prophets and missionaries.[220] Christian hospitality in the second and third centuries also extended to providing for those in prison and seeking, if possible, to free them. Cyprian, in the third century, cared for a number of Christians who were in prison during the Decian persecution.[221] Rhee notes that this care extended to those who were condemned to the mines and exile.[222] Another category of hospitality was visiting the sick. According to Rhee, providing meals for the sick along with widows and orphans was the duty of all Christians in the church.[223] These concrete acts of charity are listed by Aristides in the second century:

> And they love one another, and from widows they do not turn away their esteem; they deliver the orphan from him who treats him harshly. And he who has, gives to him who has not, without boasting. And when they see a stranger, they take him in to their homes and rejoice over him as a very brother; for they do not

---

215. Rhee, *Loving the Poor, Saving the Rich*, 107.

216. Rhee, *Loving the Poor, Saving the Rich*, 108; see also Martyr, *First Apology*, 14.

217. 1 *Clement* 59.4; *Diognetus* 5.7; Justin, *First Apology*, 15; Ignatius, *Letters: Smyrnaeans* 6.2.

218. Clement of Alexander, *Instructor* 2.1.

219. Rhee, *Loving the Poor, Saving the Rich*, 113; Martyr, *First Apology*, 67.

220. *Didache* 11–13.

221. Cyprian, *The Epistles* 5.1; 12.1; 13.2; 14.2.

222. Rhee, *Loving the Poor, Saving the Rich*, 123; Cyprian, *The Epistles* 76–77, 79–80.

223. Rhee, *Loving the Poor, Saving the Rich*, 128.

call them brethren after the flesh, but brethren after the spirit and in God. And whenever one of their poor passes from the world each one of them according to their ability gives heed to him and carefully sees to his burial.[224]

Authority in Communitas

The appearance of named positions of leadership in the communities of Christ followers in pastoral epistles and the writings of Ignatius and Clement is often cited as the transition from a charismatic, undifferentiated community to the institutionalized and hierarchical community.[225] Rapp notes that a common narrative among historians of this period is that the necessity for a centralized authority arose out of a concern for the integrity, unity, and survival of the church in the context of persecution and increasing schisms.[226] According to Rapp, in this narrative of the church, historians recount this development as the end of a period of innocence and the start of the decline of the spiritual life of the church.[227] However, there are three weaknesses in this particular narrative explanation of the development of organization and centralization in the communities. First, there was little differentiation between the function of overseer (bishop) and a position of overseer in the writers of this period. Second, as noted in the previous chapter, the early communities from the very beginning differentiated between leaders and other members in the community. Third, authority and the exercise of authority is much more complex than the simple dichotomy between charismatic and legal authority. The routinization of charismatic authority has been suggested as the explanation for the appearance of offices within the community, but this does not take into account different types of authority and its exercise.

In her study of bishops in late antiquity, Rapp suggests a more nuanced analytical framework for studying the authority of bishops, suggesting three types of authority: spiritual authority, ascetic authority, and pragmatic authority. She designates spiritual authority as authority based on the Spirit's presence in the person. Ascetic authority is defined as the efforts that focus oneself in hopes of attaining perfection. This authority was made evident in a person's appearance, lifestyle, and conduct. Finally,

---

224. Aristides, *Apology*, 15.
225. Hellerman, *The Ancient Church as Family*, 134.
226. Rapp, *Holy Bishops in Late Antiquity*, 7.
227. Rapp, *Holy Bishops in Late Antiquity*, 7.

pragmatic authority focused on actions to benefit others.[228] In my analysis of leadership in the previous chapter, spiritual and ascetic authority correspond to the embodiment of the characteristics of the community, and pragmatic authority corresponds to experiential authority in which one acts for the benefit of the community. Both of these characteristics are qualities of ritual leaders within communitas. In this section, I examine how the writers of this period described the authority of the bishops and, secondly, the exercise of authority in the communities.

The legitimization of authority for leaders of the second and third centuries was based on similar qualities for leaders of the Pauline communities. Rapp notes that communities emphasized exemplary behavior as a qualification for and exercise of authority. She states, "Bishops are always held to a higher code of conduct and their ability to exercise leadership is conditional on their adherence to that code."[229] The outline of qualifications of leaders in the pastoral epistles of the Pauline tradition became the yardstick for the moral qualifications of leaders.[230]

Rapp notes that the earliest evidence for a monarchic episcopate occurs in the writings of Ignatius.[231] However, the criteria for leadership remains anti-structural in the post-Pauline communities. In his letter to the Philadelphians, Ignatius made it clear that legitimacy for leadership came from God. The bishop owed his office to God, not because of his own efforts or the efforts of the congregation.[232] Ignatius also lists the way in which the bishop lived in a godly composure and was free from anger as part of his legitimacy.[233] The bishops embodied love.[234] Clement in his letter to the Romans also highlighted the qualities that legitimized leaders' authority. They have "ministered to Christ's flock faultlessly, humbly, quietly, and unassumingly."[235] They were men of honor and integrity.[236] In the late second century, Tertullian affirmed the same kind of characteristics: "The tried men of our elders preside over us, obtaining that honor not by purchase but by established character."[237] Origen in the third century also commented,

---

228. Rapp, *Holy Bishops in Late Antiquity*, 16–17.
229. Rapp, *Holy Bishops in Late Antiquity*, 18.
230. Rapp, *Holy Bishops in Late Antiquity*, 25.
231. Rapp, *Holy Bishops in Late Antiquity*, 26.
232. Ignatius, *Letters: Philadelphians*, 1.1.
233. Ignatius, *Letters: Philadelphians*, 1.1–2.
234. Ignatius, *Letters: Trallians*, 3.2.
235. *1 Clement* 44.3.
236. *1 Clement* 4.6.
237. Tertullian, *Apology*, 39.

"We exhort those who are mighty in word and of blameless life to rule over churches. Those who are ambitious of ruling, we reject."[238]

Other leaders in the post-Pauline community also had to have similar qualities to be eligible for leadership. In the second century, Polycarp provided a description of deacons and elders that highlighted the characteristics of the person (ascetic) and their service to the community (pragmatic). Like ritual leaders in communitas, leaders must embody the qualities of the community and use them for the common good. Polycarp writes:

> Likewise the deacons should be blameless before his righteousness, as servants of God and Christ and not of men; not slanderers, or double-tongued, not lovers of money, temperate in all matters, compassionate, careful, living according to the truth of the Lord, who became a servant of all[239]

He continues:

> Also the presbyters must be compassionate, merciful to all, turning back those who have gone astray, looking after the sick, not neglecting widow, or orphan, or one that is poor, but always taking thought for what is honorable in the sight of God and man, refraining from all anger, partiality, unjust judgment, keeping from all love of money, not hasty in believing evil of anyone, nor being severe in judgment.[240]

The legitimacy of the authority of leaders in the post-Pauline community was based on their actions on behalf of the community. This was also an indication of their own embodiment of the values of the community.[241] As noted above, leaders of schisms were noted for their wrong actions as indication of their wrong beliefs. A leader's actions validated and legitimized his authority.[242] Leaders were expected to show concern for and care for others.[243] They were to refute false teachers with gentleness but stand their ground.[244] They were not to neglect widows but to serve as their protector.[245]

---

238. Origen, *Against Celsus*, 8.75.
239. Polycarp, *Letter to the Philippians*, 5.2.
240. Polycarp, *Letter to the Philippians*, 6.1.
241. Rapp, *Holy Bishops of Late Antiquity*, 18.
242. Ignatius, *Letters: Polycarp*, 1.2.
243. Ignatius, *Letters: Polycarp*, 4.1.
244. Ignatius, *Letters: Polycarp*, 3.1.
245. Ignatius, *Letters: Polycarp*, 4.1.

There were several ways in which leaders, and bishops in particular, exercised their authority. In Ignatius' letters in the second century, he considered bishops as the sole ritual leader of the community: "Nothing must be done in the church without the bishop's approval."[246] They were to perform the Eucharist, baptisms, and love feasts.[247] However, their actions were to be in service to others. They were to be in continual prayer for others.[248] Bishops were to be concerned for everyone and willing to bear their burdens.[249]

In addition to the ritual function of the bishop, the bishop's exercise of power was not for domination but for empowerment. In the second century, the bishop's authority was allocated by members of the community through voluntary submission of the members of the community.[250] The writers of this period commanded and appealed to the communities to submit to their leaders, but this was often tempered by an appeal to common love and relationship rather than power. The appeals for righteous behavior, unity, and peace were to empower people to live a cruciform life.

Examples of these qualities are found in Clement's letter to the congregation at Corinth. He starts his letter by commending them for their previous positive actions for the community. He then provides examples of the damage that rivalry causes. He does not write ordering appropriate action but rather reminding them of their common goals and motivation. He states, "We are writing dear friends, not only to admonish you but also to remind ourselves. For we are in the same arena and involved in the same struggle."[251] He appealed for them to submit to their leader for two specific reasons. The first reason was for the good of the unity of the community. Clement's argument was that people within the community had different positions and gifts; "each in his own rank" serves under the general.[252] But he also argued that each part was important in the body. Therefore, their acceptance of their role in the community preserved the whole body.[253]

The second reason for his request that they submit to the leadership was for their own empowerment to live the cruciform life. Those who were responsible for the revolt were encouraged to submit to the leadership and learn obedience for their own benefit. Clement wrote, "For it is better for

---

246. Ignatius, *Letters: Smyrnaens*, 8.1.

247. Ignatius, *Letters: Smyrnaens*, 8.1–2.

248. Ignatius, *Letters: Polycarp*, 1.3.

249. Ignatius, *Letters: Polycarp*, 1.3.

250. The *Letters of Ignatius* and *1 Clement* are noted in the section on humility.

251. *1 Clement* 7.1.

252. *1 Clement* 37.3.

253. *1 Clement* 37.5.

you to have an insignificant yet credible place in Christ's flock than to appear eminent and be excluded from Christ's hope."[254] Clement's purpose in writing focused on this empowerment: "We have written enough to you, brothers, about what befits our religion and is most helpful to those who want reverently and uprightly to lead a virtuous life."[255]

Ignatius also used a form of mutuality when he addressed the church at Ephesus: "I do not give you orders" and "I address you as my fellow students, and I needed your coaching in faith, encouragement, endurance and patience."[256] He wrote because, as he states, "Love forbids me to keep silent."[257] In this letter, he exercised authority not from power, but from a concern for them. Authority was exercised not through domination but by seeking the best for others. In this case, Ignatius believed that disunity in the church was harmful and led them away from living a cruciform life. He wrote, "For when you harbor no dissention that can harass you, then you are indeed living in God's way."[258] Calls to submit to authority were not to promote the authority of the bishop but rather to empower people to live a cruciform life.

Later in the second and third centuries, there was still this ideal for leadership. The qualifications for Christian leaders were that they were pure of heart, had a sense of modesty, and were considerate of others. It was their character that qualified them for leadership, and God was the one who chose leaders.[259] It was not something that could be purchased or something that someone could strive to achieve.[260] Those who were ambitious were disqualified from service.[261] They were to be meek and humble in all things.[262]

Summary

In this section, I examined three dimensions of inaugurated eschatology found in the writings of second- and third-century liminal communities of followers of Christ. First, I demonstrated that the inaugurated eschatology found in Pauline traditions remained central to the self-understanding of

254. *1 Clement* 57.2.
255. *1 Clement* 62.1.
256. Ignatius, *Letters: Ephesians*, 3.1.
257. Ignatius, *Letters: Ephesians*, 3.2.
258. Ignatius, *Letters: Ephesians*, 8.1.
259. Tertullian, *Apology*, 39.
260. Tertullian, *Apology*, 39.
261. Origen, *Against Celsus*, 8.75.
262. Cyprian, *The Epistles*, 4.2.

the communities in the second and third centuries. This liminality was both temporal (they were living between the cross and the parousia) and embodied (they lived the new life of the Spirit in the flesh). Second, I demonstrated that communities embodied this liminality as a social body, the social dimension of inaugurated eschatology. People became members of this community through anti-structural criteria based on the belief in Jesus and incorporation through the Spirit. In this new liminal community, they were to relate to each other based on their common identity of being in Christ. Their interpersonal relationships were to be marked by characteristics of communitas: allocentricism and anti-structure. However, as in Pauline communities, their new identity in-Christ did not erase their statuses, but rather they were to relate anti-structurally within their structural statuses. Finally, I demonstrated that the authority of the leaders in the second-century communities was still based on the anti-structural criteria of embodiment of the values of the community and service to it. As in Pauline communities, the exercise of authority was directed toward the empowerment of the communities to live a cruciform life rather than to dominate others. In the next section, I discuss how the liminal post-Pauline communities related to the structures of the broader Greco-Roman world in which they were situated.

In the World, But Not of the World

As noted in our theoretical framework, the relationship between structure and anti-structure is an important dialectic. For the post-Pauline communities of Christ followers, this was not only reflected within their communities but also was expressed in their relationships within the broader Greco-Roman world. The second and third centuries were not only periods of transition within the communities, but their relationship with the broader society came more sharply into focus.[263] Since the post-Pauline communities cover a broad geographic area and time period, there were a variety of ways in which this relationship was expressed. However, writings of this period provide some common features. Since they were living in communitas while still in the structures of the world, the writings during this period reflect both confrontation and accommodation with Greco-Roman society. In this section, I briefly discuss the confrontations between the post-Pauline community and broader society. This is important because it helps frame some of the difficulties Christ followers faced as they sought to live in the world but not be of

---

263. Wagner, *After the Apostles*, 127–138.

the world in the second and third centuries. I then will discuss evidence of anti-structural living within structure during this period.

Confrontation—Not of the World

Although there was a vast range of opinions about the relationship of the communities to the structure of Greco-Roman society in the second and third centuries, there were two areas in which post-Pauline communities separated themselves from the broader Greco-Roman world: idolatry and morality. Although these were addressed in Pauline writings to communities of Christ followers, the writers in the second and third centuries directed their critique toward the broader society. First, they critiqued the moral failure of the broader society. As Wagner argues, this was not unique to early Christians since pagans in the second and third centuries also critiqued these same areas, particularly corruption, drunkenness, gluttony, greed, violence, and especially sexual misconduct.[264] Philosophers sought to educate people to control their passions, but early Christian apologists contrasted the moral degeneracy of pagan society with the way of Christ. The second area in which the early Christians critiqued pagan society was in its spiritual degeneracy and idolatry.[265] Christian apologists in the second and third centuries found the accounts of pagan activity devoid of moral and ethical value. Whereas Greco-Roman aristocrats sought to revitalize pagan religion, early Christians sought to replace it with Christianity. Wagner notes, "Christians repeated the pagan criticism of paganism and offered in its stead the one whom they claimed was the Way, the Truth, and the Life."[266]

The pagan community also confronted Christianity in the second and third centuries.[267] According to Wagner, the most cogent charges against early Christians were those of atheism and treason, which in Roman society in the second and third centuries could not be separated.[268] Those who did not sacrifice to the gods did not look after the well-being of the city nor support Rome and the emperor.[269] The litmus test for loyalty to the state was whether or not a person sacrificed to the gods.[270] However, persecution of Christ followers was sporadic and generally directed toward leaders until

---

264. Wagner, *After the Apostles*, 130.
265. Wagner, *After the Apostles*, 130.
266. Wagner, *After the Apostles*, 131.
267. Wilken, *The Christians as the Romans Saw Them*, 94–125.
268. Wagner, *After the Apostles*, 132.
269. Wilken, *The Christians as the Romans Saw Them*, 56–58.
270. Wagner, *After the Apostles*, 132.

Decius' reign (AD 249–251).[271] Decius was the embodiment of old Roman virtues, and he believed that the neglect of Roman gods, who had made Rome great, was the reason for the decay and the calamities that Rome was experiencing.[272] In AD 249, he issued imperial edicts to sacrifice to the gods. Those who complied were given certificates indicating their compliance.[273] Some have noted that the intent of the decree was not to crush early Christianity as a direct target, rather it was intended to revive the worship of Roman gods.[274] Those who sacrificed were restored to the broader society but were considered apostate to the church. Those who did not sacrifice were punished with fines, servitude in the mines, or death.

At an intellectual level, pagans challenged post-Pauline Christians on three points which the apologists sought to answer: novelty, ignorance, and barbarism. For Greco-Roman society, the veracity of a particular belief was based on its longevity; something new was not considered true.[275] Since Christianity was based on the Christ event that occurred in the early first century, it was very recent. The second claim was that Christianity was steeped in ignorance. The basis of Christian belief and behavior was the resurrection of Christ, and this made no sense philosophically nor experientially.[276] And finally, there was the accusation of barbarism. Pagan critics noted the appeal of Christianity to the marginalized of society: the poor, slaves, and women.[277] Pagan critics linked the validity of the message to the social status of those who adhered to it.[278]

The Christian responses to these accusations in the second and third centuries was to develop answers through the use of Greco-Roman rhetoric and thought forms.[279] In some cases, writers such as Justin Martyr and Clement of Alexandria sought to use the intellectual tools of their day to describe, defend, and advance early Christianity through philosophical and rhetorical concepts. Tertullian represented the opposite extreme by rejecting the use of philosophy and warning that the wisdom of the world was foolishness. He was convinced that society was corrupted by demonic

---

271. Frend, *The Rise of Christianity*, 294.

272. Latourette, *A History of Christianity*, 87.

273. Latourette, *A History of Christianity*, 87.

274. Frend, *The Early Church*, 97.

275. Wagner, *After the Apostles*, 134.

276. Wilken, *The Christians as Romans Saw Them*, 90, 104. Wilken particularly notes Celsus' criticism.

277. Wagner, *After the Apostles*, 136.

278. Wagner, *After the Apostles*, 138.

279. Wagner, *After the Apostles*, 138.

powers.[280] Irenaeus, on the other hand distanced himself from those who demonized the state. He had a more positive attitude toward the state and directed his writings toward heretics within the early communities of Christ followers. There was no consistent intellectual response by the post-Pauline communities to pagan society.[281]

Engagement—In the World

On the individual level, post-Pauline Christ followers were not to separate themselves from the broader Greco-Roman society. They were to live in the world but not to be of the world. However, in the ancient Greco-Roman world, one could not separate the worship of gods and the support of the state and the emperor.[282] This meant attending spectacles, sacrificing to the gods, attending celebrations, and swearing by the genius of the emperor. Early Christians, however, sought to separate pleasing God from pleasing the state or being good subjects. In the second century, Anthenagoras wrote imploring the emperor to examine the lives, the teachings, and the loyalty of the Christ followers.[283] He argued that by living according to their values and pleasing their God, they were model subjects for the emperor.[284] They submitted to one another and loved one another in the spirit of Christ. Their love and behavior was not limited to the in-group. They loved their enemies. They returned evil and harsh comments with gentleness and abuse with prayer. They were called upon to be patient with all men.[285] Justin Martyr also provided a list of characteristics that showed early Christ followers were good subjects. They avoided sexual immorality, loved all men, prayed for their enemies, shared with those in need, and fled from all anger.[286] They avoided all injustice, including exposing children to die.[287] They paid their taxes and assessments.[288] Justin Martyr summed up his view: "So we worship God only, but in all other matters we gladly serve you, recognizing you as emperors and rulers of men, and praying that along with your imperial

---

280. Wagner, *After the Apostles*, 239.
281. Wagner, *After the Apostles*, 239.
282. Wilken, *The Christians as the Romans Saw Them*, 56–57.
283. Athenagoras, *A Plea Regarding Christians*, 3.
284. Athenagoras, *A Plea Regarding Christians*, 11–12.
285. Athenagoras, *A Plea Regarding Christians*, 11–12.
286. Martyr, *First Apology*, 15.
287. Martyr, *First Apology*, 27.
288. Martyr, *First Apology*, 17.

power you may also be found to have a sound mind."[289] They were not only good subjects; they were exemplary subjects.

In the third century, Christ followers continued to support the ruler when they could. Tertullian demonstrated that communities of followers of Christ sought to please God and serve their earthly rulers. This meant finding ways to support the rulers without compromising their own beliefs. Rather than praying "to" the emperor or swearing by his genius, Christians sought to please God and please the emperor by praying "for" the emperor. Rather than fighting for the emperor, they fought with prayer.[290] They sought to be exemplary subjects by being humble in conversation, doing what was just and good with their deeds, and keeping peace with their brethren.[291] They were encouraged to support the emperor and his leaders but not if it contradicted the values of loving God and people.[292] Early Christians also declined public office so that they could pursue nobler causes and ways of serving God and the emperor.[293] However, the writers made it clear that they believed that the deeds and values of their beliefs were the best way to train up good citizens.[294]

Perhaps the most elegant description of what it meant to live anti-structurally within the structures of Greco-Roman world in post-Pauline communities was written anonymously to Diognetus in the second century. It seems fitting to end this discussion with his description:

> For Christians cannot be distinguished from the rest of the human race by country or language or customs. They do not live in cities of their own; they do not use a peculiar form of speech; they do not follow an eccentric manner of life. This doctrine of theirs has not been discovered by the ingenuity or deep thought of men, nor do they put forward a merely human teaching, as some people do. Yet, although they live in Greek and barbarian cities alike, as each man's lot has been cast and follow the customs of the country in clothing and food and other matters of daily living, at the same time they give proof of the remarkable and admittedly extraordinary constitution of their own commonwealth. They live in their own countries, but only as aliens. They have a share in everything as citizens, and endure everything as foreigners. Every foreign land is their fatherland,

289. Martyr, *First Apology*, 17.
290. Tertullian, *Apology*, 30.
291. Cyprian, *The Treaties*, 4.15.
292. Origen, *Against Celsus*, 8.75.
293. Origen, *Against Celsus*, 8.75.
294. Origen, *Against Celsus*, 8.74.

and yet for them every fatherland a foreign land. They marry, like everyone else, and they beget children, but they do not cast out their offspring. They share their board with each other, but not their marriage bed. It is true that they are "in the flesh" but they do not live "according to the flesh." They busy themselves on earth, but their citizenship is in heaven. They obey established laws, but in their own lives they go far beyond what the laws require. They love all men, and by all men are persecuted. They are unknown, and still they are condemned; they are put to death, and yet they are brought to life. They are poor, and yet they make many rich; they are completely destitute, and yet they enjoy complete abundance. They are dishonored, and in their very dishonor are glorified; they are defamed, and are vindicated. They are reviled, and yet they bless; when they are affronted, they still pay due respect. When they do good, they are punished as evildoers; undergoing punishment, they rejoice because they are brought life.[295]

They lived anti-structurally within structure.

Conclusion

During the second and third centuries, post-Pauline communities were beginning to experience some dramatic changes. Because of schisms and beliefs that challenged the unity of the early communities of Christ followers, there was an emphasis on authority: who had authority, which were authoritative beliefs, and which were authoritative writings. However, although the second- and third-century communities began to have a centralized leadership organization, they still reflected the anti-structural teaching and behavior of the Pauline traditions. Although the writers of the second and third centuries were addressing a variety of issues to a variety of audiences in a variety of genres, their writings still reflected a community in liminality with its inclusive membership and the incorporation of members by the Spirit. The members of the post-Pauline communities related to each other based on their primary identity of being in the Spirit within their structural statuses. They did not erase these statuses, but rather their interpersonal relationships were to reflect the characteristics of communitas. This identity was also central as they lived their anti-structural lives within the structures of the Greco-Roman society.

There was also a continuation of Pauline eschatology. Communities in the second and third centuries still had a strong sense of a partially realized

---

295. *Diognetus* 5.1–17.

eschatology, although there was an ongoing delay in the parousia. The writers understood followers of Christ to be already experiencing eternal life and the blessings of communion with God while they were still living in the world. Their writings reflect that they understood that they were already living in the last days, and at the return of Christ or upon their death, they would finally experience fully what they had already begun to live in the Spirit. Until then, they lived liminally on earth in the Spirit in a body of flesh until they reigned with Christ, clothed in eternity. It was this belief that allowed the early Christians to be hopeful in trials and faithful in death while living in the world but not being of the world.

Chapter 7

The End of Ancient Christianity

THROUGHOUT THIS STUDY I have used Turner's concept of liminality, structure, and anti-structure as a heuristic framework to examine the social life of early Christian communities. Using this overarching framework has allowed me to trace features that spanned from the narratives of the Jesus tradition through the traditions of the Pauline communities and post-Pauline communities. I reviewed the main features of this study topically and then made some brief observations of some of the changes that occurred as a result of Constantine's patronage.

Living in Liminality

There were three aspects of liminality that I sought to study through four different periods of writing. Liminality was expressed in terms of both a temporal liminality, embodied liminality, and the liminality of the social body. The liminality of the social body exhibited the characteristics of anti-structure in its membership, interpersonal relationships, and authority in the community. Finally, I examined the relationships of the anti-structural community to the broader social structure. In this section, I discuss the continuity and differences in the expression of liminality in the four different sets of writings of the pre-Constantine communities of Christ followers: the Jesus tradition represented in Luke's narrative of Jesus' life and teaching, the early community represented in Luke's narrative of Acts, the Pauline communities, and the post-Pauline communities.

Liminal Time

One of the main features that was consistent within all of the early Christian writings was the understanding that the reign of God was present in history. Across all of the writings that I examined, there was a general acknowledgment that Christ followers were experiencing the reign of God in the present. However, within each of the four time periods, this experience was expressed differently.

Within the Jesus tradition represented in Luke's account of Jesus and his teaching, Luke understood that the reign of God was present in Jesus' public ministry. His fronting of the Nazareth announcement and his repetition of it in Jesus' response to John's disciples indicated that Jesus' public ministry was understood by Luke as the in-breaking of God's reign in Jesus' ministry. However, Luke also framed Jesus' public ministry and the people of God in liminal phases. Jesus was the Davidic messiah but neither recognized nor enthroned. Likewise, the people of God were in liminality. They were compared to the liminal phase of Israel as she wandered through the desert, learning to be the people of God before entering the promise land.

Luke continued the story in the narrative of the book of Acts. In this narrative Jesus, as the messiah, was no longer in liminality, but through his death, resurrection, and ascension he was reincorporated as the exalted Davidic messiah, now enthroned in his rightful place. The arrival of the Spirit demonstrated that the messiah had come and the last days had begun in the present. The early followers of Christ understood that the new age had begun. However, Luke's narrative also made it clear that there would be a future culmination of some kind, a return of Christ. But the communities understood that they were already experiencing new life as they waited for his return. They were a people in liminality. The Spirit was the new common identity marker for all who were in the community.

Luke's narrative described the events that were the framework for Pauline and post-Pauline traditions. The cross was central to Paul's understanding of life as a follower of Christ. For Paul, the cross brought about a dominion change: the new age had broken into the present. He understood that the world was no longer under the dominion of sin and death, but through the cross, the dominion of righteousness and life had begun. However, although the new dominion had started, the old was still dominating the world. Like Luke's Acts, Christ followers in Pauline writings lived in the overlap of two ages in a temporal liminality. Paul adds to the understanding of this domain change through his discussions of the change that occurred in the individual with the indwelling of the Spirit. In Paul's writing, Christ followers embodied liminality. They had been separated from their former status through the indwelling of the Spirit; they were changed from what they were before. However, they lived out that new existence in their physical body. They were in transition until their reincorporation at death or at the parousia. Paul's exhortations were based on this understanding of embodied liminality. They were to live according to their new identity in-Christ rather than their former identity as slaves to sin and death.

Post-Pauline tradition reflected these Pauline traditions. They understood themselves to be living in the last days while living in the present. However, one difference in post-Pauline communities was an increasing diversity of opinion about how the end would take place and whether there would be a millennium or not. They also followed Pauline tradition in understanding that Christ followers embodied this liminality through the indwelling of the Spirit within their physical bodies. They understood themselves to be living with Christ in the present, and at death they would only experience life with Christ more fully.

Liminal Community

The second feature that was consistent throughout the study of the early Christian communities was that there was a corporate expression of being a Christ follower. When someone became a follower of Christ, they became a part of a corporate expression of the in-Christ life. There were three aspects of this corporate community. Consistently through all traditions, membership in this liminal community was determined by anti-structural criteria. In all of the traditions, one became a member through obedience to the word of Jesus. In the narrative of Acts (Pauline and post-Pauline traditions), members were incorporated into the in-Christ community through the Holy Spirit. Members in the communities had a common anti-structural identity; they were followers of Jesus. Their status in structure did not matter. Their primary common identity was obedience to and identification with Christ. In Pauline tradition, this was expressed as being in-Christ and marked by a common identity, the Spirit. There were various metaphors to depict this common identity: siblings, temple, and body. Post-Pauline traditions follow Pauline tradition in their understanding of incorporation into a corporate community, and there was still evidence of the use of sibling, temple, and body analogies in the writings in the second and third centuries.

The second aspect of the community was the character of interpersonal relationships within these communities. Across all four periods, interpersonal relationships were characterized by communitas as those of a community in liminality. They were allocentric and anti-structural. In all four periods, the sibling metaphor was used to express both their identity as family and the kind of behavior that was expected between members of the community. People in the community were expected to be involved in each other's lives through mutual commands to "one another" each other. They were to mutually encourage one another to live a new way of life.

Humility, also expressed as status reversal, was an important characteristic of these communities. The writings of these four periods acknowledged the differences between people; being in liminality did not erase those differences. There were differences in gender, economic status, social status, and even in spiritual gifts. However, instead of using those differences to exalt oneself and add to one's own honor, Christ followers were to use their status for others. They were to use their gifts, their possessions, and their positions for the benefit of the community. Members were not to treat others differently because of their status but as members of the same family—as siblings.

Finally, love was the hallmark in all of the traditions. It was "other" focused, seeking the best for another. Materially, it was expressed through the use of possessions and wealth for the benefit of others. Use of possessions was both a reflection of and contribution to the unity of the community. Unlike sectarian groups that strengthened insider/outsider boundaries, for Christ followers love had no boundaries. This other-centered concern was not only to be directed toward those in the community, but it was to be expressed in all relationships, even to those who were enemies.

The third area that was consistent across all four periods was how authority in the community was legitimized and exercised. Although the writings of these four periods express a variety of ways in which the community organized leadership roles, there were consistent expectations regarding the qualities for leaders. The authority of leaders came from anti-structural characteristics rather than from a structural position. Across all traditions, the authority of leaders in the communities of Christ followers came from their embodiment of the values of the community and service to the community. These values were central to the exercise of their authority as well. The exercise of authority was not for domination over people in the community but to empower people to live the cruciform life within and outside the community.

Anti-Structure in Structure

The feature that distinguished the early pre-Constantine Christ communities from millenarian or other sectarian groups is that they were not to separate themselves from structure, but they were to live out these anti-structural lives within structure. They also were to extend these same types of relationships to those outside the community. Although there was a consistent engagement with structure, the different geographic and historical contexts shaped what this engagement looked like.

Across all traditions, the writers encouraged early Christ followers to participate in structure. They were to pay their taxes, obey their leaders, and give honor where honor was due. They were to be exemplary citizens, not taking revenge nor insulting others but living peaceably with all. There was a general acknowledgement of the right of the government to organize and govern people.

Conflicts between the communities and structure arose when the structure prevented or hindered living anti-structural lives. Jesus confronted the structural leaders who emphasized national identity over living honorably before God. The apostles confronted structural leaders when they sought to prevent the apostles from telling people about the anti-structural way of being the people of God. The apostles also challenged people who opposed the people of God through their actions or agenda, such as Ananias and Sapphira. Paul confronted the issues of exclusion and domination based on structural statuses, which were opposed to the anti-structural, interpersonal relationships in the community. In the post-Pauline communities, the writers opposed structure when allegiance to structure (through pagan sacrifice) threated allegiance to God. In each of these confrontations, people in structure were viewed as opposing the anti-structural agenda of God.

The early communities of Christ followers lived within structure. Because they were to extend these anti-structural relationships to those outside the communities, their boundaries were mutable and permeable. Thus, early Christ followers influenced their Greco-Roman neighbors with their lives, but conversely the Greco-Roman culture also influenced their communities. This tension of structure and anti-structure could lead to either a transformation of structure or a transformation of the anti-structural communities to structure as happened under Constantine.

Anti-Structure Becomes Structure—Constantine

Few argue against the fact that Constantine through his edicts became a patron of the early Christian communities, but how much Constantine's actions changed the trajectory of the early Christian communities is contested. Some argue that changes were already taking place within the pre-Constantine communities in regard to issues of authority, orthodoxy, and the role of the church in society.[1] Others argue that Constantine's actions

---

1. Rapp, *Holy Bishops in Late Antiquity*, 13. Rapp tends to see a trajectory, particularly when it comes to the functional roles of the bishops.

created a radical break in the fundamental practices and shape of the early Christian communities.[2] However, it is highly unlikely that the church would have emerged as it did by the end of the fourth century without Constantine's intervention. As Ramsay MacMullen notes, "Christendom, the city of God, was very different in the year 400 from what it had been in 200."[3] The debate generally centers around discussion of the wealth of the early communities. Both pre-Constantine and post-Constantine, the communities controlled revenue and property as well as the role of the leaders within the communities.

Henry Chadwick points out that although early Christianity was illegal and the community as a corporate entity could not own property, there was considerable revenue that each bishop controlled in the third century.[4] Bishops were responsible for hospitality to strangers, paying stipends, and feeding the poor. He notes that at Rome a quarter of the revenue went to the bishop and three-quarters went to workers, the sick, the poor, and maintenance of church buildings.[5] Although the community itself did not own property, often property or houses that were used for meetings were held in the name of the bishop or one of the deacons he designated. Because of this, it was often difficult to determine who actually held titles to community houses, cemeteries, and common funds.[6] Rhee notes that the communities in actuality functioned as defacto owners and property managers in the third century.[7]

However, there is no archaeological evidence prior to Constantine of the type of church buildings that began to appear during the reign of Constantine.[8] Most of the buildings prior to Constantine that might have been used for community gatherings were built for a different use, usually a private home, and were adapted for use as a community meeting place. Graydon Snyder argues that there is no evidence of large meeting places before AD 300. He dates the earliest known structure built specifically for corporate use at AD 310, just before the edict of Milan.[9]

---

2. Rhee, *Loving the Poor, Saving the Rich*, 179.
3. MacMullen, *The Second Church*, 95.
4. Chadwick, *The Early Church*, 58.
5. Chadwick, *The Early Church*, 56, 58.
6. Grant, *Augustus to Constantine*, 176.
7. Rhee, *Loving the Poor, Saving the Rich*, 151.
8. Snyder, *Ante Pacem*, 299; MacMullen, *The Second Church*, 12. MacMullen points to five Eastern churches of third-century date.
9. Snyder, *Ante Pacem*, 152.

Several scholars have noted that the position of the community and clergy in the broader society began to change in the mid-third century. Rhee argues that the church as an institution was engaged in several financial functions beginning in the third century.[10] Frend also observes that early Christians were gaining numbers and wealth because the church was considered a safe trustee.[11] The third-century community at Rome, for instance, became a depository for widows and orphans.[12] There is also evidence of bishops engaging in profit-making business transactions.[13] The third-century community was able to pay out large sums of money to the poor and the sick.[14] According to Rhee, "The church and clergy played an economically significant role by serving as depositories, banks and trustees for its members and even engaged in trades apparently as 'fund raisers for charity' and business affairs for profits."[15]

However, when Constantine first gained power in AD 312 in the West and then as sole emperor in AD 324, he made several changes that impacted fourth-century Christianity.[16] First was his edict of toleration (Edict of Milan, AD 313), which put Christianity on equal footing with cults within the empire and included freedom of worship, a financial subsidy, and clerical exemption from compulsory public service and taxes.[17] Constantine also ordered the property of the communities that was seized during the persecutions returned to the communities and gave grants to build additional buildings.[18] This and his other pro-Christian decisions allowed the communities to accept endowments, which he also provided.[19] In addition, he provided a fixed distribution to the poor to be administered through the community.[20] The benefaction of Constantine was on a large scale, and the effect on Christian communities was "nothing less than revolutionary."[21] However, these actions did not just transform the scale of what the

10. Rhee, *Loving the Poor, Saving the Rich*, 155.
11. Frend, *The Early Church*, 104.
12. Rhee, *Loving the Poor, Saving the Rich*, 155.
13. Rhee, *Loving the Poor, Saving the Rich*, 156.
14. Frend, *The Early Church*, 104.
15. Rhee, *Loving the Poor, Saving the Rich*, 157.
16. Frend, *The Rise of Christianity*, 485.
17. Rhee, *Loving the Poor, Saving the Rich*, 179; Eusebius, *The History of the Church*, 10.6, 10.7.
18. Frend, *The Rise of Christianity*, 487; Eusebius, *The History of the Church*, 10.5.
19. Fox, *Pagans and Christians*, 623.
20. Chadwick, *The Early Church*, 128.
21. Rhee, *Loving the Poor, Saving the Rich*, 179.

communities were doing financially; they also radically changed the authority structure within them.

Before Constantine's patronage, the funding for the programs of the post-Pauline Christian communities fundamentally came from within the community itself, generally from wealthy members.[22] The power that leaders had to distribute the funds came from those who gave the funds. The leaders of the post-Pauline community were accountable to those who gave the funds to use for the purpose of the community The bishop did not have independent power over the funds; if he misused the funds, wealthy patrons could withdraw their support.[23]

However, when Constantine became a patron of Christianity in the fourth century, accountability shifted. In return for his gifts, Constantine gave the Christian community officials several responsibilities within the imperial administration. Constantine gave bishops judicial responsibility for the poor in civil cases.[24] He made the bishops responsible for the grain dole to the poor—all the poor, not just Christians.[25] Furthermore, Constantine provided burial services for the poor under the direction of the bishops.[26] Thus, while the community received imperial and private gifts from the imperial government, they were also accountable to the imperial government for the use of most of those resources.[27] In the Constantine administration, the leaders of communities of Christ followers were recognized as civic leaders as well as religious leaders.[28] The Christian community in essence became part of the imperial governing body, and in doing so the church became structure.[29]

---

22. Rhee, *Loving the Poor, Saving the Rich*, 140.

23. Rhee, *Loving the Poor, Saving the Rich*, 141. Rhee points out that theologically the bishop was accountable to God. God had given this stewardship into his hands, and therefore he was accountable to God.

24. Brown, *The Rise of Western Christendom*, 78.

25. Guy, *Introducing Early Christianity*, 117.

26. Rhee, *Loving the Poor, Saving the Rich*, 181.

27. Rhee, *Loving the Poor, Saving the Rich*, 181.

28. Frend, *The Rise of Christianity*, 488.

29. Constantine's patronage of the church began the process of Christianization of the empire that continued for the next several centuries. Markus, *The End of Ancient Christianity* looks at the processes that transformed the Roman Empire. Salzman, *The Making of a Christian Aristocracy* examines specifically the conversion of the elite.

A Final Word

The essence of ancient Christianity was relationships. For the early followers of Jesus, it meant exactly that—to follow Jesus. It meant entering into a new community that sought to follow Jesus' teaching about a new way of living and relating to others. Although made up of people of different statuses (e.g., economic, ethnic, sex), they treated each other as equals. The community did not erase these statuses, but Christ followers related to each other as if these statuses did not matter. It was a community in which people set aside concerns for self for concerns of the "other." There were no boundaries for the "other." They could be a fellow Christian, a neighbor, or even an enemy. For the early followers of Jesus extending love and concern, the "other" had become the "we."

Bibliography

1 Clement. In *Early Christian Fathers*, edited by Cyril C. Richardson, 43–73. New York: Simon & Schuster, 1996.
2 Clement. In *Early Christian Fathers*, edited by Cyril C. Richardson, 193–204. New York: Simon & Schuster, 1996.
Aageson, James W. *Paul, The Pastoral Epistles, and the Early Church*. Peabody, MA: Hendrickson, 2008.
Aasgaard, Reider. "Brothers and Sisters in the Faith: Christian Siblingship as an Ecclesiological Mirror." In *The Formation of the Early Church*, edited by Jostein Ådna, 285–316. WUNT 183. Tübingen: Mohr/Siebeck, 2005.
———. *My Beloved Brothers and Sisters! Christian Siblingship in Paul*. London: T. & T. Clark, 2004.
Adams, Edward. *The Earliest Christian Meeting Places: Almost Exclusively Houses?* LNTS 450. London: Bloomsbury, 2013.
———. "First-Century Models for Paul's Churches: Selected Scholarly Developments since Meeks." In *After the First Urban Christians: The Social-Scientific Study of Pauline Christianity Twenty-Five Years Later*, edited by Todd D. Still and David G. Horrell, 60–78. London: T. & T. Clark, 2009.
Agosto, Efrain. "Patronage and Commendation, Imperial and Anti-Imperial." In *Paul and the Roman Order*, edited by Richard A. Horsley, 103–125. Harrisburg, PA: Trinity, 2004.
Alikin, Valerij A. *The Earliest History of the Christian Gathering: Origin, Development and Content of the Christian Gathering in the First to Third Centuries*. Supplements to Vigiliae Christianae 102. Leiden: Brill, 2010.
Ando, Clifford. *The Matters of the Gods: Religion and the Roman Empire*. Berkeley: University of California Press, 2008.
Aristides. *Apology*. In *Ante-Nicene Fathers*, edited by Alexander Roberts and James Donaldson, vol. 9, 259–62. Peabody, MA: Hendrickson, 2004.
Arnold, Clinton. *Ephesians: Exegetical Commentary on the New Testament*. Grand Rapids: Zondervan, 2010.
Ascough, Richard S. *Paul's Macedonian Associations*. Tübingen: Mohr Siebeck, 2003.
———. *What Are They Saying About the Formation of Pauline Churches?* New York: Paulist, 1998.
Athenagoras. *A Plea Regarding Christians*. In *Early Christian Fathers*, edited by Cyril C. Richardson, 300–342. New York: Simon & Schuster, 1996.

Aune, D. E., T. J. Geddert, and C. A. Evans. "Apocalypticism." In *Dictionary of New Testament Background*, edited by Craig A. Evans and Stanley E. Porter, 45–58. Downers Grove, IL: InterVarsity, 2000.

Bakke, Odd Magne. *"Concord and Peace": A Rhetorical Analysis of the First Letter of Clement with an Emphasis on the Language of Unity and Sedition*. WUNT 2/143. Tübingen: Mohr/Siebeck, 2001.

Banks, Robert. "Church Order and Government." In *Dictionary of Paul and His Letters*, edited by Gerald G Hawthorne and Ralph P. Martin, 131–137. Downers Grove, IL: InterVarsity, 1992.

———. *Paul's Idea of Community*. Peabody, MA: Hendrickson, 1994.

Barcley, William B. *Christ in You*. New York: University Press of America, 1999.

Barker, Margaret. "The Temple Roots of the Christian Liturgy." In *Christian Origins: Worship, Belief and Society*, edited by Kieran J. O'Mahony, 29–51. JSNTSup 241. Sheffield: Sheffield Academic, 2003.

Bartchy, S. Scott. "The Apostle Paul's Vision of a Society of Siblings." *Biblical Theology Bulletin* 29 (1999) 68–78.

———. *Call No Man Father*. Grand Rapids: Baker, forthcoming.

———. "Community of Goods in Acts: Idealization or Social Reality." In *The Future of Early Christianity: Essays in Honor of Helmut Koester*, edited by Birger A. Pearson, 309–18. Minneapolis: Fortress, 1991.

———. *Mallon Chresai: First Century Slavery and the Interpretation of 1 Corinthians 7:21*. 1973. Reprint, Eugene, OR: Wipf & Stock, 2003.

———. "Table Fellowship." In *Dictionary of Jesus and the Gospels*, edited by Joel B. Green, Scot McKnight, and I. Howard Marshall, 796–800. Downers Grove, IL: InterVarsity, 1992.

———. " 'When I Am Weak, I am Strong': A Pauline Paradox in Cultural Context." In *Kontexte der Schrift*. Vol. 2, *Kultur, Politik, Religion, Sprach—Text: Wolfgang Stegemann zum 60. Geburtstag*, edited by Christian Strecker, 49–60. Stuttgard: Kohlhammer, 2005.

Bilezikian, Gilbert. *Beyond Sex Roles*. Grand Rapids: Baker, 2006.

Blasi, Anthony. "Office of Charisma in Early Christian Ephesus." *Sociology of Religion* 56 (1995) 245–56.

Blue, Bradley. "Acts and the House Church." In *The Book of Acts in Its Graeco-Roman Setting*, edited by David W. J. Gill and Conrad Gempf, vol. 2, 119–222. Grand Rapids: Eerdmans, 1994.

Bock, Darrell L. *Acts*. Baker Exegetical Commentary on the New Testament. Grand Rapids: Baker, 2007.

———. *Luke Volume 1:1—9:50*. Baker Exegetical Commentary on the New Testament. Grand Rapids: Baker, 1994.

———. *Luke Volume 9:51—24:53*. Baker Exegetical Commentary on the New Testament. Grand Rapids: Baker, 1996.

Bowie, Fiona. *The Anthropology of Religion*. Oxford: Blackwell, 2000.

Brawley, Robert L. "From Reflex to Reflections? Identity in Philippians 2:6–11 and Its Context." In *Reading Paul in Context: Explorations in Identity Formation*, edited by Kathy Ehrensperger and J. Brian Tucker, 128–146. LSNT 428. London: T. & T. Clark, 2010.

Brown, Peter. *The Rise of Western Christendom*. Oxford: Blackwell, 2003.

Bruce, F. F. *The Book of Acts*. New International Commentary on the New Testament. Grand Rapids: Eerdmans, 1988.
Bultmann, Rudolf. "Forward." In *Jesus' Proclamation of the Kingdom of God*, edited by Richard Hyde Hiers and David Larrimore Holland, xi. Philadelphia: Fortress, 1971.
———. "Jesus and Paul." In *Existence and Faith*, 183–201. Cleveland: World, 1960.
Burke, Trevor. *Family Matters: A Socio-Historical Study of Kinship Metaphors in 1 Thessalonians*. JSNT 247. London: T. & T. Clark, 2003.
Burkert, Walter. *Ancient Mystery Cults*. Cambridge: Harvard University Press, 1987.
Burridge, Kenneth. *New Heavens, New Earth*. Pavilion Series: Social Anthropology. Oxford: Blackwell, 1969.
Burridge, Richard A. *Imitating Jesus: An Inclusive Approach to New Testament Ethics*. Grand Rapids: Eerdmans, 2007.
Burtchaell, James Tunstead. *From Synagogue to Church: Public Services and Offices in Earliest Christian Communities*. Cambridge: Cambridge University Press, 1992.
Campbell, Constantine R. *Paul and Union with Christ*. Grand Rapids: Zondervan, 2012.
Campbell, William. *Paul and the Creation of Christian Identity*. London: T. & T. Clark, 2008.
Chadwick, Henry. *The Early Church*. London: Penguin, 1993.
Chilton, Bruce. *Pure Kingdom: Jesus' Vision of God*. Studying the Historical Jesus. Grand Rapids: Eerdmans, 1996.
Cho, Youngmo. *Spirit and Kingdom in the Writings of Luke and Paul: An Attempt to Reconcile These Concepts*. Waynesboro, GA: Paternoster, 2005.
Ciampa, Roy E., and Brian S. Rosner. *The First Letter to the Corinthians*. Pillar New Testament Commentary. Grand Rapids: Eerdmans, 2010.
Clarke, Andrew. *Secular and Christian Leadership in Corinth: A Socio-Historical and Exegetical Study of 1 Corinthians 1–6*. Arbeiten zur Geschichte des antiken Judentums und des Urchristentums 18. Leiden: Brill, 1993.
Clement of Alexandria. *Fragments*. In *Ante-Nicene Fathers*, edited by Alexander Roberts and James Donaldson, vol. 2, 569–88. Peabody, MA: Hendrickson, 2004.
———. *The Instructor*. In *Ante-Nicene Fathers*, edited by Alexander Roberts and James Donaldson, vol. 2, 207–98. Peabody, MA: Hendrickson, 2004.
Cohen, Shaye J. D. *From the Maccabees to the Mishnah*. Library of Early Christianity 7. Louisville: Westminster John Knox, 2006.
Collins, John J. *The Apocalyptic Imagination*. Grand Rapids: Eerdmans, 1998.
Constantineanu, Corneliu. *The Social Significance of Reconciliation in Paul's Theology: Narrative Readings in Romans*. LNTS 421. London: T. & T. Clark, 2010.
Conzelmann, Hans. *Acts of the Apostles*. Translated by James Limburg et al. Hermeneia. Philadelphia: Fortress, 1987.
Cook, Stephen L. *Prophecy and Apocalypticism: The Postexilic Setting*. Minneapolis: Fortress, 1995.
Crossan, John Dominic. *The Birth of Christianity: Discovering What Happened in the Years Immediately after the Execution of Jesus*. San Francisco: HarperSanFrancisco, 1998.
———. *The Historical Jesus: The Life of a Mediterranean Jewish Peasant*. San Francisco: HarperSanFrancisco, 1991.
Cyprian. *The Epistles of Cypria*. In *Ante-Nicene Fathers*, edited by Alexander Roberts and James Donaldson, vol. 5, 275–420. Peabody, MA: Hendrickson, 2004.

———. *The Treatises of Cyprian*. In *Ante-Nicene Fathers*, edited by Alexander Roberts and James Donaldson, vol. 5, 421–564. Peabody, MA: Hendrickson, 2004.

Daley, Brian E. *The Hope of the Early Church*. Grand Rapids: Baker, 2009.

Davidson, Ivor J. *The Birth of the Church*. Grand Rapids: Baker, 2004.

Davies, John Gordon. *The Early Christian Church*. New York: Holt, Rinehart & Winston, 1965.

The Dead Sea Scrolls. Edited by Florentino García Martínez and Eibert J. C. Tigchelaar. Grand Rapids: Eerdmans, 1999.

DeSilva, David A. *Honor, Patronage, Kinship & Purity*. Downers Grove, IL: InterVarsity, 2000.

———. "Patronage." In *Dictionary of New Testament Backgrounds*, edited by Craig A. Evans and Stanley E. Porter, 766–71. Downers Grove, IL: InterVarsity, 2000.

Didache. In *Early Christian Fathers*, edited by Cyril C. Richardson, 171–182. New York: Simon & Schuster, 1996.

Diognetus. In *Early Christian Fathers*, edited by Cyril C. Richardson, 205–12. New York: Simon & Schuster, 1996.

Donfried, Karl Paul. *Paul, Thessalonica, and Early Christianity*. Grand Rapids: Eerdmans, 2002.

Driver, Tom F. *The Magic of Ritual: Our Need for Liberating Rites that Transform Our Lives and Our Communities*. San Francisco: HarperSanFrancisco, 1991.

Duling, Dennis C. "Millennialism." In *The Social Sciences and New Testament Interpretation*, edited by Richard L. Rohrbaugh, 183–205. Peabody, MA: Hendrickson, 1996.

Dunn, James D. G. *Baptism in the Holy Spirit: A Re-Examination of the New Testament Teaching on the Gift of the Spirit in Relation to Pentecostalism Today*. Studies in Biblical Theology. London: SCM, 1970.

Dunson, Ben C. *Individual and Community in Paul's Letter to the Romans*. Wissenschaftliche Untersuchungen zum Neuen Testament. Tübingen: Mohr Siebeck, 2012.

Ehrensperger, Kathy. *Paul and the Dynamics of Power*. Library of New Testament Studies. New York: T. & T. Clark, 2007.

Ehrman, Bart D. *Jesus: Apocalyptic Prophet of the New Millennium*. Oxford: Oxford University Press, 1999.

Elliott, John H. "The Jewish Messianic Movement: From Faction to Sect." In *Modeling Early Christianity*, edited by Philip F. Esler, 75–95. London: Routledge, 1995.

Esler, Philip F. *Community and Gospel in Luke-Acts*. SNTSMS 57. Cambridge: Cambridge University Press, 1987.

———. *The First Christians in Their Social Worlds*. London: Routledge, 1994.

———. "Imagery and Identity in Gal. 5:13 to 6:10." In *Constructing Early Christian Families: Family as Social Reality and Metaphor*, edited by Halvor Moxnes, 133–149. London: Routledge, 1997.

Estrada, Nelson. *From Followers to Leaders: The Apostles in the Ritual of Status Transformation in Acts 1–2*. New York: T. & T. Clark, 2004.

Eusebius of Caesarea. *The History of the Church*. Translated by G. A. Williamson. London: Penguin, 1965.

Fee, Gordon D. *God's Empowering Presence: The Holy Spirit in the Letters of Paul*. Peabody, MA: Hendrickson, 1994.

———. "Hermeneutics and the Gender Debate." In *Discovering Biblical Equality*, edited by Ronald W. Pierce and Rebecca Merrill Groothuis, 364–81. Downers Grove, IL: InterVarsity, 2005.

———. *Paul, the Spirit, and the People of God*. Peabody, MA: Hendrickson, 1996.

Ferguson, Everett. *Church History: From Christ to Pre-Reformation*. Grand Rapids: Zondervan, 2005.

Finger, Rita Halteman. *Of Widows and Meals: Communal Meals in the Book of Acts*. Grand Rapids: Eerdmans, 2007.

Finlay, Stephen. *The Family Metaphor in Jesus' Teaching*. Eugene, OR: Cascade, 2009.

Fox, Robin. *Pagans and Christians*. San Francisco: Harper & Row, 1986.

Frend, W. C. *The Early Church*. Philadelphia: Fortress, 1982.

———. *The Rise of Christianity*. Philadelphia: Fortress, 1984.

Fuller, Michael E. *The Restoration of Israel: Israel's Re-Gathering and the Fate of the Nations in Early Jewish Literature and Luke-Acts*. Berlin: de Gruyter, 2006.

Gager, John G. *Kingdom and Commmunity*. Englewood Cliffs: Prentice Hall, 1975.

Garnsey, Peter, and Richard Saller. *The Roman Empire: Economy, Society, and Culture*. Berkley: University of California Press, 1987.

Gehring, Robert. *House Church and Mission*. Peabody, MA: Hendrickson, 2004.

Ger, Steven. *The Book of Acts: Witness to the World*. Twenty-First Century Biblical Commentary Series. Chattanooga, TN: AMG, 2004.

Glad, Clarence E. *Paul and Philodemus: Adaptability in Epicurean and Early Christian Psychagogy*. Leiden: Brill, 1995.

Goheen, Michael. "A Critical Examination of David Bosch's Missional Reading of Luke." In *Reading Luke: Interpretation, Reflection, Formation*, edited by Craig G. Bartholomew, Joel B. Green, and Anthony C. Thiselton, 229–67. Grand Rapids: Zondervan, 2005.

Goodman, Martin. *Ancient Judaism and the Roman World: Collected Essays*. Ancient Judaism and Early Christianity 66. Boston: Brill, 2006.

———. *The Roman World 44 BC–AD 180*. London: Routledge, 1997.

Gorman, Michael J. *Cruciformity: Paul's Narrative Spirituality of the Cross*. Grand Rapids: Eerdmans, 2001.

Grant, Robert M. *Augustus to Constantine: The Rise and Triumph of Christianity in the Roman World*. Atlanta: John Knox, 1970.

Green, Joel. *The Gospel of Luke*. New International Commentary on the New Testament. Grand Rapids: Eerdmans, 1997.

Gunkel, Hermann. *Die Wirkungen des heiligen Geistes nach der populären Anschanung der apostolischen Zeit und der Lehre des Apostels Paulus*. Göttingen: Vandenhoek & Rupecht, 1909.

Guy, Laurie. *Introducing Early Christianity*. Downers Grove, IL: InterVarsity, 2004.

Hall, Stuart. *Doctrine and Practice in the Early Church*. Eugene, OR: Cascade Books, 2011.

Hansen, Bruce. *All of You Are One: The Social Vision of Galatians 3:28, 1 Corinthians 12.13 and Colossians 3.11*. Library of New Testament Studies 409. New York: T. & T. Clark, 2010.

Harland, Philip A. *Associations, Synagogues, and Congregations: Claiming a Place in Ancient Mediterranean Society*. Minneapolis: Fortress, 2003.

———. "Connections with Elites in the World of Early Christians." In *Handbook of Early Christianity: Social Science Approaches*, edited by Anthony J. Blasi et al., 385–408. New York: Altamira, 2002.

———. *Dynamics of Identity in the World of the Early Christians*. New York: T. & T. Clark, 2009.

Harrison, James R. "Paul and Ancient Civic Ethics: Redefining the Canon of Honour in the GraecoRoman World." In *Paul's Graeco-Roman Context*, edited by Cilliers Breytenbach. Leuven: Peeters, 2015.

Heen, Erik M. "Phil 2:6–11 and Resistance to Local Timocratic Rule: Isa Theo and the Cult of the Emperor in the East." In *Paul and the Roman Imperial Order*, edited by Richard A. Hosley, 125–154. Harrisburg, PA: Trinty, 2004.

Hellerman, Joseph. *The Ancient Church as Family*. Minneapolis: Fortress, 2001.

———. *Jesus and the People of God: Reconfiguring Ethnic Identity*. Sheffield: Sheffield Phoenix, 2007.

———. *Reconstructing Honor in Roman Philippi*. Cambridge: Cambridge University Press, 2005.

Herzog, William. *Jesus, Justice and the Reign of God*. Louisville: Westminster John Knox, 2000.

Hill, Charles E. *Regnum Caelorum: Patterns of Millenial Thought in Early Christianity*. Grand Rapids: Eerdmans, 2001.

Hoehner, Harold W. *Ephesians: An Exegetical Commentary*. Grand Rapids: Baker, 2002.

Hogan, Pauline Nigh. "No Longer Male and Female:" In *Interpreting Galatians 3.28 in Early Christianity*. Library of New Testament Studies. New York: T. & T. Clark, 2008.

Holmberg, Bengt. *Paul and Power*. Philadelphia: Fortress, 1978.

Hopkins, Keith. "Elite Mobility in the Roman Empire." *Past & Present* 32 (1965) 12–26.

Horsley, Richard A. *Jesus and Empire*. Minneapolis: Fortress, 2003.

Howell, Martha, and Walter Prevenier. *From Reliable Sources*. Ithaca: Cornell University Press, 2001.

Hultgren, Arland J. *The Rise of Normative Christianity*. Minneapolis: Fortress, 1994.

Hunt, Stephen. "Introduction." In *Christian Millenarianism*, edited by Stephen Hunt, 1–11. Bloomington: Indiana University Press, 2001.

Hur, Ju. *A Dynamic Reading of the Holy Spirit in Luke-Acts*. London: T. & T. Clark, 2004.

Huttunen, Niko. *Paul and Epictetus on Law*. Early Christianity in Context 405. New York: T. & T. Clark, 2009.

Ignatius. *Letters of Ignatius*. In *Early Christian Fathers*, edited by Cyril C. Richardson, 87–120. New York: Simon & Schuster, 1996.

Irenaeus. *Against Heresies*. In *Early Christian Fathers*, edited by Cyril C. Richardson, 358–298. New York: Simon & Schuster, 1996.

Jackson, T. Ryan. *New Creation in Paul's Letters*. Wissenschaftliche Untersuchungen zum Neuen Testament, edited by Jörg Frey. Tübingen: Mohr Siebeck, 2010.

Jewett, Robert. *The Thessalonian Correspondence: Pauline Rhetoric and Millenarian Piety*. Philadelphia: Fortress, 1986.

Johnson, Luke Timothy. *The Acts of the Apostles*. Sacra Pagima 5. Collegeville, MN: Liturgical, 1992.

———. *Religious Experience in Earliest Christianity*. Minneapolis: Fortress, 1998.

Johnson, Marshall. *The Evolution of Christianity: Twelve Crises That Shaped the Church*. New York: Continuum, 2005.

Josephus. *The Antiquities of the Jews*. Translated by William Whiston. Peabody, MA: Hendrickson, 1987.

Joshel, Sandra R. *Work, Identity and Legal Status at Rome: A Study of the Occupational Inscriptions*. Norman: University of Oklahoma Press, 1992.

Judge, E. A. "The Social Pattern of Christian Groups in the First Century." In *Social Distinctives of the Christians in the First Century: Pivotal Essays by E. A. Judge*, edited by David M. Scholar, 1–56. Peabody, MA: Hendrickson, 2008.

———. "St. Paul as a Radical Critic of Society." In *Social Distinctives of the Christians in the First Century: Pivotal Essays by E. A. Judge*, edited by David M. Scholer, 99–116. Peabody, MA: Hendrickson, 2008.

Justin Martyr. *First Apology*. In *Early Christian Fathers*, edited by Cyril C. Richardson, 242–289. New York: Simon & Schuster, 1996.

Käsemann, Ernst. "Blind Alleys in the Jesus of History Controversy." In *New Testament Questions of Today*, 23–65. Philadephia: Fortress, 1969.

Kee, Howard Clark. *Who Are the People of God?: Early Christian Models of Community*. New Haven: Yale University Press, 1995.

Keener, Craig S. *Acts: An Exegetical Commentary: 3:1—13:28*. Vol. 2. Grand Rapids: Baker, 2013.

———. *Acts: An Exegetical Commentary: Introduction and 1:1—2:47*. Vol. 1. Grand Rapids: Baker, 2012.

———. *Paul, Women, and Wives: Marriage and Women's Ministry in the Letters of Paul*. Grand Rapids: Baker, 1993.

Kim, Yung Suk. *Christ's Body in Corinth: The Politics of a Metaphor*. Minneapolis: Fortress, 2004.

Klauck, Hans-Josef. *Hausgemeinde und Hauskirche im frühen Christentum*. SBS 103. Stuttgart: Katholische Bibelwerk, 1981.

Kloppenborg, John S. "Collegia and Thiasoi: Issues in Function, Taxonomy and Membership." In *Voluntary Associations in the Graeco-Roman World*, edited by John S. Kloppenborg and Stephen G. Wilson, 16–30. London: Routledge, 1996.

Koester, Helmut. *Paul & His World: Interpreting the New Testament in Its Context*. Minneapolis: Fortress, 2007.

Kreitzer, L. J. "Eschatology." In *Dictionary of Paul and His Letters*, edited by Gerald F. Hawthorne and Ralph P. Martin, 253–69. Downers Grove, IL: InterVarsity, 1993.

Kuecker, Aaron J. *The Spirit and the 'Other': Social Identity, Ethnicity and Intergroup Reconciliation in Luke-Acts*. London: T. & T. Clark, 2011.

Ladd, George Eldon. *The Presence of the Future*. Grand Rapids: Eerdmans, 1974.

———. *A Theology of the New Testament*. Grand Rapids: Eerdmans, 1974.

Landolt, Jean-Francois. " 'Be Imitators of Me, Brothers and Sisters' (Philippians 3.17): Paul as an Exemplary Figure in the Pauline Corpus and the Acts of the Apostles." In *Paul and the Heritage of Israel: Paul's Claim Upon Israel's Legacy in Luke and Acts in the Light of the Pauline Letters*, edited by David Moessner et al., 290–317. New York: T. & T. Clark, 2012.

Latourette, Kenneth Scott. *A History of Christianity: Volume 1, Beginnings to 1500*. New York: Harper, 1975.

Lee, Michelle. *Paul, the Stoics, and the Body of Christ*. SNTSMS 137. Cambridge: Cambridge University Press, 2006.

Lee, Sang Meyng, *The Cosmic Drama of Salvation*. Wissenshaftliche Untersuchungen zum Neuen Testament. Tübingen: Mohr Siebeck, 2010.

Lendon, J. E. *Empire of Honor*. Oxford: Oxford University Press, 1997.
Levine, Lee I. *The Ancient Synagogue*. New Haven: Yale University Press, 2000.
Libanius: Autobiography and Selected Letters. Vol. 1. Translated by A. F. Norman. Cambridge: Harvard University Press, 1992.
Lim, Kar Yong. "Paul's Use of Temple Imagery in the Corinthian Correspondence: The Creation of Christian Identity." In *Reading Paul in Context: Explorations in Identity Formation*, edited by Kathy Ehrensperger and J. Brian Tucker, 189–208. London: T. & T. Clark, 2010.
Lohfink, Gerhard. *Jesus and Community*. Philadelphia: Fortress, 1982.
Luckensmeyer, David. *The Eschatology of First Thessalonians*. Gottingen: Vandenhoeck & Ruprecht, 2009.
Lundström, Gösta. *The Kingdom of God in the Teaching of Jesus*. Translated by Joan Bulman. Edinburgh: Oliver & Boyd, 1963.
MacDonald, Margaret. *The Pauline Churches*. SNTSMS. Cambridge: Cambridge University Press, 1998.
Mack, Burton L. *The Christian Myth: Origins, Logic, and Legacy*. New York: Continuum, 2001.
MacMullen, Ramsay. *Christianizing the Roman Empire A.D. 100–400*. New Haven: Yale University Press, 1984.
———. *Paganism in the Roman Empire*. New Haven:Yale University Press, 1981.
———. *Roman Social Relations: 50 B.C. to A.D. 284*. New Haven: Yale University Press, 1974.
———. *The Second Church: Popular Christianity A.D. 200–400*. Atlanta: Society of Biblical Literature, 2009.
Maher, Michael. "Knowing the Tree by Its Roots: Jewish Context of the Early Christian Movement." In *Christian Origins: Worship, Belief and Society*, edited by Kieran J. O'Mahony, 1–28. New York: Sheffield Academic, 2003.
Malina, Bruce. *The Social Gospel of Jesus*. Minneapolis: Fortress, 2001.
Malina, Bruce, and Jerome H. Neyrey. "Honor and Shame in Luke–Acts: Pivotal Values of the Mediterranean World." In *The Social World of Luke-Acts*, edited by Jerome H. Neyrey, 25–66. Peabody, MA: Hendrickson, 1991.
Mallen, Peter. *The Reading and Transformation of Isaiah in Luke–Acts*. Library of New Testament Studies. New York: T. & T. Clark, 2008.
Marguerat, Daniel. *The First Christian Historian*. Cambridge: Cambridge University Press, 2002.
Markus, Robert. *The End of Ancient Christianity*. Cambridge: Cambridge University Press, 1990.
Matlock, R. Barry. *Unveiling the Apocalyptic Paul: Paul's Interpreters and the Rhetoric of Criticism*. Sheffield: Sheffield Academic, 1996.
McCabe, David R. *How to Kill Things with Words: Ananias and Sapphira under the Prophetic Speech-Act of Divine Judgment (Acts 4:32—5:11)*. New York: T. & T. Clark, 2011.
McCready, Wayne O. "Ekklesia and Voluntary Associations." In *Voluntary Associations in the Graeco-Roman World*, edited by John S. Kloppenborg and Stephen G. Wilson, 59–73. London: Routledge, 1996.
McKechnie, Paul. *The First Christian Centuries*. Downers Grove, IL: InterVarsity, 2001.
Meeks, Wayne. *The First Urban Christians: The Social World of the Apostle Paul*. New Haven: Yale University Press, 1983.

Menzies, Robert P. *Empowered for Witness*. New York: T. & T. Clark, 2004.

Morgan-Wynne, John Eifion. *Holy Spirit and Religious Experience in Christian Literature ca. AD 90–200*. Waynesboro, GA: Paternoster, 2006.

Moxnes, Halvor. "Patron-Client Relationships and the New Community in Luke–Acts." In *The Social World of Luke–Acts*, edited by Jerome H. Neyrey, 241–270. Peabody, MA: Hendrickson, 1991.

Neyrey, Jerome. "The Symbolic Universe of Luke-Acts: 'They Turned the World Upside Down.' " In *The Social World of Luke–Acts*, edited by Jerome Neyrey, 271–304. Peabody, MA: Hendrickson, 1991.

Nystrom, Bradley P., and David P. Nystrom. *The History of Christianity*. New York: McGraw-Hill, 2004.

O'Brian, Peter T. *The Letter to the Ephesians*. Grand Rapids: Eerdmans, 1999.

Origen. *Against Celsus*. In *Ante-Nicene Fathers*, edited by Alexander Roberts and James Donaldson, 4, 395–669. Peabody, MA: Hendrickson, 2004.

———. *De Principiis*. In *Ante-Nicene Fathers*, edited by Alexander Roberts and James Donaldson, 4, 239–385. Peabody, MA: Hendrickson, 2004.

Pagels, Elaine. *The Gnostic Gospels*. New York: Random House, 1979.

Paget, Alan G. *As Christ Submits to the Church: A Biblical Understanding of Leadership and Mutual Submission*. Grand Rapids: Baker, 2011.

Pao, David W. *Acts and the Isaianic New Exodus*. Grand Rapids: Baker, 2002.

Pate, C. Marvin. *The End of the Age Has Come*. Grand Rapids: Zondervan, 1995.

Pelikan, Jaroslav. *Jesus through the Centuries*. New Haven: Yale University Press, 1999.

Perrin, Norman. *The Kingdom of God in the Teaching of Jesus*. Philadelphia: Westminister, 1963.

Peterson, David. *The Acts of the Apostles*. Grand Rapids: Eerdmans, 2009.

Pierce, Ronald W. "Contemporary Evangelicals for Gender Equality." In *Discovering Biblical Equality*, edited by Ronald W. Pierce and Rebecca Merrill Groothuis, 58–78. Downers Grove, IL: InterVarsity, 2005.

Pilch, John J. "Sickness and Healing in Luke–Acts." In *The Social World of Luke–Acts*, edited by Jerome H. Neyrey, 181–210. Peabody, MA: Hendrickson, 1991.

Polhill, John B. *Acts*. The New American Commentary. Nashville: Broadman, 1992.

Polycarp. *Letter to the Philippians*. In *Early Christian Fathers*, edited by Cyril C. Richardson, 131–41. New York: Simon & Schuster, 1996.

Rabens, Volker. *The Holy Spirit and Ethics in Paul*. Wissenshaftliche Untersuchungen zum Neuen Testament. Tübingen: Mohr/Siebeck, 2010.

Rapp, Claudia. *Holy Bishops in Late Antiquity: The Nature of Christian Leadership in an Age of Transition*. Los Angeles: University of California Press, 2005.

Rauschenbusch, Walter. *Christianity and the Social Crisis*. New York: Doran, 1907.

Ravens, David. *Luke and the Restoration of Israel*. JSNT. Sheffield: Sheffield Academic, 1995.

Reinhold, Meyer. "Usurption of Status and Status Symbols in the Roman Empire." *Historia* 20 (1971) 275–302.

Rhee, Helen. *Loving the Poor, Saving the Rich: Wealth, Poverty, and Early Christian Formation*. Grand Rapids: Baker, 2012.

Richardson, Cyril C. "Introduction to Early Christian Literature." In *Early Christian Fathers*, edited by Cyril C. Richardson, 15–26. New York: Simon & Schuster, 1996.

Richardson, Peter. "Early Synagogues as Collegia in the Diaspora and Palestine." In *Voluntary Associations in the Graeco-Roman World*, edited by John S. Kloppenborg and Stephen G. Wilson, 90–109. New York: Routledge, 1996.

Russell, Walter Bo. *The Flesh/Spirit Conflict in Galatians*. New York: University Press of America, 1997.

Salzman, Michele Renee. *The Making of a Christian Aristocracy*. Cambridge: Harvard University Press, 2002.

Sampley, J. Paul. *Walking between the Times*. Minneapolis: Fortress, 1991.

Sanders, E. P. *Jesus and Judaism*. Philadelphia: Fortress, 1985.

———. *Paul, the Law, and the Jewish People*. Philadelphia: Fortress, 1983.

Sandnes, Karl Olav. "Equality Within Patriarchal Structures." In *Constructing Early Christian Families: Family as Social Reality and Metaphor*, edited by Halvor Moxnes, 150–166. London: Routledge, 1997.

Saucy, Mark. *The Kingdom of God in the Teaching of Jesus*. Dallas: Word, 1997.

Schäfer, Klaus. *Gemeinde als 'Brüdershaft': Ein Betrag zum Kirchenverständnis des Paulus*. Bern: Lang, 1989.

Scheid, John. *An Introduction to Roman Religion*. Bloomington: Indiana University Press, 2003.

Schweitzer, Albert. *The Kingdom of God and Primitive Christianity*. Translated by Ulrich Neuenschwander. New York: Seabury, 1968.

Scobie, Charles H. H. "A Canonical Approach to Interpreting Luke: The Journey Motif as a Hermeneutical Key." In *Reading Luke: Interpretation, Reflection, Formation*, edited by Craig G. Bartholomew et al., 327–49. Grand Rapids: Zondervan, 2005.

Scroggs, Robin. "The Earliest Christian Communities as Sectarian Movements." In *Social Scientific Approaches to New Testament Interpretation*, edited by David G. Horrell, 69–92. Edinburgh: T. & T. Clark, 1999.

Shepherd, William H. *The Narrative Function of the Holy Spirit as a Character in Luke-Acts*. Society of Biblical Literature Dissertation Series. Atlanta: Scholars, 1994.

Shepherd of Hermas. *Commandments*. In *The Apostolic Fathers*, edited by Michael W. Holmes, 504–555. Grand Rapids: Baker, 2007.

Sim, David. *Apocalyptic Eschatology in the Gospel of Matthew*. Cambridge: Cambridge University Press, 1996.

Snowden, Frank M. *Blacks in Antiquity: Ethiopians in the Greco-Roman Experience*. Cambridge: Harvard University Press, 1970.

Snyder, Graydon. *Ante Pacem*. Macon, GA: Mercer University Press, 2003.

St. Clair, Michael J. *Millenarian Movements in Historical Context*. New York: Garland, 1992.

Stambaugh, John E., and David L. Balch. *The New Testament in Its Social Environment*. Library of Early Christianity. Philadelphia: Westminister, 1986.

Stegemann, Ekkehard W. "Coexistence and Transformation: Reading the Politics of Identity in Romans in Imperial Context." In *Reading Paul in Context: Explorations in Identity Formation*, edited by Kathy Ehrensperger and J. Brian Tucker, 3–23. London: T. & T. Clark, 2010.

Stegemann, Ekkehard W., and Wolfgang Stegemann. *The Jesus Movement: A Social History of Its First Century*. Translated by O. C. Dean. Minneapolis: Fortress, 1995.

Stein, Robert H. *Luke*. The New American Commentary. Nashville: Broadman, 1992.

Stott, John R. W. *The Message of Acts*. The Bible Speaks Today. Downers Grove, IL: InterVarsity, 1990.

Stowers, Stanley K. "Does Pauline Christianity Resemble a Hellenistic Philosophy?" In *Paul Beyond the Judaism/Hellenism Divide*, edited by Troels Engberg-Pedersen, 81–102. Louisville: Westminster John Knox, 2001.

Strauss, Mark L. *The Davidic Messiah in Luke–Acts*. JSNTSup. Sheffield: Sheffield Academic, 1995.

Strecker, Christian. *Die liminale Theologie des Paulus: Zugänge zur paulinischen Theologie aus kulturanthropologischer Perspektive*. Göttingen: Vandenhoeck & Ruprecht, 1999.

Strom, Mark. *Reframing Paul: Conversations in Grace and Community*. Downers Grove, IL: InterVarsity, 2000.

Sumney, Jerry L. "'Christ Died for Us': Interpretation of Jesus' Death as a Central Element of the Identity of the Earliest Church." In *Reading Paul in Context: Explorations in Identity Formation*, edited by Kathy Ehrensperger and J. Brian Tucker, 147–72. London: T. & T. Clark, 2010.

Swete, Henry Barclay. *The Holy Spirit in the Ancient Church*. Reprint, Eugene, OR: Wipf & Stock, 1996.

Tannehill, Robert C. *Dying and Rising with Christ*. 1996. Reprint, Eugene, OR: Wipf & Stock, 2006.

Taylor, Justin. "The Original Environment of Christianity." In *Christian Origins: Worship, Belief and Society*, edited by Kieran J. O'Mahony, 214–24. New York: Sheffield Academic, 2003.

Tertullian. *Against Marcion*. In *Ante-Nicene Fathers*, edited by Alexander Roberts and James Donaldson, 3, 269–476. Peabody, MA: Hendrickson, 2004.

———. *Apology*. In *Ante-Nicene Fathers*, edited by Alexander Roberts and James Donaldson, 3, 17–60. Peabody, MA: Hendrickson, 2004.

———. *On Modesty*. In *Ante-Nicene Fathers*, edited by Alexander Roberts and James Donaldson, 4, 74–101. Peabody, MA: Hendrickson, 2004.

———. *On the Resurrection of the Flesh*. In *Ante-Nicene Fathers*, edited by Alexander Roberts and James Donaldson, 3, 545–96. Peabody, MA: Hendrickson, 2004.

———. *The Passion of the Holy Martyrs Perpetua and Felicitas*. In *Ante-Nicene Fathers*, edited by Alexander Roberts and James Donaldson, 3, 699–706. Peabody, MA: Hendrickson, 2004.

Theissen, Gerd. *The Religion of the Earliest Churches*. Translated by John Bowden. Minneapolis: Fortress, 1999.

Thom, Johan C. "Paul and Popular Philosphy." In *Paul's Graeco-Roman Context*, edited by Cilliers Breytenbach, 47–74. Leuven: Peeters, 2015.

Thompson, Alan J. *The Acts of the Risen Lord Jesus*. New Studies in Biblical Theology. Downers Grove, IL: InterVarsity, 2011.

———. *One Lord, One People: The Unity of the Church in Acts in Its Literary Setting*. New York: T. & T. Clark, 2008.

Tucker, J. Brian. "Baths, Baptism, and Patronage: The Continuing Role of Roman Social Identity in Corinth." In *Reading Paul in Context: Explorations in Identity Formation*, edited by Kathy Ehrensperger and J. Brian Tucker, 173–88. London: T. & T. Clark, 2010.

———. *Remain in Your Calling*. Eugene, OR: Pickwick Publications, 2011.

Turcan, Robert. *The Cults of the Roman Empire*. Oxford: Blackwell, 1992.

Turner, Edith. *Communitas: The Anthropology of Collective Joy*. New York: Palgrave Macmillan, 2012.

Turner, Max. *Power from on High: The Spirit in Israel's Restoration and Witness in Luke–Acts.* Sheffield: Sheffield Academic, 1996.
Turner, Victor. *Dramas, Fields, and Metaphors: Symbolic Action in Human Society.* Ithaca, NY: Cornell University Press, 1974.
———. *The Forest of Symbols: Aspects of Ndembu Ritual.* Ithaca, NY: Cornell University, 1967.
———. *From Ritual to Theater: The Human Seriousness of Play.* New York: Performing Arts Journal, 1982.
———. *The Ritual Process: Structure and Anti-Structure.* Ithaca, NY: Cornell University Press, 1969.
Van Gennep, Arnold. *The Rites of Passage.* Translated by M. B. Vizedom and G. L. Caffee. Chicago: University of Chicago Press, 1960.
Vermes, Geza. *The Religion of Jesus the Jew.* Minneapolis: Fortress, 1993.
Wagner, Walter. *After the Apostles.* Minneapolis: Fortress, 1994.
Warrior, Valerie M. *Roman Religion.* Cambridge: Cambridge University Press, 2006.
Weiss, Johannes. *Jesus' Proclamation of the Kingdom of God.* Translated by Richard Hyde Hiers and David Larrimore Holland. Philadelphia: Fortress, 1971.
Wenk, Matthias. *Community-Forming Power: The Socio-Ethical Role of the Spirit in Luke–Acts.* London: T. & T. Clark, 2004.
Wilken, Robert Louis. *The Christians as the Romans Saw Them.* New Haven: Yale University Press, 2003.
Witherington, Ben, III. *The Acts of the Apostles: A Socio-Rhetorical Commentary.* Grand Rapids: Eerdmans, 1998.
———. *Conflict and Community in Corinth: A Socio-Rhetorical Commentary on 1 and 2 Corinthians.* Grand Rapids: Eerdmans, 1995.
———. *Jesus, Paul, and the End of the World.* Downers Grove, IL: InterVarsity, 1992.
———. *The Jesus Quest: The Third Search for the Jew of Nazareth.* Downers Grove, IL: InterVarsity, 1997.
Witmer, Amanda. *Jesus, the Galilean Exorcist: His Exorcisms in Social and Political Context.* Library of the Historical Jesus Studies. New York: T. & T. Clark, 2012.
Wright, N. T. *Jesus and the Victory of God.* Minneapolis: Fortress, 1996.
———. *The New Testament and the People of God.* Minneapolis: Fortress, 1992.

www.ingramcontent.com/pod-product-compliance
Lightning Source LLC
Chambersburg PA
CBHW050439240426
43661CB00055B/2437